# 2020 Edition

# 3D Printing Failures

## How to Diagnose & Repair all Desktop 3D Printing Issues

By: Sean Aranda

Edited by: David Feeney

Material Science by: Nicolas Tokotuu, Product Manager at Polymaker

Special Thanks to:
All of my subscribers and Patrons
David Feeney and Bennett Berger
Nicolas Tokotuu of Polymaker
Timothy at TH3D
Hanna Henry for the cover design
©2020

# Table of Contents

# Introduction

When I first started working with 3D printers, I was overwhelmed by the amount of knowledge required to have consecutive successful prints. Since I was aware of the acceptable failure rate for most other manufacturing machines, I was blown away by just how inconsistent 3D printing can be without frequent, proper maintenance.

Many desktop 3D printing companies advertise a plug and play machine that can be operated consistently without any engineering background, which is generally not true. 3D printing has been marketed by many as a magical solution to manufacturing and prototyping, but anyone who has used these machines will be able to tell you different.

From the time I began in this industry roughly five years ago, up to the point of writing this book, I have amassed well over 75,000 hours of successful printing (machine run time) across over two dozen types of FDM machines. I have repaired just about every section of the printer and have even built my own. Since prints can fail up to 20% of the time without proper maintenance, you can be safe to assume I have had to fix just about every issue you will come across.

This 2020 edition of the book has been entirely re-written. Every single chapter has been updated to any new information I have run into, including the use of new software. I have also been reached out to by individuals who have purchased the previous editions with their problems not covered in their edition, which are now included in this. There are many new photos to help diagnose and fix problems and there 6 entirely new chapters. One of these chapters has been written by an industry leader, with the "Material Science" chapter being written by Nicolas Tokotuu of Polymaker. All of this information is to make sure everything is up to date.

There is also a chapter on electrical safety that was added and helped to make by Timothy at TH3D, which I think 100% of you should read. Preventing a fire should be your number 1 concern when getting into 3D printing.

I suggest everyone read the chapter on material science before just about anything else in this book. Understanding the "Material Science" chapter helps explain the "why". If you fully understand that chapter, it is likely that you will be able to diagnose and fix many of your issues without referencing the rest of this book.

I also suggest you check out the "Limitations Involved with 3D Printing" chapter if you are new to 3D printing, since FDM machines are not a one-stop solution for anything you need.

In the diagnostic section in the beginning of this book I will go over some of the visual symptoms that you may see when your printer is malfunctioning, and what could be causing the problem. Whatever failure or ugly print you are experiencing, you should be able to compare it to the problem described, and then go to the designated chapters in order to fix.

My goal with this book is to take every failure I have witnessed and put it into one resource. This book should be able to help you fix close to 100% of the problems you are going to experience with your 3D printer. If you purchased this book and it does not help you with your specific problem, I offer you to contact me anytime at my YouTube channel "The 3D Print General", or to email me at Sean@3DPrintGeneral.com. I also open you to email me with proof of purchase for higher definition colored photos, since the publishing process will often reduce the quality.

## Warnings for using your 3D printer

Since I personally believe this industry does not do a proper job of warning the dangers involved with 3D printing when advertising products to average consumers, I feel it necessary to caution you of the real possibility of a fire while operating one of these machines. This is equipment that draws a lot of power, shakes and moves for hours, and has a lot of wires that can be dislodged or frayed. Many inexpensive manufacturers do not take the proper cautions. You shouldn't run your printer next to curtains or other flammable things, and you shouldn't leave your machine printing alone for hours if you are not confident in your build quality. I personally have an AFO Fire Extinguishing Ball mounted above my printers as insurance against the worst case scenario, and suggest everyone else to do the same.

EVERYONE should check out the video by Thomas Sanladerer titled "Everything you need to know to make your 3D printer fireproof!" on YouTube. There is some complicated things that he goes over, but it is crucial that you understand this before you purchase a $200 printer with a heated build plate and leave it unattended. There is a somewhat abridged version of his video as a short chapter in this book titled "Electrical Safety" that you should read over, which some of the basics are covered.

Another concern is that not much research has been done in relation to the amount of harmful particulates put into the air from melting plastic in this fashion. You can imagine that if you threw some Lego's into an oven and inhaled the smoke that was created, you would be doing some serious damage to your health. You should make sure that your 3D printer is in a well-ventilated area, and that you do not stand over the hotend watching it while it prints. Some manufacturers have factored this issue into their build design and enclose the machine, ventilated with filters. Specific materials are worse for your health than others, but it is a good rule of thumb to assume that melting plastic and inhaling it is not going to be good for your lungs.

## Notes about different types of printers

This book will only cover FDM desktop 3D printers and will not be able to help fixing SLA machines, SLS machines, or any other form of 3D printing. There may be some generic rules that overlap, but I was only factoring in FDM 3D printing when writing this book.

## What is FDM 3D Printing?

There are quite a few different forms of 3D printing available today, but the most common used in homes around the world is known as Fused Deposition Modeling (FDM). FDM printing works by laying down consecutive layers of material at high temperatures – with each layer given time to cool and bond together before the next layer is deposited.

This can actually be thought of as the inverse of computer numerical cutting (CNC). 3D models are transformed into G-code via a slicing program, which work as instructions for the 3D printer, telling it exactly where to move next, and how much volume is required to extrude. This additive process only uses the amount of material required to create the part, versus CNC which is subtractive and requires excess material which it is then cut from. The only exception to this is the support material required for overhangs in FDM 3D printing, acting as a form of scaffolding that is broken off after printing.

**NOTE:** I have done my best to have these photos show up in high quality, but Amazon's printing process does not seem to always be up to par. Email me at Sean@3DPrintGeneral and I will be happy to send you the HD version of these photos, along with a PDF version of this book - with proof of purchase.

## Pros to Using FDM Printing

First and foremost - the most beneficial reason to use FDM 3D printing is the costs involved. FDM printers are very affordable when compared to other printing methods, and the material can be drastically less expensive.

With the expansion of 3D printing over the last few years, the amount of m options have increased rapidly. FDM printing now allows for printing nylon, and carbon fiber blends - some of which have strength tha the average individual. There are likely over one hundred types available, each with their own price, strength, heat resistance print – meaning there is something available for almost rial option is a lot less expansive when working with

## Types of FDM 3D Printing

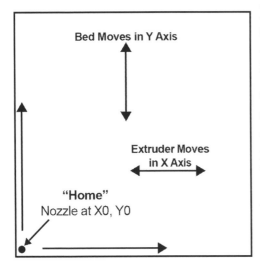

Bed Moves in Y Axis

Extruder Moves
in X Axis

"Home"
Nozzle at X0, Y0

Many of the axes and solutions I describe are for Cartesian machines. A Cartesian FDM 3D printer is one in which the build plate moves in the Y direction, the extruder moves in the X direction, and the carriage is moved up and down in the Z direction. This is how most desktop FDM 3D printers function. The photo is a digram of how most Cartesian printers find "home", though some home to their max.

A CoreXY machine is where the bed moves up and down in the Z direction, and the extruder moves in both the X and Y direction. There are some variations with this, such as an H-Bot, but they essentially work the same. While I may call all of these printers "CoreXY" that is because they were the first gantry system I was aware of, but I am actually referring to a gantry system in general. There are definitely some benefits involved with this method since you should be able to achieve some tighter tolerances, as well as avoid some Z-wobble and thin parts being knocked over from the bed rattling. Your frame should also be able to print much faster without printing issues due to the lack of the heavy bed being moved back and forth. Many prefer a CoreXY machine, including myself – they are just not as common as Cartesians.

A Delta 3D printer looks and functions quite differently than either of these, since the extruder is suspended above the build plate via three arms in a triangular fashion. These machines have their downfalls but can normally print much faster than a Cartesian with the same specs. I personally do not have much experience with these types of FDM machines.

You should be able to use all of the remedies in this book on CoreXY and Delta machines, but some of the dimensions described in the directions and firmware will be different.

There are also two types of extruder setups – direct and Bowden – both of which can have a gear ratio or not. A direct extruder is one where the stepper motor is ___ filament directly into the hotend, and is attached to the carriage. A Bowden ___ filament is fed from a stepper motor attached to the frame to the ___ Bowden extruder will reduce the weight on your carriage which ___ lly print much faster. The problem with Bowden machines is ___ith printing unique materials and fine nozzles, with some ___ry fine nozzles being entirely impossible. You will also ___ettings in order to prevent a "hairy" print, which is

___ edition of the book, but in general I am dis-
___ prefer those.

# Good Practice

Before I get into the specifics of fixing particular failures, I feel it necessary to go over some good practices to maintain your printer in top condition. Since 3D printers are mechanical machines that experience frequent rattling and movement, they require constant maintenance in order to continue performing at their peak. Look over the "Mandatory Maintenance" chapter as well to make sure you properly take care of your printer.

## Keep a clean environment

If you do not make sure to always clean up your printer work area, you will be surprised just how quickly everything can get out of hand.

Make sure you always throw away excess material since it can eventually get in the way of your gears turning properly. Since there are fans blowing on different sections of your printer, you could even blow some stringy old material onto your current print.

Keeping your printer clean includes your build plate. This does not need to be cleaned after every print and will be determined by your specific build plate and adhesion method (as described in the "Bed Adhesion" Chapter). I like to clean off my build plate every couple of prints to make sure I have a proper first layer.

If you have an air compressor it can help immensely with cleaning the different parts of your printer from debris and dust.

## Print replacement parts that are likely to break in advanced

You really don't want to wait for a printed part on your machine to break and to not have a replacement on hand. If you only have one 3D printer, you are going to have to order replacements, when it could have been as easy as printing an extra set when you first got your machine.

The first thing I do when I get a new machine is I print a replacement set of printed parts, the files for which are normally provided by the manufacturer. If not, you can likely find them on Thingiverse. This is not much fun because the first day or two of printing will just be these parts, and not anything cool for yourself.

Keep these parts to the side and hope you will never need them, but you will be happy you did this if you ever do. I have kicked myself plenty of times in the past when I did not do this.

## Slow your printer down

Many printing issues can be fixed or diagnosed easier if you run your machine a bit slower. There are possibilities you can run into a nozzle clog by doing this, but in general, you will have a much higher success rate by printing a bit slower.

You can do this by reducing your print speed in your slicer settings and by reducing your machine's acceleration, both of which are described later in this book.

I personally run my machines much slower than the manufacturer advertises and what many makers say they print at.

## Save slicer profiles as you go

Every time you make a tweak to your slicer settings, you should save it as a new file, organized somewhere on your computer. This is a good practice so that you can go back to profiles you know have worked in the past and can save you an immense amount of time when printing a unique material you know you have successfully printed in the past.

You can personalize profiles to specific machines and for each material you are printing with. This is the best way to hone in and perfect your settings for any given filament.

If you don't do this, you can still load a profile from a G-code. You should save your G-codes in a manner that can easily be remembered if the particular slicer settings are needed in the future. Don't just call your G-codes "Print 5" in a generic folder, since you will not be able to easily recall it later in the future.

## Properly store your filament

Filament, especially nylon mixtures, can absorb and maintain moisture when kept in a humid environment. This is why when you purchase a new spool, the filament will always be vacuum sealed with desiccants.

If you do not plan on using your filament for some time, you should properly store it with a dehumidifier or vacuum seal it. If you do not, you may start to experience failures on a spool you have used successfully in the past.

Almost all filament wants to be stored in as close to 0% humidity as possible. I would set my dehumidifier to the lowest setting – 20% - which always worked great. I used to live in a very dry area where humidity rarely gets above 30%, so I did not have to deal with this nearly as much as someone living in a very humid area of the world. Now that I have moved to Texas I have to be much more careful in preserving my material.

## Always watch the first layer of your print before leaving unattended

This is a very important tip. Never start a print and just walk away before watching that first layer print. Even with a $5,000 machine with auto levelling, and a technician with a lot of experience, it would be inadvisable to not watch this first layer print.

Any issue with finding the proper Z-height can lead to a failed print that can damage your machine. If the print starts too close to the build plate, you may have to kiss your build plate and nozzle goodbye. If the print starts too far from the build plate, you are going to have a massive cleanup on your hands.

I would guess that 75% of the failures I experience can be diagnosed from the first layer. This is the fastest set of failures to diagnose, but if you don't watch the first layer printing, you will be left with quite a lot of headaches. To this day I watch 100% of my prints first layer before leaving the machine unattended.

# Dedicate specific machines to particular materials if possible

If you happen to be able to own a few printers, I suggest designating particular machines (or at least hotends) to specific materials. If a machine only prints PLA, it will run into less issues than the same printer that runs many different materials. Switching materials can leave debris, different printing and build plate temperatures can require Z-height calibration, and different abrasive materials can cause the need for different types of nozzles.

I understand this is not possible for those who only have 1 or 2 printers, just keep in mind that every time you switch to a different type of material you will have different tweaks you need to make.

# Don't get frustrated

3D printing can involve more annoyances than you may have first imagined. It might take you 20 re-prints just to hone in the proper Z-height and to level your build plate, if you are not used to the machine. Or you may start a 28 hour print that decides to clog 26 hours in.

There are countless ways that 3D printing can end up leaving you frustrated, but it is key to keep calm. Remember that there is a solution to the problem you are having and you just need to properly diagnose it.

# Diagram of a 3D Printer

** *Reminder* ** All photos in this book, including the diagram below, may have been printed in poor quality for your edition, which was out of my control. If you would like high definition color photos, as well as a PDF version, just email me at Sean@3DPrintGeneral.com with proof of purchase and I will send them your way.

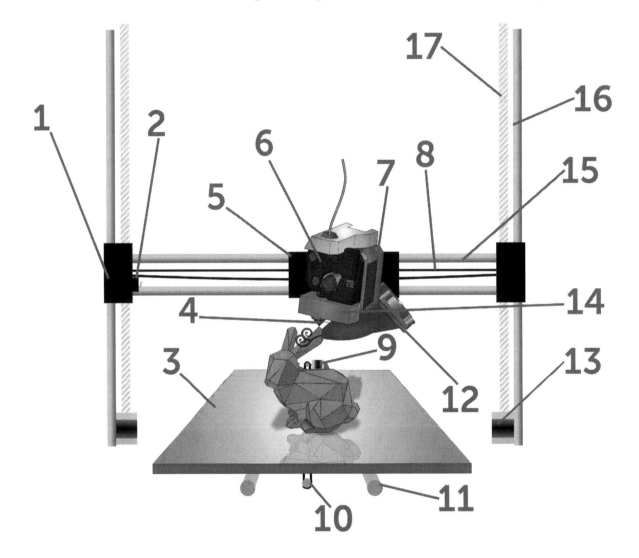

    **1. Z Carriage.** This connects to both the Z rod and threaded rod/leadscrew. The leadscrew then turns due to the stepper motor it is attached to, which then moves the x carriage up and down. On Bowden machines this is often where the extruder is attached.

    **2. X Endstop.** This is what tells the hotend to stop when homing. There is also a Y and Z endstop not shown in this picture which have the same function (though a Z endstop may be replaced by an auto bed leveler).

**3. Build plate.** This can be either glass, PEI, or another form of build plate. This is where the prints stick to.

**4. Nozzle.** Filament is fed through a heated nozzle in order to form your print. These can be found with different diameter holes, with the smaller the hole, the finer the detail. Nozzles range from 0.15mm – 1.4mm in diameter. They also come in brass, hardened steel, and ruby tip, with each becoming more abrasive resistant and more expensive.

**5. X Carriage.** This is where the hotend (and printers with direct extruders) attach to. The X carriage is attached to the X rods and belt which then in turn move the hotend in the X direction. This carriage should be very secured and not have any rattling.

**6. Extruder.** This is how the filament is fed into the nozzle. In this example I am showing a non-geared direct extruder. A geared extruder will have a gear-ratio allowing for less stress to be placed on the stepper motor, also adding a mechanical advantage for more torque, allowing the filament to be fed faster. The extruder includes a tooth drive attached to the stepper motor that pinches the filament against a bearing that freely spins. There are dual drive extruders as well which replace this bearing with another tooth drive. This extruder can also be placed on the Z carriage in a Bowden fashion.

**7. Extruder Stepper Motor.** The extruder stepper is what turns and feeds filament through the extruder. This would be placed on the Z carriage when on a Bowden setup. This is what you are controlling when you set the E-Steps. When using a geared-extruder, you put less strain on this stepper motor by giving it a mechanical advantage, which would result in less extruder motor skips. It would be smart to place a heat sink on this in order to disperse heat.

**8. X Carriage Belt.** This is what is connected to the X carriage as to move it left and right in the X direction. This belt should be tight/springy to the touch as to reduce Z-wobble.

**9. Y Stepper Motor.** This stepper motor moves the bed back and forth in the Y direction by controlling the Y carriage belt. This is only present in this fashion on Cartesian machines.

**10. Y Carriage Belt.** This is the belt that is connected to the build plate and is controlled by the Y stepper motor and spins freely on a bearing on the other side. Just as with the X carriage belt, this should be tight and springy to the touch.

**11. Y Smooth Rods.** These rods are what the Y carriage are attached to via bearings and are smooth to the touch. They help to make sure the build plate moves smoothly back and forth without rattling. These rods should be lubricated with white lithium grease so that the build plate can move without resistance. These can be replaced with a rail system instead on particular machines.

**12. Active Cooling Fan.** This fan is used to cool prints as layers are being laid down. This is crucial to use to get clean prints with particular materials, including PLA. This can lead to decreased layer adhesion on other particular materials, so you need to confirm the material you are using before turning it on in your slicer settings.

**13. Z Stepper Motor.** On some machines there is only one Z stepper motor, but there are dual steppers in this example. This stepper motor turns the Z leadscrew (or thin threaded rod) and moves the X and Z Carriage up and down, via where it is connected to the Z carriage (1 in photo). This is different on CoreXY machines, since those move the build plate up and down instead of the hotend.

**14. Heaterblock of Hotend.** This is the part of the hotend that gets hot and is attached to the heater. This is attached to the nozzle below it, and the barrel above it (with a heatbreak in between). The barrel should always have a fan blowing on it to prevent heat creep, though one is not shown in this picture.

**15. X Smooth Rods.** These rods are what the X carriage holds onto via bearings and are smooth to the touch. They help to make sure the hotend move smoothly left and right without rattling. These rods should be lubricated with white lithium grease so that the carriage can move without resistance. These can be replaced with a rail system on particular machines.

**16. Z Smooth Rods.** These are what your Z carriage is attached to via bearings in order to ensure the Z carriages are moved up and down smoothly without rattling. They should remain lubricated just like the X and Y smooth rods as to ensure there is as little friction with the bearings as possible. These can also be replaced with a rail system on particular machines.

**17. Z Leadscrew (or threaded rod).** These are threaded rods ranging from 5mm-10mm in diameter, with 8mm seeming to be the most common. Many inexpensive machines only have one of these, but I have found when there are dual leadscrews you get more consistent results. These are turned via the Z stepper motors which then thread into the Z carriages – moving the Z and X carriages up and down. These have essentially the same function for the Z carriages as the belts have for the X and Y carriage. They are threaded rods though because more weight is placed on these parts, and less frequent moving is required out of the Z direction. In general, the thicker these leadscrews are, the better. Thin 5mm threaded rods can become bent and do not last long on 3D printers. This is what moves the build plate up and down on CoreXY machines.

# Diagnosing Failures

Don't forget to email me at Sean@3DPrintGeneral.com with proof of purchase for HD photos.

## Nozzle Too Close To Buildplate

**Check Chapters:**
- Z-Height Calibration (p. 264)
- Unlevelled Build Plate (p. 242)

## Nozzle Too Far From Buildplate

**Check Chapters:**
- Z-Height Calibration (p. 265)
- Unlevelled Build Plate (p. 242)

## Uneven Build Surface

**Check Chapters:**
- Unlevelled Build Plate (p. 242)

## Spaghetti Monster

**Check Chapters:**
- Bed Adhesion (p. 18)
- Parts Being Knocked Over (p. 174)
- Z-Height Calibration (p. 264)

## Built Up Material On Nozzle

**Check Chapters:**
- Built Up Material in Nozzle (p. 35)

## Nozzle Clogs

**Check Chapters:**
- Nozzle Clogs (p. 157)
- Settings Issues (p. 207)
- Bed Adhesion for Above Issue (p. 25)

## Ghost Printing

**Check Chapters:**
- Nozzle Clogs (p. 157)
- Stripped Filament (p. 237)
- Settings Issues (p. 207)
- Material and their Settings (p. 106)
- Mandatory Maintenance (p. 104)

## Filament Snaps

**Check Chapters:**
- Filament Snaps (p. 58)
- Settings Issues (p. 207)
- Material and their Settings (p. 106)

## Running Out Of FIlament

**Check Chapters:**
- Running Out of Filament (p. 204)

## Endstop Not Engaging

**Check Chapters:**
- Not Finding Home (p. 153)

## Error: MINTEMP

**Check Chapters:**
- Hotend Not Reading Correct Temperature (p. 78)

## Hotend Not Heating

**Check Chapters:**
- Hotend Not Heating (p. 74)

## Hotend Cannot Reach Set Temp

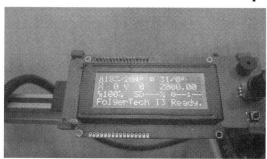

**Check Chapters:**
- Hotend Cannot Reach or Maintain Temperature (p. 69)

## Build Plate Not Heating

**Check Chapters:**
- Build Plate Not Heating (p. 29)

## Build Plate Not Reading Temp

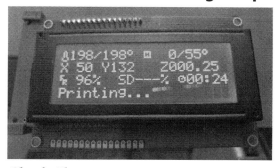

**Check Chapters:**
- Build Plate Not Reading Correct Temperature (p. 33)

## LCD Screen Dark

**Check Chapters:**
- LCD Blank or Dark (p. 97)

## Black Spots On Print

**Check Chapters:**
- Built up Material in Nozzle (p. 35)
- Material and their Settings (p. 106)

## "Wobbly" Print

**Check Chapters:**
- Z-Axis Wobble (p. 254)

## Single Layer Shift

**Check Chapters:**
- Layer Shifts (p. 87)

## Multiple Layer Shifts

**Check Chapters:**
- Layer Shifts (p. 89)

## Over Extrusion

**Check Chapters:**
- Over and Under Extrusion (p. 165)

## Under Extrusion

**Check Chapters:**
- Over and Under Extrusion (p. 167)

## Parts To Wrong Dimensions

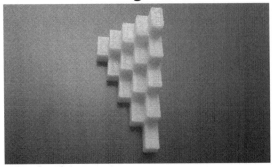

**Check Chapters:**
- Parts Not Mating Together (p. 179)

## Parts Not Mating Together

**Check Chapters:**
- Parts Not Mating Together (p. 179)
- Over and Under Extrusion - Over Extrusion (p. 165)

## Warping

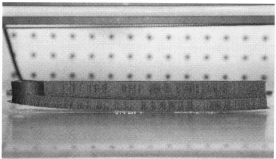

**Check Chapters:**
- Warping (p. 248)
- Material Science (p. 123)
- Bed Adhesion (p. 18)

## Layer Delamination

**Check Chapters:**
- Warping (p. 248)
- Material Science (p. 123)
- Over and Under Extrusion - Under Extrusion (p. 167)

## Poor Layer Adhesion

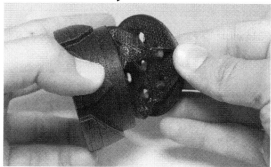

**Check Chapters:**
- Poor Layer Adhesion (p. 185)
- Over and Under Extrusion - Under Extrusion (p. 167)
- Settings Issues (p. 208)

## Ugly Top of Print

**Check Chapters:**
- Settings Issues - Lift Head Cooling (p. 219)

## "Pitted" Top Side Of Print

**Check Chapters:**
- Settings Issues - Shell and Fill Settings (p. 210 p. 212)

## Ugly Underside Of Print

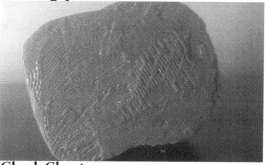

**Check Chapters:**
- Settings Issues - Support Settings (p. 220)

## "Hairy" Prints

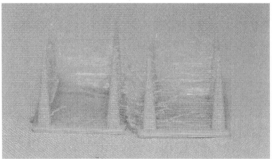

**Check Chapters:**
- Settings Issues - Material Retraction (p. 214)
- Material and their Settings (p. 106)
- Material Science (p. 123)

## Droopy/Ugly Undersides

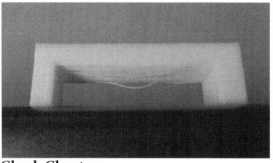

**Check Chapters:**
- Settings Issues - Support Settings (p. 220)
- Material and their Settings (p. 106)
- Material Science (p. 123)

## Text Not Legible

**Check Chapters:**
- Parts Not Mating (p. 179)
- Over and Under Extrusion - Over Extrusion (p. 165)
- Quality Options (p. 200)

## "Veiny" Print

**Check Chapters:**
- Settings Issues - Infill Overlap (p. 212)
- Ghosting (p. 65)

## Ghosting

**Check Chapters:**
- Ghosting (p. 65)

## Stripped Filament

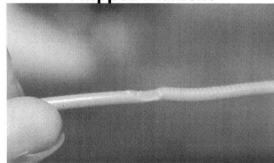

**Check Chapters:**
- Stripped Filament (p. 237)

## Elephant Foot

**Check Chapters:**
- Elephant Foot (p. 46)

## Gaps in Walls

**Check Chapters:**
- Gaps in Walls (p. 61)

## Missing Layers

**Check Chapters:**
- Missing Layers (p. 144)

## House on Fire

**Check Chapters:**
- Electrical Safety (p. 41)

# Bed Adhesion

Having proper bed adhesion is crucial to any successful print. Using different materials, nozzle diameters, layer heights, and 3D models can lead to the need for different slicer settings and manual calibration for proper bed adhesion. While the issue may be frequent, it can normally be diagnosed early on into the print. The few times you lose bed adhesion mid print, it can lead to big issues, so make sure you take the proper precautions.

These tips are also crucial in avoiding any warping on your parts, as mentioned in that chapter.

## Understanding the material you are using

Not only does each material affect your bed adhesion and settings required, each manufacturer can as well. I highly recommend against using low quality filament brands since their tolerances, humidity, and reliability are frequently subpar. I personally use Hatchbox, Overture, Polymaker, or AIO Robotics for PLA, Fiberlogy and MatterHackers for PETG, 3DXTech and MatterHackers for carbon fiber blends, taulman3D and Polymaker for unique nylons, and NinjaTek for their various flexible materials. There are many other reputable manufacturers as well, but I have found I like these companies best out of the ones I have personally tested. Read reviews before buying any material. Further information in this regard are included in the "Material and their Settings" chapter, as well as the "Material Science" chapter.

You may also be able to switch to a different material with similar mechanical features but with better bed adhesion properties, as gone over further in the "Warping" chapter.

## Slow down the speed on your first layer and turn off active cooling fan

Having your first layer extrude properly is needed to making sure that the rest of the print follows suit. Even after 5 years of experience and using higher end FDM machines, I will always watch the first layer to make sure it prints properly. If you just decide to start a print and walk away, you can come back to a very messy or warped print.

You will want to confirm that your first layer is running very slowly compared to the rest of your print (30%-60% print speed or ~20-30mm/s), and that no active cooling fan is on.

This makes sure that the first layer has its best chance of sticking to the bed, which is the most difficult layer for adhesion on any material.

# Have a heated build plate

If you want the best adhesion possible, you are going to need a heated build plate. You may be able to get away with printing specific materials without a heated build plate, but even PLA sticks better when the bed is heated to around its glass transition temperature.

The glass transition temperature of a material is always lower than the extrusion temperature and relates to when the material starts to become viscous without actually going through a phase transition. When the material becomes slightly viscous, it will be able to stick to the build plate much easier. This may cause an "Elephant Foot" issue, so refer to that chapter if experiencing this problem.

Below are the temperatures I set my heated build plate for various materials. Please keep in mind you will need to have your board actively cooled in order to have your bed reach and maintain some of these temperatures, and always refer to your specific manufacturers recommendations.

**PLA:** 50 - 60°C

**ABS:** 105°C

**PETG:** 50 - 80°C

**CFR-ABS:** 105°C

**CFR-Nylon:** 80°C

**Cheetah by NinjaTek:** 40°C

**Ninjaflex:** 50°C

**PCTPE:** 45°C on a glass bed with a coat of PVA

**Nylon 910:** 45°C on a glass bed with a coat of PVA

**Polymaker PolyMide CoPA:** 60°C

**Polycarbonate ABS:** 120°C bed (and can only print in an enclosed machine)

# Clean your bed before applying anything

Fingerprints and residue from previous prints on the plate can prevent the first layer from sticking to the plate properly. Isopropyl alcohol is used to properly clean uncoated glass and PEI beds, while acetone can be used on glass (most PEI beds will be ruined with acetone, so be careful when using that material). As mentioned below, when cleaning a PVA solution you should only use soap and water, since that is what it is soluble in.

PEI beds require a clean surface in order to stick properly, and glass will always perform better after being cleaned, so make sure you clean this plate every 5-10 prints.

# Having a proper initial Z-height

This is likely the most important step in getting a good first layer. The initial Z-height refers to how far the nozzle is from the build plate. You can easily imagine that if you start a print with your nozzle an inch off of the build plate that the material will not stick.

This is also covered in the "Unlevelled Build Plate" chapter, but essentially the distance from the nozzle to the build plate needs to be honed in based off the initial layer height. A good starting point should have the nozzle roughly the thickness of a piece of paper in distance from the build plate.

This means that you can home your printer and grab a piece of computer paper. You should be able to slide the piece of paper under the nozzle with a slight amount of drag. If you cannot slide the paper under the nozzle, it is likely too close to the build plate, and if you get no resistance, the nozzle is likely too high.

While this is a go-to method, it does need tweaking depending on your initial layer height. I have actually gotten to the point where it is easiest for me to visually determine the proper layer height. Below are a couple of comparison photos, but essentially if the material is spreading out, the nozzle is too close, and if there is a gap between layer lines, it is too far. (Remember that if you have difficulty seeing the photos to contact me at Sean@3DPrintGeneral.com with proof of purchase and I will send high quality photos).

Too Close          Just Right          Too Far

# Glass bed

When printing, I personally use a glass bed. Glass is far superior to acrylic due to its ability to remain flat and its lack of warping while heated. I prefer to use a 1/4" thick glass bed rather than the standard 1/8" glass, though it will add weight to your Y carriage on a Cartesian machine.

There are various methods to get your part to stick to a glass bed, since heating alone will not do the trick. These are NOT needed when printing with a PEI build plate.

*Hair Spray:* This is my preferred method since it seems to work quite well and allows for the bottom of the print to retain a high quality shine. Honing in on the right hair spray is important and I have settled with Aqua Net Unscented Extra Super Hold. Make sure to always proceed with caution though, because hair spray is very flammable.

Apply a thin coat as if you were spray painting your bed. You should do this with your machine off, or with all fans covered as to not have the ambient spray be sucked into your hotend assembly. If possible, remove the glass plate and add the hair spray away from the printer, so that the sticky substance does not get onto the rest of your machine. Be sure to avoid spraying the rods, because they should remain as lubricated as possible.

Allow the hair spray to dry, heat the bed, and your parts should now stick with a lot more ease. Removal of these parts is normally quite easy as well, just wait for the bed to cool to room temperature. If you wait until room temperature, and you start your print the proper distance from the build plate, it will actually pop off without much effort at all.

You will run into issues on large ABS and other high internal stress materials when it comes to warping. Applying hair spray will work for most circular shaped ABS parts, but any model with corners and a high density will experience warping, unless you switch to a different material or method of bed adhesion.

**Blue Painters Tape:** I do not use this method any longer but it will definitely work if you are having a lot of issues with your print sticking to the bed. This method is pretty much required if you are printing on a non-heated build plate.

Just grab a roll of blue painter's tape and apply it evenly to your build surface, while it is at room temperature. Apply as flat as possible and remove all bubbles. You may have to raise your Z-Height if you were previously printing straight onto the build plate, since your nozzle will now drag on the tape during its first layer.

Most materials will stick great to blue painters tape, but removal of these parts can be quite a hassle. Not only will the underside surface not maintain a high quality look, attempting to scrape off the part can come to the point where you rip the tape along with the print, creating quite a lot of post cleanup.

You will still run into difficulty with large ABS parts, but not as much as you would with only hair spray.

**Glue Stick:** I really do not recommend this method, but if you are extremely frustrated after using the above two methods, you can give this a go. Parts stick very well when you evenly rub a glue stick onto surface of your build plate.

This method requires a lot of cleanup, does not allow for a clean underside, and makes the parts quite hard to remove.

This can also be used for some nylon prints, assuming the glue stick is a PVA base.

**ABS Slurry:** If you are printing a large, dense, and rectangular ABS part without any enclosures or special build plates on your machine, you will almost certainly need an ABS slurry. Please keep in mind I almost never do this anymore, since I have switched to either PETG, PolyMide CoPA, or other materials rather than printing in ABS in order to avoid this annoyance. ABS is not nearly as common in the 3D printing world as it once was due to the emergence of these materials over the past few years.

To make an ABS slurry, grab a clean non-chemical reactant bottle, such as a disposable water bottle or glass mason jar (must have a sealed lid) , then toss in bits of ABS. You will want to use the same color ABS of the print you will be fabricating. You can use failed prints, past support material, or just break parts of the filament up right off the spool.

You will want to then add roughly 100mL of acetone per 10g of filament. This is why it is crucial that you are using a container that is not reactant to acetone. Then seal the container tight and wait a few hours until the large chunks of filament are dissolved, and you are left with a nice slurry.

You will then brush this slurry onto a room temperature build plate. Make sure it is not heated because acetone vaporizes at low temperatures, is flammable, and is not good for your health.

You can now print large ABS parts without much issues. The bottom of these parts will not be clean and you will still experience layer separations if printing a tall piece in an unenclosed printer. You will only get one print from this coat of slurry, so you will then have to clean the build plate and reapply. Cleaning consists of acetone and a decent amount of scrubbing.

Be very careful when using this method with a glass bed. The adhesion to the bed will be extreme and it is not uncommon for glass beds to shatter or chip when attempting to remove a part that is particularly stuck to the surface. Use safety glasses and cut resistant gloves if using this method with a glass plate.

To be honest, due to the extreme difficulty of printing ABS without warping, I have essentially switched to PETG and Carbon Fiber blends when I need a strong mechanical part. I haven't made an ABS slurry in nearly 3 years.

*Coat of PVA:* As mentioned above, most of the nylon materials you work with will require a coat of PVA being applied to a glass plate. I personally just use Elmer's glue mixed with water.

While I have read mixtures of up to 8 parts water to 1 part PVA, I actually go all the way up to 1 to 1. Get a cup and add some standard Elmer's glue, and then add roughly the equal amount of water. Mix this up thoroughly and then paint it onto the build plate when at room temperature.

This will be very liquidity so you will want to then heat your build plate to 45°C (or whatever temperature your print material calls for), and the water will evaporate slowly. Do not start your print until you have a dry surface. It will take about 5-10 minutes to evaporate entirely.

Your nylon parts should now stick much easier. You can also use this method for PLA and ABS, though I personally do not. In order to clean off this PVA you do not want to use alcohol or acetone, since it is not soluble in those. Just use soapy water to clean PVA off your build plate.

I have had difficulty on a couple of nylon mixtures, and ended up resorting to a glue stick, so keep that in mind as backup.

***Third Party Sticky Sheets:*** There are a few companies that make sheets that are applied to your glass build plate. These advertise high bed adhesion with easy removal. But, from what I have found, most of these products allow your part to stick very well, but do not allow for easy removal.

The majority of these products will only last for around a dozen prints because it is extremely difficult to remove parts without damaging the sheet. I do personally use these though for when I have a lot of prints that have a very small surface area touching the build plate (imagine a print bed of 100 skinny posts). I would normally have to use a brim for these types of prints, but it can literally add hours of cleanup when across hundreds of parts.

Using these sheets allow for me to print these specific parts without any brim or fear that anything will get knocked over.

I have a BuildTak bed sheet on one of my machines, and while it works pretty well, I almost never use it, the only exception being the thin small parts mentioned earlier. Removing parts is very difficult and I have found that glass with hair spray works easiest. Keep in mind that these sheets will likely not work with Nylons.

TH3D Studio offers EZMats which are similar to Buidtak, but should be easier to use. I personally have not tested these though.

# PEI bed

Some printers come with what is called a PEI bed, or you can purchase one separately. These can be full beds or sheets that you apply, but they must be used on heated build plates only. A PEI bed will essentially create small suction cups when heated - which will help parts to stick, and then become flat when cooled - allowing for very simple removal. The major benefit to using a PEI bed is that, unlike glass, it does not require surface preparation before printing (aside from keeping it clean from normal dust and debris).

You will always want to wait until your part is easy to remove or until the build plate is at room temperature before attempting any removal. If you do not, you will be far more likely to damage this very delicate material. I have broken a few PEI beds in the past, so be careful. You will definitely want to make sure you have the proper initial Z-height, since printing too close can really damage the material.

You will also want to periodically clean this bed with alcohol, otherwise you will slowly lose adhesion properties. I suggest cleaning every 5 prints. If you notice parts are not sticking like they once did, cleaning can normally fix this. Do not ever use acetone to clean a PEI bed, since it will remove the adhesion properties.

High quality PEI beds are normally pretty expensive, can be easily scratched by the nozzle and will all eventually degrade from normal use over a few hundred prints. Lower cost PEI films will bubble up, and eventually will get torn from repeated removal - but over the course of a hundred prints you will likely need to replace this part. I personally do not use PEI beds any longer, but some of the best printers come with these stock. There have been improvements in this regard since the last time I used one, so it may be worth trying one out if you are inclined to.

## Using a brim

A brim refers to the lines around the print that act as an anchor. This will be needed for all high internal stress materials such as ABS, and for most parts that have a very small surface area touching the build plate.

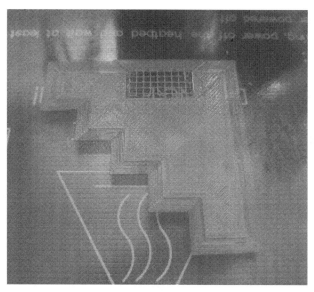

You can add a brim in your slicer settings, as explained further in the "Settings Issues" chapter. As you will read there, I prefer to only print a brim on the outside of a part. I do this because a standard brim will add anchor lines to every section of the print touching the build plate, including small holes. This adds for a lot of cleanup, and most prints only require this anchor to be applied to the outside perimeter.

How thick the brim is will be based off of the nozzle diameter. A brim of 15 lines will be twice as thick with a 0.8mm nozzle vs. a 0.4mm nozzle. For most parts requiring a brim I will use anywhere from 10-30 lines. Anything more than this is unnecessary.

If this brim doesn't help with very small parts being knocked over, you can try using a raft, as explained further in the "Settings Issues" chapter.

## Initial layer thickness (horizontal expansion)

You can also increase the thickness of the first layer of the print in order to help bed adhesion. This is not preferred because it will tweak the tolerances of the bottom of your print by the amount you increased. If you have pieces that must mate together, you should not proceed with this method.

If you are OK with the bottom layer being slightly thicker than the rest of your print, this method definitely works to help anchor your part and increase bed adhesion.

You can also make this number negative, reducing the elephant foot issue, as covered in that chapter.

## Initial Layer Height

Rather than tweaking the initial layer thickness, you can tweak the initial layer height to help the first layer lay down properly. If you are printing at 0.1mm layer heights, it is very difficult to get the first layer to stick. The lower the layer height, the more precise your Z-height needs to be. If your bed is not perfectly flat, (which is extremely common, particularly on larger printers) then you may need to use this parameter to get any successful prints to adhere to the bed.

I have standardized to having the first layer be 0.25mm – 0.3mm on a 0.4mm nozzle, so that I have a lot more leeway on the initial Z-height. This means my first layer will be 0.25mm - 0.3mm, while the rest will be lower for a higher quality print.

The rare times I use a 0.15mm or 0.25mm nozzle, this number is much lower, but still roughly 3x the layer height of the rest of the print. Getting the first layer to stick on a 0.15mm nozzle and 0.05mm layer heights is a task that will definitely give you a headache.

## What to do when this happens

What you see above is the result of an overnight print that lost its bed adhesion a couple of hours in. The ways to prevent this from happening are all of the methods mentioned earlier in this chapter, but once it happens, you have quite the cleanup on your hands.

If your issue is not quite as bad as mine, you can just heat the nozzle to a bit higher than extrusion temperatures, and clean up using a set of pliers. If it is as bad as mine, you may end up needing to purchase some new parts.

You will need to disassemble all of the parts affected. If you do not want to spend time torching material, you can just purchase a new hotend, thermistor, and heater and assemble them in. You will actually want to try and use a heat gun before a torch, it is just the material that I am using in my example has a very high melting temperature. Make sure to use a heat gun if you can in order to have a much higher chance of salvaging parts.

To salvage as many parts as possible, you will need to get to a well-ventilated area with a mask and torch. Make sure your affected areas are disconnected from the printer, or that the machine is off and disconnected.

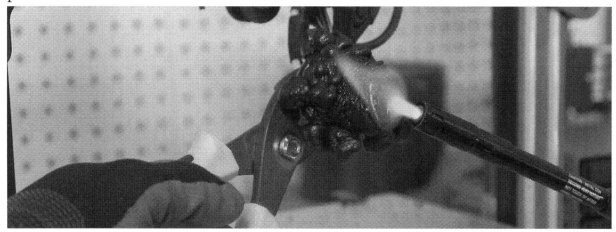

You need to clearly take the proper precautions here, but there isn't really an easier way to get this stuff off when it's this far gone. Make sure you avoid ALL wires, unless you just plan on replacing them. Essentially you just need to use your heat gun and slowly pull everything off. If you can't use a heat gun, torch for a couple of seconds, and then use your pliers to dig in.

After digging in for a few passes, you should be able to eventually get the entire chunk off at once. If you are able to heat your hotend, make sure it is hot for easiest removal (which is obviously not possible if you already cut the wires for replacement). Using a heat gun increases your chance of salvaging everything.

It ends up that I needed to use a new heater block, heater, and thermistor in this instance. Even after taking the time to remove the material from the heater block, I was unable to remove the heater and thermistor because the screws were stuck in place. I could have spent another couple of hours torching until everything could be removed, but I figured it was not worth the time.

You can purchase a replacement heater block, heater, and thermistor on Amazon or MatterHackers, and you will then need to re-connect it all. You can just cut the wires and then solder the new set. Please check the "Important Accessories and Replacements" chapter of this book for ways to connect wires.

Be careful assembling again, and reprint any parts you may need. It ends up I also needed a new barrel cooling fan, so make sure you purchase all replacement parts required. This need for new parts is why it is really important to get your bed adhesion right before walking away from it for hours at a time. Avoiding this 2 hours cleanup and $25 in parts is definitely the preferred method.

It is very possible you have a clogged nozzle or barrel after this, so if you do – follow the steps in that chapter.

I also have a video on this exact issue where I go into further detail – titled "Repairing a Gunked Up Hotend" on my 3D Print General YouTube channel.

## Summary of Fixes and Precautions:

- Know the material you are using (what are the print settings and limitations, including warping chances)
- Heat your build plate to either the glass transition temperature of the material you are using, or to a specific temperature suggested by the filament manufacturer
- Frequently clean your bed before applying any extra adhesion to remove fingerprints and residue from previous prints.
- Use either a ¼" glass build plate with a coat of hair spray, or a heated PEI bed without any extra adhesive substance
- Hone in the proper initial Z-height, since the first layer requires the nozzle be a proper distance from the build plate
- Create an ABS Slurry if you are printing a large ABS part in a non-enclosed printer on a glass bed
- Slow down the speed and turn off active cooling for your first layer
- Print with a brim if the corners are curling, parts are being knocked over, or if

you are experiencing warping

- Print with a raft to help even more than a brim
- Increase the initial layer thickness if having lots of problems with bed adhesion – though this is not really suggested on normal parts
- Increase the initial layer height to max out your nozzle diameter (75% the nozzle diameter) so that the tolerance on your initial Z-height is a lot easier to hone in.
- If you are left with an overnight mess on your hotend, use a heatgun to remove and clean everything.

# Build Plate Not Heating

As with your hotend not heating, this failure is very easy to diagnose since your build plate will not heat up, or will turn off instead of maintaining a temperature. It seems that this issue comes up more frequently than your extruder not heating because more power is required to heat your build plate due to its size. This is particularly true for Cartesian printers which require the bed to have high acceleration moves in the Y axis, which can accelerate wear on the wiring.

After you confirm you are using the correct volt/amp for your heater/board combination, you can move forward to checking the following issues.

Many of these instructions are similar to the "Hotend Not Heating" chapter in this book.

## Heater malfunctioning

The heater for your build plate is normally either a thick material stuck to the underside of your bed, or is its own separate surface. This heater will have thick gauged wire soldered onto it, which will transfer the power to provide heat.

The easiest diagnosis for when your heater is malfunctioning is to see if this connection has been frayed or destroyed. Frequent usage of your machine (especially Cartesian ones) or other unforeseen problems, can cause this cord to be pulled and tugged from its connection on your heater. Make sure your power is turned off and your machine is unplugged, then take your build plate off so you can easily see the underside of the heater. If you notice that a wire has been pulled from the bed, or is not connected strongly, you will have to solder it back on properly, or purchase a replacement connector.

Most heaters are very simple resistive elements, so it is pretty rare to find that the heater itself is not working. It is recommended to proceed to the next steps before purchasing a new one.

DO NOT REPLACE A HEATER CORD WITH A NORMAL SMALL GAUGED WIRE (thinner than 14 gauge) YOU WILL BE SUSCEPTIBLE TO A FIRE AND FURTHER BURNT OUT WIRES. KNOW THE AMPERAGE OF YOUR HEATER AND SIZE YOUR CORDS ACCORDINGLY.

## Burnt out connectors or wires

If the wires are connected to your build plate properly, you will want to check the cords for any disconnections or burnt out areas. When a build plate goes out, it is common for this to happen. When a connector or wire is burnt out you will not get any heating out of your build plate, unlike what I describe in the next section. This is something that has occurred on a few of the machines I have worked with.

If you find any burnt areas, you will have to cut that section off and solder the wires back together – making sure you get continuity on your multimeter after. Make sure to have your machine off and unplugged, and use the proper shrink wrap or correct gauge solder seal connectors. Absolutely no metal can be exposed after this process. Then confirm that the build plate can reach its farthest point from the board, because you just made the wire shorter than it was.

If your newly soldered wire cannot reach the board at the build plate's farthest point, you will experience layer shifts on large builds. In this case, it would be recommended to replace the entire wiring harness or add a length of wire to the harnesses after cutting out the burnt section. Avoid accumulating multiple solder joints on a single wiring harness as that will lead to increased resistance on the line and lower heating times. If replacing the wire, grab the correct gauge and see if you can get a wire with flexible silicone insulation to help prevent this from occurring in the future.

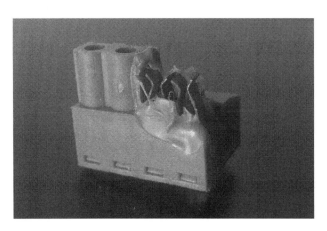

If you see that the connector that is plugged into the board is burnt out, you will need to replace it.

This is extremely common on the power input for RAMPS boards, and can be referred to as a design flaw. The connector that comes with the board is easily overheated and can melt, which is exactly what happened to me on one printer that I built. I had no active cooling fan on the board, so if I didn't notice it early, I could have had a real issue on my hands.

Historically, RepRap boards don't use connectors that are rated high enough. If you are using a RAMPS board, I can't suggest enough that you upgrade the board terminals to a well-made 16A replacement (which can be found at Digikey or Mouser). This should not be an issue on most pre-built machines, and more common if you were to build one yourself.

Remember that the area you are replacing may have some melted plastic, so you will need to clean it out entirely before attempting to reconnect. If replacing the connector does not fix this burnt out area, you may unfortunately need to replace the entire board.

Only after everything is wired properly and there is no exposed metal should you plug everything back on and test to confirm the build plate is heating again.

## Board overheating

During this particular failure the bed will normally start to heat - and then randomly turn off. This may not even cause a failed print at all - depending on when the heater goes out, how large your model is, what bed adhesions you are using, and what material you are printing with. When your board overheats mid print, you likely will not have a lot of cleanup on your hands -as you would when the hotend loses heat - but you can experience a warped part.

If you only pay attention to the beginning of a print and then come back when it is completed, you may not even notice that your board overheated. Run a print on a hot build plate (such as printing in ABS) and pay attention to when, and if, the heated build plate starts dropping in temperature.

You can normally tell if this is happening by checking the temperature of your board when the heater cuts out. Be careful though, because if the board is overheating, it will be hot enough to burn your fingers.

I go over a few of these methods elsewhere in this book, but if you are experiencing a board that is overheating, you will need to get 1-3 active fans blowing right onto it. If your board is enclosed with the rest of the machine, the build plate heating will drastically affect the ambient air temperature, causing much more frequent times your board can overheat. This is why you will want your board located outside of any enclosed printers. Small heat sinks will always help affected areas, but from what I can tell, setting up some active fans make the biggest difference.

Most manufacturers come with fans blowing on the board stock, but they can go out or not blow as fast as they should over time. Make sure to regularly check that any active cooling fans are free from excessive dust and debris, which can cause them to fail.

If your board is constantly overheating, or you are using a RAMPS board with thousands of hours of printing on it, you will want to replace it entirely. RAMPS boards are normally extremely cheap at under $10, but higher end boards such as a Rambo board may be closer to $150. These higher end boards will experience less overheating when wired correctly.

Purchasing a printer from a reputable manufacturer, such as the ones covered in the "Resources" chapter, should not experience these issues, though you will periodically want to confirm the fans are blowing properly.

## Purchase a new heated build plate

As mentioned earlier, it is very rare that you will need to do this. In fact, I have used over 20 machines for over 75,000 hours of printing and have only had to replace two heated build plates. Since these are normally a bit more expensive than replacing many other parts, confirm that you have tested all of the above methods before purchasing a replacement.

## Build plate will only heat

I decided to throw this in even though it is a bit of the exact opposite problem as the rest of this chapter, I just wasn't sure where to include it. If your build plate decides to start heating when you turn on the machine, without telling it to heat, then you have a faulty MOSFET. The MOSFET that controls the board failed, and when they fail they normally turn to "ON", which means the board will attempt to heat right when you turn on the printer.

If the MOSFET is attached to your board, you will unfortunately need to swap the entire board. If the MOSFET is external, you can go ahead and change it.

## Summary of Fixes and Precautions

- Confirm you are using the correct Volt/Amp for your heated build plate/board.
- Check to see if cords have been ripped off or have poor connection to the build plate.
- Check for visual damage (burnt out cords/connectors).
- Solder or rewire sections of wire that are disconnected or burnt out – always using the proper gauge.
- Confirm you have connectivity in the wires from the board to the heated build plate via a multimeter.
- Replace any burnt out connectors to the board.
- Actively cool your board.
- Replace board if overused or burnt out.
- Replace MOSFET if your build plate will start heating without you telling it to, and replace the whole board if the MOSFET is onboard.

# Build Plate Not Reading Correct Temperature

At times this problem can be pretty difficult to diagnose, and just like when your hotend isn't reading the proper temperature, if left unattended it can lead some serious issues.

These instructions are very similar to the "Hotend Not Reading Correct Temperature" chapter.

## Build plate reading 0° or you receive a bed not heating error

There is a thermistor for your heated build plate that works as a thermometer - and just with the hotend's thermistor - it can become damaged or disconnected. These thermistors are not very expensive, but can be difficult to replace on certain setups - so while it is good to have a spare, you will likely want to test everything else first.

If your thermistor has no physical damage that you can see, you will want to check for continuity in the wire. If there is a frayed wire, or a section of a wire you can diagnose has no continuity via a multimeter, you can cut and solder skipping the section – or rewire entirely. If your thermistor is still intact, replacing the wiring will likely fix your issue. When repairing the wiring you will then need to confirm that the build plate can reach its farthest point from the board, because you just made the wire shorter than it was.

If your newly soldered wire cannot reach the board at the build plate's furthest point, you will experience layer shifts on large builds.

Note: if you are in a pinch, soldering the thermistor line will work but it may lead to additional process issues since you are changing the resistive value of that line and therefore the temperature that the board is reading. Your material profiles may require slightly different temperatures after doing this. It is typically recommended to completely replace this section of the wiring if possible.

## Confirm thermistor is attached properly

Well-built machines will have their thermistors attached snugly to the build plate, but cheaper machines may only be held onto your heated platform by some Kapton tape. Constant moving and shaking of your build plate can make it so this tape becomes disconnected, and your thermistor will inevitably shake out of its holder.

This will cause your thermistor to read a lower temperature than your build plate actually is, since it is not actually touching it. This problem can become severe if the thermistor gets far enough from the build plate, which can cause your heated platform to continue to rise in temperature until your board overheats.

You need to confirm that your thermistor is attached properly to the build plate and that there is no chance of it being ripped out mid print.

Having a build plate that is off by 5 degrees typically will not really affect the quality of your print, but it can definitely become an issue when the differential gets more than this.

## Still experiencing issues

If you are still experiencing issues, or you notice that your bed is continually 10 or more degrees off from where it should be, you will likely want to replace your thermistor and rewire it from the build plate to the board.

If the problem continues, flash your machine with the original firmware, and then replace the board if necessary. Replacing the board should be a last case solution.

## Summary of Fixes and Precautions

- Make sure the thermistor is actually connected to the build plate and not hovering next to it.
- If thermistor is noticeably damaged, replace it.
- Check for breaks or frays in your wire and solder or rewire as needed.
- Make sure that if you do rewire, you give enough slack to allow the build plate to move to its farthest point.
- Replace and rewire thermistor from the heated platform all the way to the board.
- Flash firmware to factory settings.
- If still malfunctioning - replace board.

# Built Up Material in Nozzle

If you do not have a specific hotend for every material you are using, you will likely experience some black dots on your prints from time to time. Even when you are using only one material, this can still be a frequent occurrence.

One of the biggest issues with this failure is that you will often not be able to diagnose it until it happens. This means that a black spot might show up on an important section of your piece 10+ hours in. This is why it is crucial you maintain the cleanliness of your hotend by frequently purging and cold pulling out any residue from your nozzle, along with using a nylon brush.

## Ensure your hotend and nozzle is set up properly and tight

Every hotend setup needs to be assembled in a slightly different fashion, but nearly all of them require you to not over-tighten. This precaution to not over-tighten can lead to gaps between the nozzle and heater block if you assembled everything while at room temperature.

When the heater rises in temperature, the metal expands and can cause your once tight nozzle/heater block to actually have minor gaps. This gap can cause material to ooze out and make its way onto your print. Since this material has been stuck on a hot nozzle before finally being pushed onto your model, it will likely be black and burnt, regardless of the color you are using.

If you notice that your heater block is loose when hot, or that you constantly have to brush off the nozzle or hotend from excess material, you will likely need to tighten these parts.

I always suggest doing the final tightening of your nozzle and heater block when heated to 240°C, using proper gloves and tools. Remember that you have a high chance of burning yourself, so only do this with extreme caution.

You also want to make sure to not over-tighten anything. I have broken quite a few heater blocks, nozzles, and heat break barrels due to over-tightening and not being careful. These parts, especially when hot, can easily snap under pressure. When you are doing this, make sure to only tighten until you know that the nozzle and heat block are not loose, and will not unscrew during the print.

If you still are experiencing material oozing from the gap between your nozzle and heater block you will likely need to upgrade or replace your nozzle, heater block, or entire hotend. Poorly made or worn out parts will not have tight tolerances, and can lead to these gaps in your threads. I have seen images of cheap knockoff products cut in half showing just how poor their tolerances are.

This is why it is important to only purchase name brand parts and not to buy Chinese aftermarket knock-offs. For example, if you want an E3D hotend, only purchase from verified dealers such as E3D, Filastruder or Matterhackers because there are many counterfeit products on the market. Matterhackers is a good source for most 3D printing parts.

## Purging material

Every time you switch filaments, after very long prints, or when switching between different materials, you are going to want to purge out the material that may have oxidized inside of the hotend. There are a couple of ways that you can do this.

If you are using the same material, you can go ahead and heat the hotend to its printing temperature. You then push down the filament for about an inch, and then pull up quickly. Cut off the end and you should be good to go with your next print. Repeat this step as necessary if you are switching to a different color in order to ensure that you do not get any mixed colors during your print.

If you are switching to a material that prints at a higher temperature (such as switching from PLA to ABS) purging is normally simple. You will want to do the same procedure as above, just perhaps do it multiple times in order to confirm that no remaining residue within the hotend. If this hotter material is in a different color, then you will follow the same procedure, it will just be more apparent when you haven't purged enough. Since you are printing at a higher temperature, the majority of the previous material should be removed.

A real issue occurs when you are switching to a material that prints at a lower temperature than your previous filament (such as switching from ABS to PLA).

It is likely you will not be able to purge all of the residue material with the above method, because the ABS needs to be purged at a temperature it can properly extrude at.

If you like to live dangerously, you can purge this material by pushing the colder filament through the hotend when it is set to the higher temperature (such as extruding PLA at 235°C when switching from ABS). Push the material through at a steady pace and then pull it out very quickly, making sure to not let it sit. If you attempt this method, you are going to have a higher chance of a nozzle clog, and you may not get 100% of the residue material.

The proper way to get rid of this material would be to do a Cold Pull as described below, or to purge by using a cleaning filament/nylon material.

Purging with cleaning filament or nylon can be done by heating your extruder to a temperature of around 240°C – 250°C, and then extruding the cleaning filament through as you would with the examples above. Quickly pull the filament out as to not leave any residue, and you will see just how much gunk cleaning filament was able to pull out.

Though less common when using cleaning filament than with other printing materials, you still run the risk of leaving residual material in the hotend that will come out later as a black, burnt spot.

## Cold pull

When switching to a material that prints at a lower temperature than your previous filament you will likely want to do a cold pull. Cold pulls are also very beneficial to do as regular maintenance on your machine regardless.

I personally like to perform cold pulls with either a cleaning filament or Nylon mix, but you can perform them with the material you are trying to clear out. My favorite material to do this with is actually Nylon 910 by taulman3D. Not only is that material great to print with, it seems to work even better than cleaning filament I have used in the past for removing the oxidized material in the hotend.

What you will want to do is heat the hotend to the temperature of the material you are using to do the cold pull (250°C for Nylon 910). Push the filament through for an inch, or as much is required for you to no longer see the previous material coming out the nozzle.

Then quickly set your hotend to 140°C - 160°C. You don't want to leave the material sitting in the hotend for a long period of time because it can oxidize itself, or even cause heat creep in your barrel. Once the nozzle cools to this newly set temperature you will want to pull out the filament. This can be difficult if there is a lot of built up residue material, but it normally doesn't require too much effort.

Once you pull you should see excess burnt or colored material on the filament you just cold pulled. Repeat this process until you no longer see this residue.

This is the best way I know of, other than purchasing a new hotend/heater block, to get rid of the excess and oxidized material.

## Use a wire brush to clean nozzle and hotend

You should have a brass or copper brush on hand to clean the nozzle and hotend periodically. Before a print, especially one where you see material has built up on the heater block/nozzle, you will want to clean it with a wire brush (when heated). When the nozzle is hot you can brush off any excess material that has built up.

Many people suggest using a nylon brush instead of a wire brush since it is far less abrasive. I will use a nylon brush frequently and only periodically use a wire brush on a very dirty hotend. If using a metal wire brush it is better to use one made of copper or brass as opposed to steel to reduce the amount of nozzle abrasion that occurs.

If you use a brass brush, make sure you heat the hotend and then cut the main power before brushing. If not, you can short out the thermistor and/or kill the board. Don't just turn off the heating, turn off the entire printer as to prevent a board from shorting.

This is crucial in maintaining a clean nozzle and reducing the amount of burnt spots experienced on a print.

## Don't leave filament resting in a heated hotend

You shouldn't heat your hotend until you are ready to extrude. If you leave filament in a heated hotend for long periods of time you will increase your chance of nozzle clogs and oxidization of the material. This is a surefire way to increase the amount of times you will see burnt black spots on your print.

Make sure all of your end G-codes have the script M104 S0, which turns off your hotend after completing a print.

## Use a silicone sock if available

One great improvement done by E3D for their hotends is adding a simple silicone sleeve for the heater block and nozzle. This blue sleeve fits right over their heater block and does not melt at normal extruding temperatures. Many other manufacturers now also offer this feature due to the success from the E3D socks.

As mentioned in the "Hotend Can't Reach or Maintain a Temperature" chapter, these socks help to keep the hotend from sporadically changing temperatures, but that is not their best feature. The greatest part about these sleeves is the extreme reduction in black burnt spots on your prints. Your heater block and nozzle will remain in shiny clean condition so long as you print using the sleeve.

Black burnt spots are still possible due to the fact you can have oxidized material built up in the heater block, but the problem should be vastly reduced. The only negative I have found from these sleeves is when attempting to print with a large diameter nozzle in a draft resolution. When I print on a 0.6mm nozzle at 0.4mm layer heights I always remove this sleeve. This is because the thick layer heights increase the probability that the sleeve will get in the way of the print and be knocked off.

E3D now makes silicone socks with a large hole for the entire nozzle to fit through, which can be used when printing at these larger layer heights.

## Excess material built up on nozzle

The two examples shown above have an extreme amount of material stuck to the nozzle. This is caused via letting a part that is not stuck to the build plate continue to print. Once a part is knocked off or does not have the proper bed adhesion, your printer will continue to print, and thus, build up material all over the hotend.

Please refer to the "Bed Adhesion" and "Parts Being Knocked Over" chapters for ways to prevent and clean this, since this isn't exactly the same problem described in this chapter.

## Summary of Fixes and Precautions

- Make sure you have a well-made hotend and that everything is tightened when heated to 240°C. Take proper precaution to not over tighten.

- Purge old material by pushing down new material an inch and pulling out quickly. Cut off any old material that is stuck onto the filament and repeat the process until there is no longer any excess residue.

- Use cleaning filament or Nylon 910 since it works best for this process.

- Cold pull by extruding cleaning filament/ Nylon through the hotend at 250°C. Allow the nozzle to then cool to 140°C – 160°C, and pull the filament out. Repeat this process until you no longer get discoloring.

- Don't leave filament in a heated hotend for extended periods of time.

- Use a silicone sock to reduce black spots on your print.

# Electrical Safety

Let me first state my thanks to Timothy over at TH3D since he does quite a lot for the 3D printing community. One area of his expertise resides in upgrades and proper precautions for 3D printers, which many 3D printer manufacturers overlook. Please also refer to Thomas Sanladerer's video "Everything you need to know to make your 3D printer fireproof!" on YouTube for an even more detailed description of everything in this chapter.

Always remember, 3D printers are machines and not toys, regardless of how they are advertised. Inside the electronics of your machine you will have high voltage coming from the wall (AC power) and then lower voltage that comes out of your power supply (DC power). When working on your machine you should always have the power disconnected and AC cord unplugged from the wall.

While the lower cost 3D printers are great bargains and are helping millions of people get into 3D printing who weren't able to in years past, there are some key wiring issues present on most lower end brands that should be addressed before using them long term.

## Build of your printer

While the actual frame of your printer will likely not be the catalyst for a fire, it can help to contribute to it. This really isn't a problem anymore with the advancements in the industry, but many low end printer frames used to be made out of wood or acrylic. Wood would obviously make the situation worse, and acrylic also burns quite well.

You can help to mediate any issues when using an all metal frame. Not only are all metal frames preferred for their sturdiness, they also contribute to electrical and fire safety. Luckily, the majority of 3D printers built today have a metal frame.

Even on a metal frame there are plastic printed and injection molded parts that are not flame retardant. As an extra precaution, it is recommended to print in a flame retardant material when making parts for the frame of your machine. Anything that helps to slow down and prevent the potential of a fire spreading is beneficial.

The next part of your printer that needs to be checked is how the wiring is travelling from your board to the parts on your machine. Not only should these wires be organized so they cannot be tugged on during printing, but they should be insulated with a flame retardant material if possible. This can drastically help to prevent any fire that may begin.

You must also consider the operating environment of the 3D printer. Making a wooden box enclosure is not a smart idea. Keeping your printer right below curtains is also not a smart idea. Having your printer in an area that is well ventilated and not next to flammable objects is the best move you can make in this regard.

## Make sure your screw terminal connections are not tinned

The first thing that should be checked on your machine is to ensure that the wires going into the screw terminal connections are not "tinned". These power connectors are on your board and where your wires from your printer motherboard connect to.

Tinning is the process of dipping the ends of the wires into solder to make sure the wires stay together. This speeds up assembly for the manufacturer and cuts costs down. The issue is that screw terminals should be used with either bare wires or crimp ferrules. Crimp ferrules are ends that you can place on bare wire that compress the strands into a metal end. These are the best case scenario but require the ends and a special crimp to install them. The free alternative is to cut off the tinned ends and strip the wire to expose the bare wire. You can then install the bare wires directly into the screw terminals.

The issue with tinned wires is that when you tighten down the screw terminal it will deform and crack the solder. Then, as current is going through the wire, the solder heats up, expands, and then contracts - leaving a gap inside the terminal. This means that there is little to no contact between the wires and the terminal, which will make a weak connection. Once this happens the electricity will arc inside the terminal, creating a large amount of heat that will melt the terminal. This can result in the printer not working correctly, or even worse, starting a fire.

All wires that are connected to a screw terminal need to be very tight, to the point you are unable to pull them out with your hands. Check your terminals every so often if you are concerned about this, and if they continually need to be tightened, you do not want to use them. You can get some crimp ferrules, or worst case, solder directly to the board bypassing the terminals entirely.

## Underpowered Connectors

As mentioned in other chapters, this is extremely common on the power input for RAMPS boards, and can be referred to as a design flaw. The connector that comes with the board is easily overheated and can melt, which is exactly what happened to me on one printer that I built. I had no active cooling fan on the board, so if I didn't notice it early, I could have had a real issue on my hands.

Historically, RepRap boards don't use connectors that are rated high enough. If you are using a RAMPS board, I can't suggest enough that you upgrade the board terminals to a well-made 16A replacement (which can be found at Digikey or Mouser).

This is actually a very common reason for 3D printer fires. As with other fire potential problems, you should first search the model of your printer and read forums if anyone has had problems with underpowered connectors or fires (just as I mentioned the common flaw in the RAMPS board). This will help you save time if you are not super educated with electronics.

You can also check manually if your connector is under powered by finding the part number and looking up what it is rated for. These ratings will include voltage, current, and temperature. The temperature of your enclosed board will be increased, meaning that the connector needs to work in these increased temperatures.

If you are using a standard 40-80w heater at 12V, and you wanted to make sure it's good for any situation, all connectors for that heater should be rated at least 8amps at 12 volts, which will allow for anything the heater can throw at it.

This is actually one of the benefits of 24V printers, since it reduces these issues. A 24V heater will run half of the amperage when compared to a 12V heater of the same wattage.

Make sure all of your connectors are from reputable manufacturers and are rated high enough for the power you are putting through them. A good design rule is that you should not be using connectors that are rated less than 120% of the maximum amperage you intend to put through them.

# Build plate wiring

Just as with your phone charging cable, the wires coming out of your build plate will be damaged over time (especially on Cartesian machines where the bed is consistently rattling). You can get to the point where the build plate is only being heated by a few strands of wiring that is left, with the current still being the same across those strands, they begin to heat up more and more. Severe fraying caused by repetitive motion over long periods can create a real potential for a fire.

You can help prevent this by creating a strain relief for all wiring harnesses that experience movement during the print. This will allow the stress on the wires to be spread out over a distance and prevent a specific section from having an increased potential of being worn down. Something like flexible conduit or spiral wrap will work great. Drag chains are the best option, but they are a bit more difficult to install.

Finally, you can prevent this by using a good silicone flexible insulation for the wiring. You can purchase new wiring for your build plate and then rewire it all with this flexible insulation as to help prevent this fraying from ever occurring.

# Heated build plate MOSFET

A MOSFET is essentially a digital switch that turns power on and off. Most printer build plates will use them on their board to turn on and off heaters.

The issue is that they need to be designed properly for the current you are trying to drive. A lot of times boards will include an under powered MOSFET that is not rated for the frequency or amperage it needs to drive, or are very close to the limitation, without engineering any sort of safety factor. This can cause a thermal runaway. This is particularly dangerous when attempting to print in high temperature or poorly ventilated areas.

These MOSFETS can get hot when pushing more power than they are rated for, and when hot they are also working outside their designed temperature range. One of the best ways to help reduce this issue is to add a heatsink to your MOSFET and to add a cooling fan to your electronics. Keeping the temperature down on your MOSFET will drastically improve your chances of not getting a fire.

Technically, the MOSFET should not be so hot that this becomes an issue to begin with. Thermal issues with the MOSTFET would indicate that the board isn't using the correctly rated MOSFET. A heatsink and a fan should help to not make this an issue, but the manufacturer should have been using a different MOSFET to begin with. You can de-solder and re-solder a new MOSFET rated for your build plate if this is the case with your printer, but this isn't an easy process, and I only suggest doing this if you are comfortable with electronics. This is why a heatsink and a fan is normally the easiest solution.

Some build plates on larger printers work on 115V or higher. It is important to understand the potential dangers of working with AC voltages and are comfortable working on 115V or higher before touching this equipment. I don't suggest this for people not experienced in electrical issues.

## Thermal protection in the firmware

Marlin firmware, especially new versions, have thermal protections built in. This means it can detect if temperatures are outside of the expected ranges and will automatically turn your printer off. These can be found in the configuration.h section of your firmware and should be enabled.

One example of thermal protection would be with the MOSFET. Your MOSFET can fail either when on or off, and this thermal protection can protect for both. The board checks to make sure the temperature is going down when the MOSFET is turned off, and if the temperature isn't decreasing, the machine will turn everything off as a safety procedure. It also checks the temperature when the MOSFET is turned on, and if it doesn't see any temperature raise, it will cut everything off since your wires could be dislodged.

Many manufacturers have these disabled but it is a great protection from anything ever occurring.

# Fire extinguishing ball

Finally, the last bit of insurance over your machine getting on fire, is a fire extinguishing ball. This is a ball that you can hang above your printer that will explode with fire extinguisher when it reaches a certain temperature, guaranteed to put out a small flame.

These balls are only around $40 each and I personally have an AFO Fire Extinguisher Ball above my printers as a last line of defense. You can take all of the proper precautions but nothing will make you feel quite as safe as using one of these. You can at least rest assured that your entire house will not burn down with these above your printers. Remember that many home insurance providers will not cover for a fire caused by your printer, so $40 is the cheapest insurance you will ever buy, and I recommend it to 100% of people using a 3D printer.

# Elephant Foot

Elephant foot is an issue where the bottom few layers of your print are much thicker than the rest of your print. Almost as if the material was mushed out before correcting itself after a couple of layers.

This is a fairly straight forward issue to fix as there can only be a couple of causes.

## Nozzle too close to build plate

This issue is covered in the "Z-Height Calibration" chapter, but can result in an ugly elephant foot if not dealt with. When the first layer has the nozzle too close to the build plate, material is built up, smashed out, and presents itself as thicker than the dimensions of the actual part. Without enough distance between the nozzle and the build plate, this issue is going to be hard to avoid.

The elephant foot would course correct after about 5-10 layers, but the bottom section of your part will definitely be the incorrect dimensions. Refer to the Z-Height Calibration chapter to fix this.

## Build plate too hot

Another reason this elephant foot failure can occur is from running your build plate too hot for the material being extruded. I never run PLA with a build plate hotter than 60 degrees Celsius (sometimes only 50 degrees), but if you do, you can have a distorted bottom of your print.

This is because you are setting the build plate higher than the materials glass transition temperature. This means that the material on the bottom few layers becomes deformed as material is deposited on top of them. While it is easier to get good bed adhesion at these high bed temperatures, the deformation causes this elephant foot.

Make sure you are using the proper build plate temperature for the material you are using by referring to the manufacturer suggestions. If you know you have the proper Z-height and are operating within the suggested temperature range, and are still getting an elephant foot, you should attempt reducing your build plate temperature a bit further. Otherwise you can try out the next suggestion to make sure this problem is eliminated.

## Use a raft

It is rare that I use a raft on my standard DIY machines, but if elephant foot is a consistent issue, a raft should make this failure disappear. A raft can cure having your nozzle too close to your build plate, and it can also fix having the build plate be too hot. This raft acts as a barrier between your print and the bed and should mean you no longer have any elephant foot issues.

The photo above has before and after removing the raft on the same print, and below is this print with a raft (on the right) next to the version with the elephant foot issues (on the left).

Many printers are meant to use a raft standard in order to help with bed adhesion, and so long the settings are dialed in, a raft can be a great solution. It is just something I do not personally use that often because I prefer the underside of my print to be smooth and glossy.

## Negative initial layer horizontal expansion

This is a feature in Cura and may be called something different in other slicers. The initial layer horizontal expansion can cause the first layer to have a thicker or thinner expansion. Having a thick expansion can help with bed adhesion, but will increase your elephant foot issues. Setting this number negative can help to mitigate elephant foot on parts you are just having a ton of problems with.

I personally use a raft when this becomes an issue, but going this route should help as well.

## Summary of Fixes and Precautions

- Make sure your nozzle is not too close to the build plate by referring to the "Z-Height Calibration" chapter.

- Confirm you are running your build plate within the suggested temperature range for the material used.

- Utilize a raft to mitigate the problem entirely.

# Extruder Stepper Skipping
## (Extruder Making a Clicking Noise)

Your extruder stepper motor skipping can happen on any setup, but it seems to be most common on non-geared extruders. A geared extruder allows for a mechanical advantage that will have your motor spin faster, but have much less resistance against it.

When using a non-geared extruder you will be forced to run your prints slower than you could otherwise, so that you do not experience these skips. Please keep in mind I have never experienced extruder motor skipping on the dual-drive geared Bondtech BMG extruder, which is just one of the many reasons I suggest using one.

## Is your nozzle too close to the build plate?

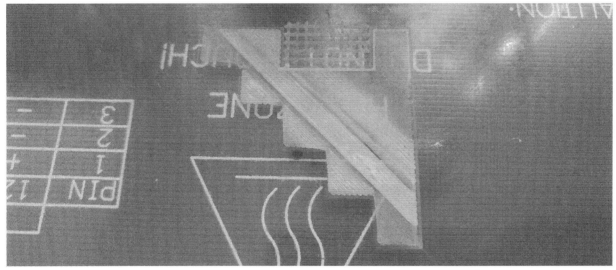

If you hear this skipping on your first layer, it is very likely your nozzle is too close to the build plate. When the nozzle is too close on this first layer, there is no room for the material to extrude. Not only will this cause damage to your nozzle and can even crack your printer bed, it will cause you to hear frustrating clicking noise. This can also lead to stripped filament on geared extruders that do not have the stepper motor skipping.

As mentioned in the "Z-Height Calibration" chapter, confirm your nozzle is homing at the proper height from the build plate before starting any print. Giving enough room for the filament to be laid down properly on a build plate can reduce the strain on your extruder and reduce the amount of times it skips.

## Slow your prints down

A common reason your extruder might be making that skipping noise is that you are running your prints too fast. Your nozzle can only push out so much filament depending on its diameter. So, just as with bottlenecking in traffic, you will experience stoppage if you try to push too fast (especially on non-geared extruders and small nozzle diameters).

This can result in grinding of your filament or extruder stepper skipping. The general rule of thumb is to not print faster than 100x the nozzle diameter on non-geared extruders. So if you are using a 0.4mm nozzle, you should limit your print speeds to 40mm/s, and adjust according to your performance. This may be slow to some experienced people in the industry, but is the rough estimate I use for printing on a non-geared extruder. I run closer to 60mm/s on a good geared extruder such as the Bondtech BMG.

You can test this out mid print if you have a LCD screen on your machine. Most LCD setups are designed so that when you turn the knob mid print, it will change the feed rate (speed). If you hear clicking and would like to see if reducing the speed can fix the issue, turn this knob counter-clockwise. Go to 90% and lower to see if the skipping is decreasing.

If you still are seeing this problem, you may want to check there is not too much moisture in your filament, as covered in the "Stripped Filament" chapter.

## Reduce acceleration

The acceleration of your machine is something that is set in the firmware, but can also be tweaked with certain slicing software - including Cura. You can tweak this mid-print though if you have an LCD display. Under Control – Motion you should find the option for Acceleration, depending on how your board was flashed. You likely do not want this number over 1000 for an inexpensive machine, and for some Cartesian machines you won't want this over 500. Manually reduce this number and see if it helps. This will also help with ghosting, as covered in that chapter.

If you do not have an LCD screen, or you would like to permanently change this number, you can find the acceleration in your printers firmware in Marlin, under the configuration.h tab.

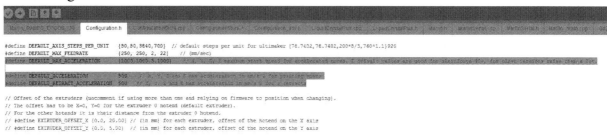

It is easiest to tweak this in the slicing software, as covered in the "Settings Issues" chapter.

## Nozzle Clog

If you have a clog in your barrel or hotend, then you may come across this issue. Your extruder will be trying to push filament down but will click when it is unable to do so. Make sure you check the "Nozzle Clogs" chapter if you are experiencing this.

I have even had minor residue left from switching from ABS to PLA cause extruder motor skips, especially when working with underpowered, non-geared extruders. So if you are working with one of these, a cold pull is suggested after every material change.

## Increase the extrusion temperature

Before attempting this, make sure that your issue isn't being caused by heat creep (refer to the "Nozzle Clogs" chapter of this book). If you are experiencing a clog in your barrel due to heat creep, increasing your extrusion temperature will only make the problem worse.

If you are not experiencing any heat creep and the barrel of your machine remains close to room temperature, you can try increasing the extrusion temperature a bit to decrease the chances of your stepper motor skipping. You will normally not want to go outside the recommended print temperatures, but there has been a few times I have had to do this to print properly.

This increase in temperature, so long as you are still within the materials accepted extrusion temperature range, will allow more filament to feed through the nozzle at a faster rate.

## Loosen the tension on your idler

Most extruder setups have an idler that allows for you to adjust tension – pinching your filament against the hobbed gear or bolt. This tension is necessary to prevent filament grinding and to make sure the proper amount of material is being pushed through the extruder.

While a decent amount of tension is required, you can of course go too far and have this idler be too tight. When too tight you can actually flatten the filament, making it too wide to feed. When material is too fat to too feed you will experience similar issues as you would with Heat Creep in the "Nozzle Clogs" chapter, or you may experience stripped filament, but it can also result in the skipping of your extruder motor.

Pinching too tight on a motor that does not have a lot of torque can also cause skipping at the point of contact. While a tight idler allows for good grip on your filament, it is harder for the extruder motor to spin, especially on non-geared setups.

If you notice that the tension on your idler is very tight and you are experiencing skipping of your stepper, try loosening it a bit. Just keep in mind if you go too loose, you can experience under extrusion as the hobbed gear or bolt will begin to slip on the filament.

## Making sure filament path is clear

The first step in making sure your filament path is clear is to check for nozzle clogs and residue in your hotend setup. Any problem you find in the "Nozzle Clogs" chapter of this book can lead to extruder motor skipping, so you will want to make sure the path in your barrel is clear from old material and debris. You can do this by torching out the old plastic in a well-ventilated area as described in that chapter.

Aside from old material and debris, I am also talking about the actual pathway that your filament is traveling before being fed through the extruder. If you have a 3D printed carriage that is warped, or one that is not to tolerances, you may have a pathway that does not allow your filament to pass smoothly through it. Any big turns that are required to get your filament to go down your barrel will add to the difficulty involved with feeding material. Resistance at the spool or pathway leading to the extruder will also cause problems.

You may need to print parts (or purchase parts) for a new extruder on your machine with tighter tolerances and a clearer path to the hotend. This is yet another reason you only want to buy hotends from reputable manufacturers that have tight tolerances.

All metal hotends allow for heating without the need of Teflon tubing. This Teflon tubing can become deformed over the course of a lot of heating, making the filament path not clear. I always suggest using/upgrading to an all metal hotend (such as E3D or Micro-Swiss).

## Adjust the current to your extruder stepper

If you are running a board with digital current control, when you flash firmware onto your printer there is a section that tells the board how much current is flowing to the steppers. You will essentially want this to the minimum possible that still gets the job done. This is because going too high can cause overheating, the driver to run less efficiently, cause wear on the stepper motor, and results in an increase in noise.

Other boards have a manual current control, including the common RAMPS board. For these you will need a multimeter and a screwdriver. Please keep in mind this is only something I have had to do a couple of times and is very rare that you will need to change. This is only when you know that there is just not enough power being driven to the extruder stepper. It is likely smart to switch to a geared extruder before doing this.

You first want to have your machine turned off and disconnect the stepper motor cable from the board. You then need to look up both the stepper motor you are using, as well as the stepper driver.

Current limits are determined in the motor and driver data sheet. You will not want to run higher than either the driver continuous current limit, or the motor current rating limit, so it is often good to have a driver that has a higher continuous current rating. I suggest going off of the continuous current limit of the Motor.

Once you know what current limit you want, you then need to find out the calculation for your stepper driver to determine a Vref. I had always assumed the calculations are the same, but they definitely are not. You can go to the current limiting section of your stepper driver data sheet in order to figure out the VREF you will want. Current limit will equal Vref x 2.5 for standard A4988, and Vref x 2 for DRV8825. There is then another option by TMC where the calculation is slightly different, where Vref= (Motor current x 2.5)/1.77. To find out your ideal Vref, there is a handy calculator that someone made online which you can search for by typing "Stepper Driver Vref Calculator", where you just enter the rated current of your motor and it will read out the ideal Vref numbers for each driver type.

I understand this is very confusing for someone who is new to this, just as it was for me. But essentially the Vref is the power that is being sent to your motors and it can be tweaked depending on your motor and stepper driver setup. So if your max current limit on your motor is 1AMP, and you are using the standard A4988 driver, you will have a Vref of roughly 0.4. This is because 0.4 x 2.5 = 1. This 0.4 would be your target number that your multimeter will read out. If your Vref is lower than 0.4, you will not be having enough power sent to the motors, meaning they can result in layer shifts and motor skips. Going higher than 0.4 can result in an overheated motor.

To test this out, you will actually need to plug back in your power and turn the machine on, while you still have access to the board. Be careful now that everything is on. Make sure the driver you are testing has the stepper motor unplugged from the board. You would then grab your multimeter. No real way to do this without a multimeter.

Set your multimeter to 20V DC, and touch your black negative lead to a ground pin on the stepper driver (titled GND). If you are unaware which the ground pin is, you can also touch the black negative lead to the negative section of your power supply. Just make sure to only touch a ground section.

You can then clip the positive lead of your meter to the metal shaft on the screwdriver to help read everything out while you change it. If you do not have a clip to connect the lead to the screwdriver, you will need to test, tweak, and test again. You then touch the positive lead (or the screwdriver if you have it clipped) to the potentiometer on the stepper driver. This is a very tiny screw like object on the driver. You will then see a voltage number on your multimeter. This is your Vref, which you want to make sure equals your calculation above.

You can turn the screwdriver clockwise to increase the voltage, and counterclockwise to decrease (which is actually the opposite on the TMC driver, so just make sure you are testing after each small turn). A 1/8 turn of the potentiometer will make a drastic difference in your Vref – so make sure to not turn too fast.

If you experience overheating after this process, you will want to reduce this current, but increasing it should help with skipping on underpowered extruders – just make sure to not go over the rated limits. I suggest you make sure you have upgraded to a geared extruder and tend to the notes below before going this route.

## Clean the teeth on your hobbed gear/bolt

Your filament is constantly being pinched to geared teeth that grip it and push it downward. Over time these teeth can be filled with material, causing them to be smooth rather than to have a grip. You will want to get a very small wire brush or metal pick and clean this out periodically. Having a good grip on your material is essential to avoiding stepper skipping and material slippage.

Please check the "Stripped Filament" chapter for further information if you continually experience debris on the teeth of your extruder.

## Too small of a nozzle

The smaller the nozzle you use, the more likely you will experience stepper motor skipping. I had a near impossible time printing with a 0.25mm nozzle and a non-geared extruder. While I didn't hear clicking (since I was running the print extremely slow), minor motor skips led to a print looking as though it was grossly under extruded. E-steps were right on, yet the print looked as though it was under extruded.

This is due to an increased bottlenecking effect at the point of the nozzle. I was forced to upgrade to a geared extruder to print with these finer nozzle diameters. E3D actually advertises that their lower diameter nozzles require a geared direct extruder to work.

Now that I use a Bondtech BMG extruder, I have zero issues with printing on nozzles as low as 0.15mm in diameter.

## Upgrade to a geared extruder

If you are using a Creality style printer, it is likely the extruder that came with your machine is a plastic and non-geared. One great upgrade would be to purchase an all metal extruder, but even better than that would be to purchase an extruder with a gear ratio.

As mentioned elsewhere in this chapter, a geared extruder, such as the basic Greg's Wade extruder, will help to prevent the stepper motor from skipping. In fact, a geared extruder is pretty much mandatory for printing flexible materials and for using very fine nozzle diameters.

These gears add a mechanical advantage for increased torque without adding pressure on the stepper motor - though you will need to increase and re-adjust your e-steps after switching (Refer to the "Over and Under Extrusion" chapter in this book).

Upgrading to a geared Greg's Wade extruder requires a very minimal amount of extra parts. You can likely find the required printed parts for your printer and hotend assembly on Thingiverse. These parts normally include a large herringbone gear, a small herringbone gear that is connected to your stepper, mount for your hotend and stepper, and some minor hardware purchases.

Along with various washers and bolts, you will need three 608ZZ regular skateboard bearings and an 8mm hobbed bolt. Hobbed bolts can be purchased from NewEgg for about $2, or you can spend a bit more from places like Amazon or specialty 3D printing stores. You can even make one yourself by looking up a "how to" online.

Assembly is very easy and all of the printed parts can be completed in about 24 hours on a standard Prusa I3. You will just need to recalibrate your e-steps after upgrading, but you will want to factor in some basic gear ratios first. A classic Greg's wade with a 39:11 gear ratio has e-steps of 500 or more, unlike 90 where a standard direct drive starts at. If you start checking your e-steps before changing from 90 to 500, you will drastically under extrude on your first attempt.

Personally, I now only use purchased extruders. I have standardized to either an E3D Titan, or my current favorite - a Bondtech BMG extruder. The Bondtech BMG has a dual drive, meaning that both sides pinching the filament have teeth that grab onto the filament, rather than just one pushing against a bearing. This increased grip really helps to have proper extrusion and ease to print with smaller diameter nozzles and flexible filaments. As mentioned in the first section, I have had 0 extruder stepper skips whatsoever since switching. These unfortunately currently cost $100, and can be purchased over at MatterHackers.com, but I definitely think they are worth the money for the expanded material and printing options, with reduced headaches.

## Overheating extruder stepper motor

All stepper motors can get overheated, especially when running fast and in an enclosed machine. It is very smart to purchase some heat sinks and add them to all of your stepper motors. If you are hearing a clicking noise from your extruder,

and the motor itself is too hot to touch, you will need to reduce this temperature. A heat sink is the easiest way to do this, and is another reason working with an enclosed machine can add to printing failures when not done properly. You can also wire a fan to blow on this stepper motor if still too hot after adding a heat sink.

In the photo to the left, I have two heat sinks on the side of the extruder stepper motor, and a fan for the front, as to make sure there isn't any overheating on this pancake stepper.

You can also reduce the Vref from your stepper driver, as I went over earlier, since that will reduce how hot your motor gets in the first place.

## Upgrade to a more powerful stepper/driver/board/ power supply

This isn't needed unless you are still experiencing problems or just want to run your machine faster than the settings I suggest. Of course, if you have a malfunctioning stepper, driver, board, or power supply you will need to replace it - but upgrading these parts will not be needed if you took the steps listed above. That is unless you would like to run your printer at extremely high speeds and print temperatures. Printing at 270°C extrusion temperatures and speeds above 200x the diameter of the nozzle will likely require a 24v machine, and possibly an upgraded board/ driver/stepper combination.

But you can of course also just order a more powerful board, stepper driver, and stepper so that you can run more current, causing far less skips in the motor. Just make sure you understand and purchase everything for the current voltage provided by your power supply.

## Upgrade to a Volcano or SuperVolcano for large nozzle diameters

This is covered in depth in the "Speed Limitations" chapter, which I suggest you read if you plan on using a larger diameter nozzle (0.8mm and higher).

## Summary of Fixes and Precautions:

- Confirm your first layer isn't too close to the build plate.

- Slow your prints down (manually change during print with the knob on the LCD screen to see if this fixes the problem).

- Reduce acceleration.

- Print at a slightly higher extrusion temperature.

- Loosen the tension on the extruder idler.

- Have a clear, straight filament path. Reprint or find more suitable extruder carriage on Thingiverse if required.

- Increase the current to your stepper if not at limit and not experiencing overheating.

- Maintain a clean hobbed gear/bolt.

- Increase nozzle diameter if using smaller than a 0.4mm nozzle.

- Upgrade to a geared extruder such as a Greg's Wade Extruder. Designs can be found on Thingiverse and minor parts purchased on Amazon, eBay, or NewEgg.

- Purchase an upgraded geared extruder such as the E3D Titan or my favorite Bondtech BMG.

- Make sure your extruder stepper motor is not overheating and add a heat sink and/or fan to help prevent the issue.

# Filament Snaps

Another easy to diagnose issue that can be extremely frustrating since it can happen hours into a print.

## Understand the material you are using

Certain materials have lower elongation than others, meaning they will snap easier on the spool. Almost all of the carbon fiber blends snap extremely easily on the spool and will require you to use Teflon/PTFE tubing to guide the filament and help prevent breaks mid print.

Teflon tubing to guide your filament to the extruder will generally help with filament breaks and tangles.

PLA has a much lower elongation than ABS, so you will experience more frequent snaps during the print with it. You can test this yourself since you should be able to snap a piece of PLA off of its spool, while ABS will require a tool to cut.

3.00mm filament is also far more likely to experience these issues than 1.75mm filament, as explored in the "Upgrades and Purchasing a New Printer" chapter. 3mm (or rather 2.85mm) PLA near the end of the spool can be impossible to print without snapping occurring, which is definitely a benefit for the thinner diameter.

## Properly store your filament

Depending on the climate you live in and material you are using, not properly storing your filament can cause it to not print properly or break very easily. If you do not plan on using a spool of filament for a week or longer, you should store it in a controlled environment. This is likely the most common reason for filament snapping when it shouldn't.

You can store this opened filament in an enclosed environment with a dehumidifier, or vacuum seal it with a desiccant bag. The dehumidifier should be set to as low as you can (normally around 20%). This is even more important if you live in an area of the world with high humidity.

This is extremely important when using nylon filaments because they can easily absorb moisture within hours of being exposed to a high humidity environment. Low humidity filament containment and feeding systems are also manufactured for use of highly hygroscopic materials such as nylons.

If you do not properly store your filament, you will need to go through the steps required to get the moisture out, or even purchase a new spool.

## Change manufacturer

If the manufacturer of your filament does not have high reviews, you may experience frequent breaks. This is when spending a bit more for a name brand can pay for itself. Hatchbox, E-Sun, Polymaker, Matterhackers, ColorFabb, IC3D, taulman3D, AIO Robotics, Overture, and Proto-Pasta are just a few of the filaments providers that should have no problems straight from the manufacturer.

Without naming any brands, I have had consistent failures and filament breaks from a few specific lower priced companies.

## Loosen idler tension

The tension on your extruder idler may be pinching your filament too tight. If this is the case, the grinding of filament may lead to your material snapping entirely.

This would normally lead more to stripped filament, as discussed in that chapter, but it is possible for it to grind until snapping.

Most extruder setups allow for the adjustment of this tension. You want it to be tight enough for there to be plenty of pressure, but not too much that it grinds into the filament or deforms it. If you think this may be too tight, see if loosening the idler fixes your problem.

## Check for nozzle clog

You can be experiencing a nozzle clog if your filament is snapping, so if this is the case, be sure to read the "Nozzle Clogs" chapter in this book.

## Summary of Fixes and Precautions

- Know the possibility that the specific material you are using might break.
- Switch to a 1.75mm extruder and hotend setup for less frequent filament snaps.
- Properly store your filament. Using old or improperly stored material is likely the most common reason for this happening.

- Always buy from a well-respected manufacturer for 3D printing filament.
- Replace your spool and try a new manufacturer if needed.
- Check for a nozzle clog and fix if that is the underlying culprit.

Filament Snaps

# Gaps in Walls

This particular issue is something I have personally noticed to happen less frequently on Cura, but it could happen on just about any slicer. This is when the walls of your print do not connect and can result in gaps.

## Why it's happening

If you're walls are not designed to be a multiple of the thickness of your layer lines, you can imagine why this happens. Let's say your walls are 1.8mm in thickness, and you have your layer lines set to 0.4mm. Your slicer will either attempt to create 2.0mm walls (5 shells), or it will error on the lower side of 1.6mm (4 shells), causing a 0.2mm gap. I believe that all slicers go with the latter, as to avoid printing a part that is too thick.

This gap is normally filled via your infill percentage, or by top layers, but you may run into issues when it doesn't.

Each slicer seems to deal with this in a different way. Most will bunch the shells together on each side of the print, with a 0.2mm gap in the center. I believe Slic3r does what you see in the photo above, just spreading each wall out with a smaller gap, though I may be wrong. I personally do not use Slic3r, but the photo above is from someone who purchased the 2019 edition of my book using Slic3r who had this issue.

If you want your shell walls to fill the entire area of your print, then you would need the walls to be a multiple of your layer line width. If not, you can try the following solution.

# Fill Gaps Between Walls

Luckily Cura has the ability to fix this issue:

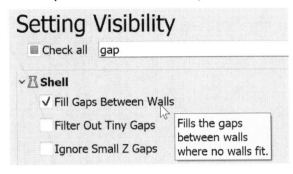

As you can see by the description, this is meant to fix this exact problem. If the gap between walls is thinner than your layer line width, this should fill in that area. Simplify3D should have a similar feature called "gap fill".

This doesn't always do the job, but when it doesn't, normally your infill percentage will.

This may cause blobs to appear on the side of your print, so if you are experiencing blobs, you can choose to "Filter Out Tiny Gaps". Very tiny gaps, ones you likely wouldn't notice on your final print, will then be avoided.

# Make your walls a multiple of your line width

The ideal solution would be to redesign the wall in question to be a multiple of your desired line width. If this isn't possible for you, you can slightly tweak your line width to work.

As with the example in the beginning of this chapter, if you need your shells to fill up a 1.8mm wall, using a 0.4mm line width will cause a 0.2mm gap. You can go around this issue by upping your line width to 0.45mm instead. You will then have 4 lines at 0.45mm, which will be exactly 1.8mm without any gaps being created.

If you go into your "preview" section of your slicer after slicing, and you see there is a minor gap in your walls, you can adjust your line width accordingly. While I normally prefer to keep my line width the same as the nozzle diameter I am using, you can go up to 120% the nozzle diameter and not lose much quality, if at all.

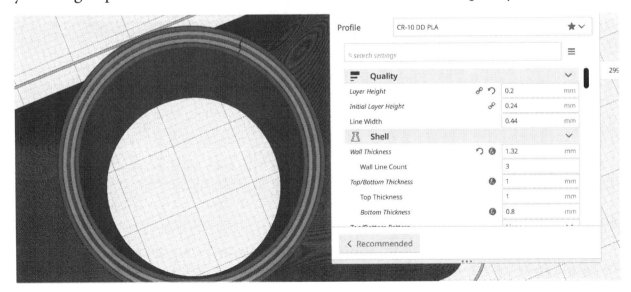

The example above has the line width to 0.44mm and it can only fit two shells (two inner, two outer – making 4 walls), so there is a gap in the middle of these walls. This part is 2.0mm thick, so you can see why this is happening. This is even with the "Fill Gaps Between Walls" checked on. This does go away if you have infill % on, but the above example is with 0% infill. If you require the line width you have selected, then you will need to have infill fill in that gap.

You can now see what this same print looks like with 0.4mm line width and no infill:

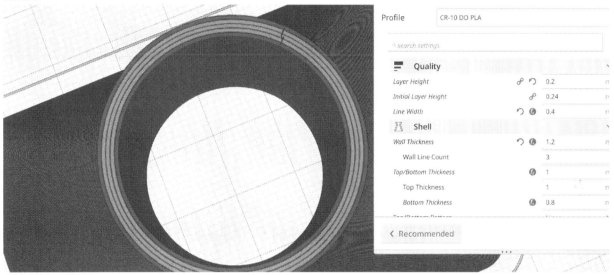

You can see how that gap disappeared, since at 0.4mm line widths the printer is able to fit another wall. You then have 5 walls making 2.0mm, the exact thickness of the part.

You can actually just change the line width of the walls if you choose, so that it doesn't affect the rest of your print. Cura allows you to just tweak the wall line width, or even just the inner or outer wall line width – which is located in the "Quality" section. This means for the example above, you can have just your wall line widths set to 0.44mm, and the rest of your print be 0.44mm. You could also set your inner and outer walls at different thicknesses if it helps you to fill in all gaps with a line width you prefer.

The photo above is showing off an example just like this. The one on the left was using a 0.4mm line width and the one on the right was using 0.44mm line widths. The math worked out that the 0.44mm line widths fit without leaving any gaps like the 0.4mm version did.

## Potential under extrusion

When none of the walls are touching, similar to the photo at the beginning of the chapter, you could actually be under extruding. As explained by Ultimaker on one of their guides for Cura:

"If the walls are not touching each other at all it is an extrusion issue. Cura is asking your printer to create a series of 0.4mm lines and is spacing them so that they fuse together. However, if your printer is under extruding slightly, the lines will be marginally thinner and they no longer fuse together properly. The solution could be as simple as reducing your print speed slightly or increasing your temperature a few degrees."

You can check the "Over and Under Extrusion" chapter for further attempts to see if this is the issue if just reducing print seed or increasing your temperature does not fix the issue.

## Gaps between infill and walls

This is a different issue than the one explained in the rest of this chapter. The most common reason for there being a gap between your infill (or top/bottom layers) and the walls, is the infill overlap percentage being set too low. I normally will keep my infill overlap percentage around 7 or 8%, but some people suggest going up to 30%.

I normally don't suggest doing this since it can lead to a "veiny" print, but you can also choose to print "Infill Before Walls", which should help to make the infill attach to the shell walls.

## Summary of Fixes and Precautions

- Choose to "Fill Gaps Between Walls" on your slicer.
- Attempt to make your walls a multiple of your line width.
- Check to see if you are under extruding, and perhaps slow down the speeds of your shell walls.
- Check your infill overlap percentage when dealing with gaps between your main part and the shell walls.

# Ghosting

Ghosting in printing essentially refers to an "echo" where details in your print can be seen outside where they should be, which may also be called "ringing".

The number one reason this occurs is having your acceleration and jerk settings too high. This is extremely common in 3D printing, especially since many printer manufacturers will auto set the default value for these numbers too high, since it will allow them to advertise faster printing times.

A part with some minor ghosting is still entirely useable, so printer manufacturers may get away with calling something a successful print that we as makers would be upset with.

Keep in mind this issue should be reduced on a CoreXY or Delta machine, since the increased weight of moving the print bed on Cartesians will make this problem worse.

## Reducing jerk and acceleration

As you can tell from the photo above, there is a drastic difference in ghosting between the two examples. These parts were printed with every slicer setting being the same, except for Jerk and Acceleration.

Acceleration is pretty self-explanatory, but jerk refers to something you may not know unless you are involved in the 3D printing sphere. Jerk refers to the initial speed after a directional change. After stopping and starting again, your printer will start instantaneous at your jerk speed before then accelerating to your print speed.

The failed print on the left had accelerations of 3,000 m/s $^2$ and a jerk of 30 mm/s while the print on the right had accelerations of 500 m/s$^2$ and a jerk of 12 mm/s – all other settings being the same. It has become clear to me that jerk and acceleration are the key factors when it comes to reducing ghosting.

The print on the left took 1 hour 36 minutes and the print on the right took 1 hour 50 minutes, so it is clear you will need to wait longer for your print to finish, but it is definitely worth it to have the quality you expect.

## Controlling jerk and acceleration right in Cura

As mentioned elsewhere in this book, the newer versions of the Cura slicing software is updated frequently, and it now allows for jerk and acceleration control.

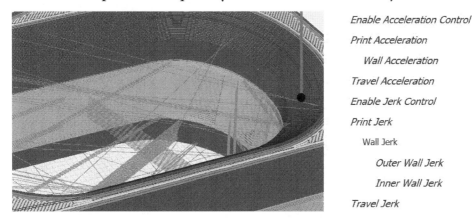

This allows you to change these numbers without having flash your firmware. In Cura, this is located under the "Speed" section. If you prefer not to use Cura, then you will have to check within your slicer if this option is available. If it isn't, you will have to manually change the Jerk and Acceleration within Marlin and reflash your firmware. These numbers are right within Configuration H:

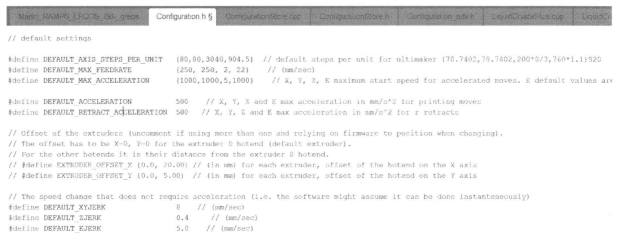

You can also find out your current acceleration numbers by typing "M503" into Repetier Host or Octoprint, which will read out all of your current firmware settings.

## Add small cushions under printer feet

This is a very minor, but easy addition to your printer to help reduce ghosting. Part of the problem with ghosting is the rattling that occurs within the printer without anywhere to disperse it. If you have a very sturdy printer on a sturdy print area, most of the rattling ends up locating within the machine.

An easy fix is to grab some small foam cubes and place them under your printer feet. This will help to disperse vibrations through the machine into the pads, allowing you to print higher acceleration and jerk speeds with reduced ghosting.

While I have these pads on my printer, I still do not print faster than roughly 800m/s² accelerations and 15mm/s jerk on my Cartesian setup. Remember that CoreXY can have much higher acceleration and jerk settings without an increase in ghosting.

## Having a lighter carriage

The lighter the carriage, the less ghosting you will experience. This means ghosting will be more of an issue on a direct extruder than a Bowden. I will still always prefer direct extruders to Bowden due to the extra amount of materials available to print, but one of the benefits to Bowden is the reduced weight.

You can also reduce the weight on your carriage via a smaller/lighter extruder stepper and/or carriage. In fact, as of editing this book E3D just announced their brand new Hermes extruder/hotend, which may be available by the time you are reading this. Hermes is an extruder and hotend built in one package, with dual drive gears for the extruder, all of it being much lighter than having them as individual parts.

## Belts too tight

Having belts too loose can cause Z-wobble (or even layer shifts), but going too tight can cause ghosting. There is no specific standard for how tight a belt should be, but I generally say they should be tight enough to have no droop and be springy to the touch. If they are so tight it is actually stretching out the belt, it can cause a reduction in dampening and add to your ghosting problems.

As mentioned elsewhere in this book, I have had far more problems with belts being too loose, so I would test the other suggestions in this chapter before you go loosening belts.

## Having too tight of a frame

You almost always want to have a well-built, strong frame. Unfortunately, if you do not have any dampeners for your axis, this means that the vibrations from your machine won't be as dispersed, resulting in increased ghosting.

Having this be too loose can result in Z-wobble – as covered in that chapter. This means you are going to be trying to find the happy medium where you get no Z-wobble and no ghosting, something fairly hard to achieve (and a reason CoreXY is preferred over Cartesian).

You don't want to go loosening screws on your machine in order to allow more dampening, which means it may be difficult to do much about this, other than adding cushions below the printer.

Please refer to my video titled "Reduce Ghosting in 3D Printing" on YouTube for further information.

## Summary of Fixes and Precautions

- Reduce your acceleration and jerk via Cura or your preferred slicing software.
- If not available in your slicing software, reduce via marlin and re-flash.
- Add small foam cushions below your printer feet to help disperse vibrations.
- Reduce weight on carriage if possible.
- Have dampening for your axis if possible.
- These problems are less of an issue on CoreXY and Delta machines.

# Hotend Can't Reach or Maintain Temperature

This problem can arise in a couple different fashions. Your printer may be able to reach its set point but then cannot hold it during the middle of the print, or your hotend may not ever be able to reach the temperature you give it.

## Confirm you are using the proper wattage heater

I had a consistent issue on one machine where it had extreme difficulty holding 230°C, and could never reach 250°C. I had done all of the tests mentioned below but the hotend just couldn't make it. It turned out I was using a 30W heater instead of 40W, which the machine was rated for (Lulzbot TAZ 5 in this example).

Replacing the heater with the proper wattage fixed this problem instantaneously. Wiring for the heaters is typically color coded by wattage, so make sure the colors match and the rating on the cartridge are the same when changing out your heater. You can check the resistance on the heater to determine if everythign is correct. 12V 40W should be around 3-4 Ohms, 24V 40W should be around 14-15 Ohms.

## Check firmware for MAXTEMP

It is also smart to confirm that the maximum temperature for your extruder is set higher than you will be printing in your firmware. Your printer will be restricted from reaching any temperature higher than this.

```
// When temperature exceeds max temp, your heater will be switched off.
// This feature exists to protect your hotend from overheating accidentally, but *NOT* from thermistor short/failure!
// You should use MINTEMP for thermistor short/failure protection.
#define HEATER_0_MAXTEMP 270
#define HEATER_1_MAXTEMP 245
#define HEATER_2_MAXTEMP 245
#define BED_MAXTEMP 200
```

This should be automatically set to a safe number for your machine and hotend, but if it was ever turned to 230, you would not be able to reach any temperatures above that. If you were to upgrade to a high temp hotend, you would likely need to tweak this number to what the new hotend is rated for. Don't set this to a high number if you are unsure of your hotend setup.

## PID autotuning

PID refers to a proportional integral derivative controller that is used in 3D printing to control the temperature of the nozzle. When the PID settings are not correct, a fan can drastically change the temperature of the hotend.

An active cooling fan, or even something as minimal as the barrel fan, can drop a hotend from 210°C to 160°C if the PID settings are off.

This rapid cooling will make the nozzle too cold for the filament to feed, or may even prevent your print from starting at all.

If you notice that the temperature is fluctuating consistently around the set point that is also a sign that the PID settings need to be tuned. Erratic fluctuation is more likely to be a sign of intermittent electrical failure or the temperature sensor getting lodged from its cavity.

You can change your overall PID settings for your machine in your firmware, but I actually suggest getting a specific PID number for the particular material and fan settings you are attempting to print. You can then add these PID numbers into your start G-code.

I actually don't really do this anymore since the machines I am using now are able to maintain most temperatures without unique PID settings, but it may be needed on your printer.

The first thing you will want to do is to mimic the material you will be printing with (or at least the material you are having difficulty with). If you will be using an active cooling fan, manually turn it on.

While still cold, you will then want to give this command through your printer terminal (Repetier, Octoprint, etc.)

**M303 E0 S**temperature

So if you are testing out PLA, and you want to print the PLA at 200°C, you would type in:

**M303 E0 S200**

This will run a PID Autotune. After a decent amount of time your program will feedback values for P I and D:

```
bias: 92 d: 92 min: 196.56 max: 203.75
Ku: 32.59 Tu: 54.92
Clasic PID
Kp: 19.56
Ki: 0.71
Kd: 134.26
PID Autotune finished ! Place the Kp, Ki and Kd constants in the configuration.h
```

As mentioned in that readout, you would open up marlin and go to your configuration.h tab in order to change the PID settings for your entire machine.

```
bias: 92 d: 92 min: 196.56 max: 203.75
Ku: 32.59 Tu: 54.92
Clasic PID
Kp: 19.56
Ki: 0.71
Kd: 134.26
PID Autotune finished ! Place the Kp, Ki and Kd constants in the configuration.h
```

Some machines also let you change this within the EEPROM of the LCD screen. Just make sure you store settings if you go this route.

You can also change the PID settings using G-code commands, which I explain shortly.

As mentioned earlier, I actually suggest getting a separate PID value for each material you plan on using for the most precise results, if this issue is becoming a nuisance. This is because the numbers you are inputting may be drastically different when printing at 200°C without an active cooling fan vs. printing 250°C with an active cooling fan. This is particularly true with lower end machines and may not be needed on well-built printers.

If you would like a specific PID setting for a specific material, run the exact same M303 code mentioned above in the settings desired. For example, if you would like to get a good PID number for PETG, turn on your active cooling fan and run

## M303 E0 S250

Once you are read out a number go to the start G-code section of your slicing program. You will then want to add this line before your G90 input:

## M301 H1 P##.## I##.## D##.##

Here is an example Start G-code for PLA with an active cooling fan I was read out for one of my machines. Remember that each machine will vary:

**Printer Settings**

| | | |
|---|---|---|
| X (Width) | 200 | mm |
| Y (Depth) | 200 | mm |
| Z (Height) | 150 | mm |
| Build plate shape | Recta... | |
| ☐ Origin at center | | |
| ☑ Heated bed | | |
| G-code flavor | RepR... | |

**Printhead Settings**

| | | |
|---|---|---|
| X min | 20 | mm |
| Y min | 10 | mm |
| X max | 10 | mm |
| Y max | 10 | mm |
| Gantry height | )999999800 | |
| Number of Extruders | 1 | |

**Start G-code**
```
G90 ; absolute positioning - this line w
M82 ; set extruder to absolute mode - th
G28 ; home all axes
M301 H1 P18.39 I1.26 D66.91
G1 Z0.2 F1200 ; raise nozzle 0.2mm
G92 E0 ; reset extrusion distance
```

**End G-code**
```
M104 S0 ; turn off extruder
M140 S0 ; turn off bed
G28 X0 Y0 ; Homes X and Y axis
G0 Y180 ; Moves the heated bed to the fr
M84 ; disable motors
```

You would then save this .ini profile so that whenever you are printing with this material in the future, you will not experience dropping or difficulty maintaining the nozzle temperature.

The final way you can set your PID is by using Repetier Host, Octoprint, or another way you can give direct G-code commands to your printer (just as you did when you tested for PID). You would then type "M301 H1 P### I#### D####". You would then need to type "M500" as to save those settings. You can then type "M503" to confirm the settings have saved.

If your PID Autotune has failed, and you have confirmed you are using the correct wattage heater, you can try the next solution

## Get a new heater

This normally isn't needed, but I have had a printer shipped to me that just couldn't maintain its temperature straight from the manufacturer. I ran PID autotune a dozen times and still the temperature fluctuated all over the time. Well it ends up it was just a malfunctioning heater. Replacing the heater fixed the issue instantaneously.

## Readjust or reprint active cooling fan

The most common culprit for hotend temperatures dropping mid-print is that your active cooling fan kicks on and it is blowing directly onto your nozzle. With your hotend at room temperature, turn on your active cooling fan. Then place your finger onto your nozzle and hotend and see if you feel a lot of cool air. If you are, this air may be what is dropping your hotend temperature during your print.

You may be able to overcome this differential by running your PID tuning while the active cooling fan is on, as mentioned above, but it doesn't always work. The best active cooling fans are ones that go around your hotend and blow directly downward. You only want the air to be blowing onto your print and not onto your nozzle.

If your active cooling fan is blowing directly onto your hotend, you will need to print a new duct. Search on Thingiverse and elsewhere for a file that will fit your extruder/hotend setup. There are likely dozens already created. Make sure that this duct angles the air downward as to avoid the heater block and nozzle.

These fan ducts can get in the way of your printer finding home, or can even get in the way of raised bed clips, so be careful and confirm your machine can move to all areas of your build plate before starting a print.

## Add a silicone sock

As mentioned in a couple chapters in this book, you should add a silicone sleeve to your heater block/nozzle, if the manufacturer makes one. Not only does this silicone sock prevent burnt black spots on your print, it can actually help insulate the hotend. Any air blowing around the heater block will not have as much effect on cooling a nozzle that has a silicone sleeve around it.

If you have confirmed you are using the proper wattage heater, that your machine can reach the temperature you are trying to reach, air is not blowing onto your heater block, you've added a silicone sleeve, and your PID Autotuning is still failing, you will likely need to replace and re-flash. Buy a new heater and thermistor, rewire to your board, and flash your machine again. Then attempt to run the PID Autotuning code.

If still failing you may actually require a new board or power supply. There is a problem that exists with the CR-10 boards where it has difficulty holding temperatures of 230 degrees and above. TH3D Studios can fix this easily over at TH3DStudio.com. I don't claim to be an expert on why this board was faulty, which is why a company like TH3D is great to use.

This is precisely what happened with my CR-10 and Timothy at TH3D helped fixed it for me quickly.

## Summary of Fixes and Precautions

- Confirm you are using the proper wattage heater for your machine.
- Check that you're not exceeding the MAXTEMP for your firmware.
- Run the PID Autotune sequence for the temperature you are having difficulty holding, along with turning on any fans that will be running during the print.
- Change the PID in marlin to set the standard for your machine, add the code to your start G-code for each given profile, or just set via G-code commands.
- Make sure your active cooling fan isn't blowing directly onto your heater block and nozzle. If it is, you will need to adjust it or reprint a new fan duct so that it aims directly onto your print.
- Add a silicone sock if available.
- If all else fails, replace heater and thermistor.
- Flash firmware.
- Absolute final solutions would include replacing your board and power supply, but this should not be necessary in the vast majority of times you experience this problem.
- CR-10 printers have this issue on some boards and it can be fixed via TH3DStudio.com

# Hotend Not Heating

This failure is not common but easy to diagnose, since your extruder will not heat up. If the temperature is reading out properly, then this is an issue with your heater. Many of these instructions are similar to the ones in the "Build Plate Not Heating" chapter in this book.

After you confirm you are using the correct Volt/Amp for your heater/board combination, you can move forward to checking the following issues.

## Heater malfunctioning

The heater is the cartridge attached to thick wires (normally red or blue) that is connected to the heat block of your hotend. As with all parts on a printer, this cord can wear out and malfunction. Luckily, replacement heaters are fairly inexpensive.

It is best to have a spare heater available so that you can easily test if it is your heater or your board that is malfunctioning. All you would need to do is to disconnect the heater from the board and connect your replacement heater, and then see if heats up without any issue. If it does, then it may not be worth your time to even figure out what is wrong with your old heater. This is why it is great to have all of your important parts use a connector. This way you do not have to cut wires if you just want to test a part out.

If you do not have a spare heater, you can start by checking the continuity of the wires from the cartridge to the board using a multimeter. This may be difficult for you if you do not have any connectors or exposed wires that you can access near the cartridge, which is why I suggest testing by using a spare. Even if you do find that one of the wires has a break in it, you will likely need a replacement cord, since it needs to be a thick gauged wire. For a 12V 30A heater, you will want at least a 14 gauge wire.

DO NOT REPLACE A HEATER CORD WITH A NORMAL SMALL GAUGED WIRE (thinner than 18 gauge) YOU WILL BE SUSCEPTIBLE TO A FIRE AND FURTHER BURNT OUT WIRES

## Burnt out and/or disconnected wires and connectors

This is far more common if you are experiencing issues with your build plate not heating, but can occur with your extruder heater as well. You should easily be able to see any burnt out connectors on your board with the naked eye, and if you can't, you will be able to once you disconnect the hotend from the board.

When a connector or wire is burnt out you will not get any heating out of your hotend, unlike what I describe in the next section. If there is a wire you can easily see was burnt out in one section, you can often fix this without replacing the entire wire.

A disconnect may be as simple as noticing that a connector had vibrated loose. When there is a partial or intermittent break in the wiring, typically referred to as fraying, this issue can be much more difficult to diagnose. This should only ever be an issue on older machines with many printing hours, and on machines where the wires aren't organized. When this does happen, try to replace the entire wiring harness with a new one if available from the manufacturer. When one section of wiring begins to fray the rest typically will follow shortly thereafter. Make sure to rewire in an organized fashion.

With the printer off and unplugged, cut off the burnt section out of the wire, and then solder the two sections that are not burnt out back together (or use solder seal connectors). Be sure to use the proper shrink wrap because absolutely no metal can be exposed after this process. I mention what I use in the "Important Accessories and Replacements" chapter. Then you will need to confirm that the extruder can reach its farthest point from the board, because you just made the wire shorter than it was.

If your newly soldered wire cannot reach the board at the extruder's furthest point, you will experience layer shifts on large builds.

If you see that the connector going from your hotend heater to the board is burnt out, you will need to replace it.

This is extremely common on the power input for RAMPS boards, and is referred to as a design flaw. The connector that comes with the board is easily overheated and can melt, which is exactly what happened to me on a printer that I built. Since I had no active cooling fan, if I didn't notice it early, I could have had a real issue on my hands.

Historically RepRap boards don't use connectors that are rated high enough. If you are using a RAMPS board, I can't suggest enough that you upgrade the board terminals to a well-made 16A replacement (which can be found at Digikey or Mouser). Make sure to refer to the "Electrical Safety" chapter for more information.

Remember that the area you are replacing may have some melted plastic, so you will need to clean it out entirely before attempting to reconnect. If replacing the connector does not fix this burnt out area, you may actually need to replace the entire board.

Only after everything is wired properly and there is no exposed metal, plug everything back on and test to confirm the hotend is heating again.

RAMPS boards are actually quite out of date now and MKS or SKR boards are now the standard  Popular boards include: MKS GenL, MKS SGEN L, and SKR V1.3.

# Board overheating

Just as with the section above, this is more common with the build plate not heating, but you will normally notice this issue if your heater starts to heat and then cuts out at a certain point.

Remember that this is different than your printer not being able to maintain a specific temperature, which I go over in the "Hotend Can't Reach or Maintain a Temperature" chapter. Rather, this will occur when your hotend is heating up just fine and then entirely cuts out, going all the way back to room temperature.

Not only will this cause a failed print, it will likely cause a severe nozzle clog if your printer continues to try and cold extrude.

You can normally tell if this is happening by checking the temperature of your board when the heater cuts out. Be careful though, because if the board is overheating, it will be hot enough to burn your fingers.

I go over a few of these methods elsewhere in this book, but if you are experiencing a board that is overheating, you will need to get 1-3 active fans blowing right onto it. If your board is enclosed with the rest of the machine, the build plate heating will drastically affect the ambient air temperature, causing much more frequent times your board can overheat. Small heat sinks will always help affected areas, but from what I can tell, setting up some active fans make the biggest difference. Whenever using active cooling fans, make sure to keep them well maintained. Check for dust accumulation and make sure the area around them is free of debris (use a filter/grill if possible to protect the fan blades). Broken fan blades can add a lot of noise to your system and if the cooling fan fails, your board will end up overheating again.

If your board is constantly overheating, or you are using a RAMPS board with thousands of hours of printing on it, you will want to replace it entirely. RAMPS boards are normally extremely cheap at under $10, but higher end boards such as a Rambo board may be closer to $150. These higher end boards will experience less overheating when wired correctly.

## Summary of Fixes and Precautions

- Confirm you are using the correct Volt/Amp for your Heater/Board.
- Check for visual damage (burnt out cords/connectors).
- Test out a new heater if you do not see anything noticeable.
- Solder wires or rewire any section that is not connected or burnt out - always using the proper gauge.
- Replace any burnt out connector to the board.
- Actively cool your board.
- Replace board if overused or burnt out.

# Hotend Not Reading Correct Temperature

This failures refers to your hotend being a different temperature than what it actually is due to issues with your thermistor, and can lead to bigger problems if not properly addressed. This is noticeable when filament feeds at different temperatures than it is supposed to, or if you are receiving a message of "Error Min Temp".

These instructions are similar to the "Build Plate Not Reading Correct Temperature" chapter.

## Error Min Temp (or Error Stopped Temp Sensor)

If your thermistor is not connected properly your printer, it will stop working and read "Error Min Temp". This is most common on fragile, non-cartridge thermistors, but can happen on just about any setup.

If your printer is reading this error you will need a new thermistor the majority of the time. You can order replacement thermistors from your hotend manufacturer. I personally use E3D hotends, and you can easily order replacement cartridge thermistors from their website, or from Filastruder.com or Matterhackers.com for US orders.

You can measure your thermistors resistance to see if it is working correctly as well. It should be 80-100K resistance depending on your room temperature.

If your thermistor has no physical damage that you can see, you may be able to fix this without buying a new one. This is when there is an easily recognizable break in the wire, or if you can diagnose that there is no continuity.

If there is a frayed wire or a section of a wire you can diagnose has no continuity, you can cut and solder the wire skipping this section - or rewire entirely. If your thermistor is still intact, replacing the wiring will likely fix your issue. You will then you will need to confirm that the extruder can reach its farthest point from the board, because you just made the wire shorter than it was.

If your newly soldered wire cannot reach the board at the extruder's farthest point, you will experience layer shifts on large builds, or you can just rip the thermistor off the hotend.

Other possibilities include your readout showing a negative temperature. I have had this happened instead of an "Error Min Temp" when working with the CR-10.

## Not reading proper temperature

This issue is extremely difficult to diagnose if you are not looking for it and when the differential is not extreme. When drastically different from the actual heat you can have a major problem on your hand if the hotend does not stop heating. If entirely not reading correctly, or if your thermistor is hovering an inch next to your hotend, your printer will think that its hotend is not able to reach its set temperature and will just continue heating it. Many machines have safety settings to turn off your heater if it does not reach its target temperature after a few minutes, but not all do. I have personally seen melted metal from a heater block that never recognized it was actually getting hot, since the thermistor was not connected to it.

Other less severe symptoms may include consistent nozzle clogs or over/under extrusion. If you are only printing PLA you may not ever notice the temperature is reading incorrectly, due to the fact most PLA has such a wide extrusion temperature range.

If you have a device on hand that can read temperatures back to you up to 200°, then you can obviously use this to test the accuracy of your thermistor. If you don't, and you aren't experiencing issues, a simple way to test this is to try and extrude another material that has a small extrusion temperature range.

Using a material that has a smaller temperature range of let's say 220°C - 240°C will allow you to notice this problem a bit easier than with PLA. MAKE SURE you are using a spool that is reliable and has no moisture in it. Set your hotend to 220°C in this example, and if you cannot extrude any of the material, it is likely that your thermistor is reading hotter than it actually is. Do the opposite test if your hotend seems to be heating too high, by attempting to feed the filament at 240°C. If the material crystalizes, bubbles, clogs easily, or comes out extremely burnt, your thermistor is likely reading a lower temperature than your hotend actually is.

For this issue you will want to confirm that the thermistor is properly connected to the hotend. If the thermistor is hovering right next to the hotend, and not inside its holder, it will likely read out a temperature lower than the hotend actually is.

If connected properly, and there are no breaks in your wire, you will likely have to replace the thermistor by purchasing a new one, as mentioned above. This is why having a spare on hand is very beneficial

If none of these fix your problem, there is a small chance that your board itself is malfunctioning and needs replacement. Flash your firmware to factory settings, and if that doesn't work, replace the board

## Summary of Fixes and Precautions

- Keep a spare thermistor for your hotend on hand if possible. I have gone through dozens and dozens of thermistors over the years.

- Make sure the thermistor is actually connected to the hotend. If hovering next to it your hotend may not stop heating and can cause serious problems.

- If thermistor is noticeably damaged, replace it.

- Check for breaks of frays in your wire and solder or rewire as needed.

- Make sure that if you do rewire you give enough slack to have the extruder move to its farthest point.

- Check that your hotend is reading the proper temperature by extruding a low temperature range material at its low and high temperature ranges.

- Replace and rewire thermistor from the hotend all the way to the board if all else fails.

- Flash firmware to factory settings.

- If still not reading proper temperature, you may need to replace your board. Make sure you try replacing the thermistor before going this route.

# Important Accessories and Replacements

You should always have a few accessories and replacements on hand so that you do not need to order parts every time something breaks down. Some of these tools I use every single day, while others are needed a lot less frequently.

You can visit 3DPrintGeneral.com for more parts that I suggest and have personally used, with direct links on how to buy them.

## Accessories:

I consider all tools that are frequently used on 3D printed parts and the machine itself as a 3D printing accessory. I actually have a video similar to this chapter titled "Mandatory Accessories for a 3D Printer" on my YouTube channel if you wish to see more.

**Pliers:** I can't think of anything more important to support removal than a set of pliers. You will use these just about every time you print with support.

**Razor Blade:** Something you need to be extremely careful with, but cleaning up a print will always be easier with some razor blades. I use them just about every time I print with a brim, and it also helps to clean off any "hairy" residue and pop off support interface.

**Model Cutters:** These sharp, thin scissors are a lifesaver when it comes to printing very thin parts. If you have a very thin part of your print that is being held up via support material, just going at it with a set of pliers will likely break that fragile area. Using model cutters will allow you to cut this support material off without damaging your print.

**Scraper:** A scraper will come with just about any 3D printer you buy, but it is smart to have one that you prefer. I like a very strong metal that comes to a thin, flat front. I have tried out flimsy scrapers that will bend on difficult parts, and thick scrapers that are difficult to get under your print without damaging it. Get a strong metal scraper that tapers at the very front. I like the set by AMX3D if you wanted a suggestion.

**Metric Allen Screwdriver Set:** Just about every printer on the market uses a lot of Allen screws. Having an Allen wrench set is smart, but having an Allen screwdriver set is even better. It can be difficult to get to some of your screws via a normal Allen wrench, but is far easier with an Allen screwdriver.

The most common size of screw used an M3, but it is smart to have an M2.5, M3,

M4, and M5 Allen screwdrivers. I don't know of any 3D printers that use standard sizes, almost all use metric. In order to make just about any fixes or repairs to your printer, you will need this screwdrivers/wrench set.

**Solder Set or Solder Seal Wire Connectors:** Wires become frayed, and you will often need to cut them to attach new parts. There are plenty of times in this book where I go over how to fix parts on your machine, and most of them require to you cut and fix frayed wires.

The most common way to do this is to get wire strippers, solder, a soldering iron, heat shrink, a heat gun, and maybe some tin. There are plenty of tutorials on how to solder wires, which involve stripping the wire, adding some tin to help solder stick, and then using your soldering iron to melt the solder to the two exposed wires. This makes a strong connection which you cover with some heat shrink so that no wires are exposed. I personally use a wireless soldering iron by Iso-tip since I prefer it that way, but just about any soldering iron would work.

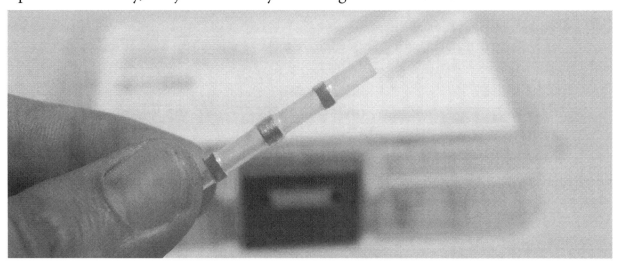

I discovered solder seal wire connectors about a year ago, which have become my new favorite way to do this. With solder seal wire connectors you do not need any soldering iron, solder, tin, or heat shrink – just wire strippers. These connectors have solder in the middle where you push the two stripped wires to. You then use a heat gun (or even a lighter if you are careful) to melt the solder and shrink the wrap around the wires. I definitely suggest having a set of these for when you need to connect wires if you do not want to pay for a full soldering kit, or are just not good at soldering like myself.

You will still need a soldering iron and solder to connect wires directly to parts, such as with a heated build plate, but these connectors work great anytime I need to connect two wires.

You will actually want to make sure you buy the more expensive version of these, with me suggesting the DX Engineering ones. These are more expensive than others you may find on Amazon, but they are worth it. Inexpensive ones will have solder that melts at too low of a temperature and can add resistance to your printer. If you do not want to purchase the more expensive version, you will likely want to just go with a standard soldering iron kit. You can also purchase these at auto stores.

**Zip Ties:** Obviously zip ties are not ideal for important parts on your machine, but they can definitely help out in a pinch. They can also help to clean up your wires by zip tying them all together. I always have a large box of different size zip ties on hand since I use them quite frequently, and never know when I will actually need them.

Make sure you actually buy well-made zip ties by reading reviews first.

**Calipers:** Calipers help immensely to accurately measure parts and filament. If you are doing any sort of designing, you are definitely going to want calipers. They also help to properly figure out your E-steps.

**Multimeter:** A multimeter has a ton of features and uses, but I really just use the continuity setting for the majority of my 3D printing needs. You can check voltage, amperage, and much more, but just figuring out if a wire is working properly is its best function.

You can easily touch a metal tip to one side of your wire, and the other metal tip to the other side, and you will be told if there is continuity with a beep. This can help immensely when trying to diagnose what isn't working on your printer, as mentioned in many chapters.

**Loctite Super Glue Gel:** My personal favorite way to combine parts strongly was actually Devcon plastic welding, but Loctite Super Glue gel is the easiest to use. I believe this has become the favorite of most 3D printing enthusiasts to combine plastic parts together. Keep in mind combining different types of materials may require different adhesives, but Loctite Super Glue Gel works wonders on PLA, and it dries extremely fast.

You will have to remove the outer container when running low, since there is still about a quarter of the gel left in the tube after you are unable to get any more out.

I have also used Starbond very recently though and they may be my new favorite method. Starbond Thick is very similar to Loctite Super Glue Gel and seems to hold just as well (if not better). Starbond also has an accelerator spray that allows the glue to dry within a few seconds, meaning you don't need to hold parts together for very long.

I have yet to find a good way to glue two nylon parts together.

**White Lithium Grease:** There are different preferences when it comes to lubing up important rods on your machine, but my favorite is white lithium grease. Periodically lubing threaded and smooth rods on your printer will help to get consistent clean prints.

**Wire and Nylon Brushes:** Nylon brushes are key to cleaning up a dirty nozzle and heater block. The only issue is that the nylon may melt on hot heaters. I really like to use brass brushes, but the added abrasion is not great for the hotend. If you have a very dirty heater block and nozzle, go ahead with a brass brush, but try to use nylon brushes when possible.

It can be quite difficult to clean up a dirty heater block and nozzle without a set of these brushes.

**Heatsinks:** As mentioned in the "Stepper Motors Overheating or Malfunctioning" chapter, it is very smart to have some heat sinks on any parts that may be getting too hot. They help to disperse heat and are very smart to add to the extruder, X, and Y stepper motors. Use with a thermal transfer adhesive backing or paste to attach.

**Something for organization:** This is pretty vague, but keeping your important accessories organized in a place near your machines will help a lot. I personally have a strong magnetic bar by my machines that have all of my tools attached to it. This way when I need something fast I can easily grab an Allen key, pliers, tweezers, scraper, etc.

You could also use some small containers that are labeled, just make sure it is all right next to your machine and organized so you don't go crazy looking for that part you need right now.

**Fire Extinguishing Ball:** It's hard to say this is really a 3D printing accessory, but it is something I can't stress enough to have in case of emergency. Hopefully it is never needed, and it will likely never be needed, but if it is, you will be happy you had one.

I have read too many stories about someone's printer catching fire, sometimes bringing down the entire house. If you are using the proper electronics on a well-built machine, it should never happen, but you want to idiot-proof yourself for something this serious. I have an AFO Fire Extinguishing ball mounted above my printers, and considering it will act as insurance on your house, $40 is well worth it. Make sure to check out the "Electrical Safety" chapter for more information.

## Replacements:

While it is nice to have replacements for every part in your machine, this is clearly not practical. Below are a list of inexpensive parts that should be held on reserve in case you were to ever need them.

**Thermistors:** Thermistors essentially act as thermometers for your hotend, making sure the heater goes to the proper temperature. These are very fragile parts, and many heater blocks just hold them in via a small screw and washer. These are very inexpensive and nice to have backups in case you ever get an "ERR: MINTEMP" or negative temperature readout.

I have gone through dozens of thermistors over the years, and they cost less than $5, so I definitely recommend a few spares for your hotend.

**Heater:** Heaters do not need to be replaced very often, but it is another inexpensive part that may come in handy. It can help to save you time diagnosing any hotend heating issues.

**Nozzles:** This is probably the most important replacement to have on hand. Brass nozzles wear out quite easily, and even hardened steal ones will eventually need to be replaced. If you are ever having difficulty diagnosing why your prints are coming out ugly, it is well worth swapping out your nozzle. Brass nozzles cost under $5 and hardened steel ones are closer to $15, but you will be extremely happy once you change your nozzle and it fixes your problems. I believe hardened steel versions are worth it, since you will not need to swap nozzles nearly as often. Personally, I have standardized to Nozzle X by E3D.

I have a video titled "The Importance of Replacing Nozzles" which goes over this further if you wish to learn more.

It would also be smart to have a few different nozzle diameters on hand. A good set would be a couple 0.25mm, 0.4mm, and 0.6mm nozzles, and maybe a 0.8mm for large prints.

**Fans:** Brushless fans can become damaged if accidentally hit when spinning, and may just burn out over time. If this is your barrel cooling fan, you are destined for repeated clogs. Make sure you have a couple of spare fans on hand for when you need them. The majority of fans on a printer are 40mm x 40mm x 10mm, but some use different sizes. E3D setups use a 30mm x 30mm x 10mm fan on their barrel. Just make sure you purchase the correct voltage for your machine.

**Silicone Socks:** These silicone sleeves go over your heater block and will help to prevent black spots on your print and to maintain print temperature. I definitely suggest to always print with these silicone socks, and to have a couple backups. These will eventually degrade and break over hundreds of hours of printing.

**Teflon (PTFE) Tubing:** Teflon tubing is used to help guide your filament to the hotend. It helps to prevent filament tangling and to make sure everything is guided correctly. Every so often these can be damaged when pushed into your hotend, so having some extra tubing on hand would be a smart idea.

**Endstops:** Endstops are another inexpensive part that will every so often need replacement. This doesn't necessarily need to be purchased before needing it, but can save you a couple of days when you run into an issue.

# Layer Shifts

Layer shifts refer to when the print looks fine other than the fact that one or multiple layers are shifted in the X or Y direction. Layer shifts can be something as simple as a loose wire or can be as difficult as recognizing that your stepper motor pulley is not functioning properly.

This can result in a print that has one, or multiple layer shifts.

## Single Layer Shift

This issue is normally a bit easier to diagnose and fix than a print with multiple layer shifts.

### Obstruction during print.

The most common cause of a single layer shift is that there was an obstruction during the printing process. This can be from tangled or too tightly wound filament, or from a cord that is the way of an axis from moving properly. You will see this occur more frequently on larger prints than small ones.

It is another reason I suggest only buying highly made filaments from reputable manufacturers. I have actually had brand new filaments that had a tangle in the middle of the spool, causing a layer shift mid print. I have heard people say this is impossible – but it has definitely happened to me.

You will want to make sure that your printer has a clear path before starting a print, and that all cords and wires are not in a position to obstruct after moving throughout the entirety of your print area. Confirm your filament is tight on its spool and that you maintain it in a way that will not allow it to tangle. If you have a spool that is becoming unwound during the print, get some Teflon tubing and mount it to your frame as tight as possible to help.

Zip tie all cords in a fashion that get them out of the way of the toolpath. Anything in the way of the extruder or build plate that is stronger than your stepper motor will cause a skip, and then result in at least a layer shift.

## Endstops in wrong spot or frame not set up properly

You will run into issues with a single layer shift if you are printing something large and your full print area is not set up properly. If you are using a slicing program where your machine settings are not to the proper dimensions of your printer, the machine will think that it can print further than it actually can. The stepper will skip when your extruder or bed hits its max build area, and the print will continue, assuming that it went the entire tool path.

You can check to make sure everything is set up correctly by homing your machine. When you home the printer and it goes to the very corner of your build plate, you likely have everything set up properly (or the center for printers with a home at center).

When you home the machine, if there is accessible print area in front of or to the side of the build plate (depending on your homing setup), you are not going to be able to use the entirety of your build area.

This can easily be fixed if your X or Y endstop is just in the wrong position by slightly adjusting their location. If these endstops are fixed on your machine, the frame itself may not be set properly. Adjust any t-nuts that may be holding your bed in the position it is in and slide until in the proper homing position. Retighten and make sure nothing can rattle. You need to make sure that your printer homes in the correct spot in order to take advantage of the entire build area. You would never know there is an issue on small prints until you decide to go with a large G-code.

## Errors in G-code or model

You will want to check out the "Model Errors" chapter for a further description, but essentially files can be corrupted or exported improperly. While in your slicing program check the model layer by layer to see if there are any holes or missing walls. Also be sure to check for actual errors on software such as Cura or the old version Netfabb.

Your G-code can actually be corrupted as well. This is not common but I have had prints that just would not print properly no matter what I did. This normally happens if you transfer a file before it has completely saved.

This is a lot harder to diagnose, but if you have a part that has caused a layer shift in the exact same spot after reprinting, then it is worth your time to reslice and reupload to your machine. It would be very unlikely to experience a layer shift in the same position if it were just caused by an obstruction.

## Too thick of layer heights - turn combing off/use

## lines for infill

This should not be an issue when working with standard nozzle sizes and layer heights, but can become an issue when going over 0.4mm layer heights. When I tested out the SuperVolcano with a 1.4mm nozzle and 1mm layer heights, my nozzle would drag over the previously laid infill when traveling.

Turning off combing allowed for the hotend to z-hop after every movement and avoid this infill. I also switched from triangular infill to lines, in order to avoid the same problem. When I did not do this – I got a layer shift from the nozzle hitting the infill and skipping the stepper motor.

# Multiple Layer Shifts

## Belts too loose (or too tight)

Belt harnesses on many machines are built in a way that will cause loosening over frequent printing. Some inexpensive machine harnesses only hold the belt tight via a zip-tie.

A loose belt will cause slippage and excess play. This is a very common problem when you are using a heavy bed that moves back and forth frequently (you will see frequent layer shifts in the Y-axis).

You will want to make sure your X and Y carriage have belts that are very tight. You can actually over tighten them, but from my experience, a loose belt is far more common than one that is overly tight. If your belt is too tight it may cause binding and ghosting (as covered in that chapter).

It is smart to print an adjustable belt tensioner for your carriages. This will allow for easy tightening when things get lose over time – otherwise you will likely have to disassemble. I go over this further in the "Z-Wobble" chapter. After adding one of these you actually can over-tighten, so be careful.

There is no specific measurement to judge if your belts are properly tight, I usually just say you don't want any droop and want the belt to be springy to the touch. If the belt feels as though it's stretching and has no real give – you've gone too tight.

## Bed corners tightened to their max

This is actually far more common than you would think. When attempting to get a level build plate you may run into a time that you end up over-tightening one or multiple corners. You do not want these corners at their maximum spring tightness because over time it can actually warp the metal plate. These warps will make your problems even worse.

You will notice an issue when you try to move the Y carriage (on Cartesian setups) with the printer off and stepper motors disabled. When one or multiple corners are over tightened, the bed will be difficult to move.

I suggest starting fresh by loosening all of the corners until they have equal minor tension on the springs. If you now notice a big difference in how easily your bed moves, then this is likely the culprit. Get the Z-rods even by checking the distance differences for the nozzle to the bed in the X direction. Just hold one rod in place while you twist the other, leveling the X-carriage (as explained further in the "Un-levelled Bed" chapter).

Only then should you adjust the corners for a level build plate. If you have a very warped metal plate you can experience certain corners that will just not get level no matter what you do. In this instance you will actually need a new metal plate. This is why you do not want to leave any corner over-tightened for long periods of time. You will be slowly putting pressure on an item that may get bent over time. Using a thicker ¼"glass build plate helps to make this issue less common.

This is just one of the many reasons an auto bed levelling device (such as the EZ-

ABL by TH3D) may be worth your time.

## Dry rods or broken bearings

Most printers have self-lubricating bearings for their carriages, but even those can get dry over frequent machine use. If you are having difficulty manually moving the X or Y axis when the machine is not printing and stepper motors are disabled, check to see if the rods are extremely dry or if the bearings are broken. A broken bearing is easily replaced and a dry rod can be fixed with some white lithium grease. Also check to make sure that the rods themselves do not have scarring from the bearing wearing down. If the rod is heavily scratched, then that may need to be replaced as well.

Just rub a minor amount of white lithium grease to the rods (both threaded and smooth) and then move the carriages around so that it spreads. If you notice a drastic increase in smooth movement of your axes, then you may have fixed your issues of multiple layer shifts. I have actually noticed some big difference and reduction in layer shifts after doing this in the past on machines with thousands of hours of run time.

Reapplying lithium grease and checking the resistance on the rods/bearings is good practice regardless of experiencing layer shifts, since it can help to allow for consistent clean prints.

## Bent rods

Rods, especially thin threaded 5mm Z-rods, can become bent over time. This bent rod can cause one or multiple layer shifts as the carriage or bed travel over these bends.

If you notice any rods that are bent, replace them immediately.

## Level Build Plate

If one side of your X-axis is much higher than the other, your printer may have difficulty evenly moving the extruder. Having one side of your machine be unleveled from the other could end up causing your stepper to skip multiple times, leading to many annoying layer shifts. This will also put unnecessary pressure on your rods which may cause them to bend and need to be replaced. Make sure took keep your X-axis level.

The same thing is true with the build plate. If it is angled and the rods aren't straight, the build plate won't move freely, and can cause multiple layer shifts.

You will notice that moving your carriage with steppers disabled will be hard if the rods aren't straight. You want to make sure that the bed and carriage can move very easily when steppers are disabled.

## Acceleration or speeds too high

Your motor's torque at a given speed must be greater than the force needed to accelerate or decelerate the carriage at a given acceleration rate and maximum speed. If you require a higher torque than the motor can supply at that given speed or acceleration, the layers will shift via the motor skipping (similar to how it is explained in the "Extruder Motor Skipping" chapter).

You can decrease the speed in your slicer settings, or by manually turning down the knob on your LCD screen. Acceleration can be decreased on the LCD screen as well, but to permanently change it you will want to go into your firmware. You can also just change the acceleration right in your Cura slicing. You will see this in the "Speed" section of Cura, as explained in the "Settings" chapter.

As mentioned in the "Extruder Stepper Skipping" chapter, you likely do not want this number over 1000, and for some machines you won't want this over 500. Manually reduce this number and see if it helps. I actually have my machine set to 500m/s/s acceleration even though it can likely handle higher, since I want consistently good quality, non-ghosted prints and am willing to wait the extra time required. CoreXY machines can handle a higher acceleration than Cartesian.

If you do not have an LCD screen, it is not offered in the slicing program you are using, or you would like to permanently change this number, you can find the acceleration in your printer's firmware in Marlin under the Configuration.h tab.

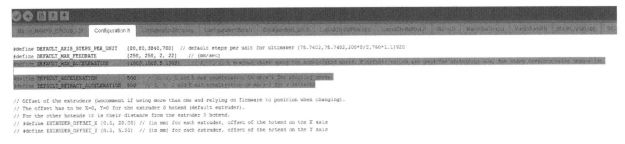

You can also find these numbers via a G-code command through Repetier Host,

Octoprint, or another terminal you are using. You will be fed out the current numbers if you type in the command "M503".

You can then set each of the numbers via their relevant G-code commands, and type another M500 to save the settings.

If you are ever having extreme difficulty with a printer and want to flash back to factory settings, but you do not have the version of Marlin for your printer, you can also type "M502", which is a factory reset. Remember you will lose any settings you may have changed (such as E-Steps), but this has saved me in the past when I was unable to determine why my motors were performing improperly.

## Driver current is too low or too high

Having the current going to your stepper drivers too low can cause insufficient motor torque and result in layer shifts/stepper skips. A driver current that is too high may overheat the stepper and cause a thermal shutdown. This shutdown will result in that stepper no longer working until it is cool once again. The same is true if the driver on your board is too hot.

Make sure that you have a fan on your board, a heat sink on your stepper motor, and a small heat sink for your stepper drivers. You can then check the current via the method described in the "Extruder Stepper Skipping" chapter, but with the X or Y motor in question. This should not be an issue with factory made machines, but will be more common on the inexpensive DIY ones, though I have had to change the stepper driver on one machine that was experiencing this overheating issue.

Remember to try previous methods before moving forward. This is only if you can tell your motor does not have enough power going to it. You may even want to test swapping the motor itself before to see if it is the motor itself that is faulty.

You first want to have your machine turned off and disconnect the stepper motor cable from the board. You then need to look up both the stepper motor you are using, as well as the stepper driver.

Current limits are determined in the motor and driver data sheet. You will not want to run higher than either the driver continuous current limit, or the motor current rating limit, so it is often good to have a driver that has a higher continuous current rating. I suggest going off of the continuous current limit of the Motor.

Once you know what current limit you want, you then need to find out the calculation for your stepper driver to determine a Vref. I had always assumed the calculations are the same, but they definitely are not. You can go to the current limiting section of your stepper driver data sheet in order to figure out the VREF you will want. Current limit will equal Vref x 2.5 for standard A4988, and Vref x 2 for DRV8825. There is then another option by TMC where the calculation is slightly different, where Vref= (Motor current x 2.5)/1.77. To find out your ideal Vref, there is a handy calculator that someone made online which you can search for by typing "Stepper Driver Vref Calculator", where you just enter the rated current of your motor and it will read out the ideal Vref numbers for each driver type.

I understand this is very confusing for someone who is new to this, just as it was for me. But essentially the Vref is the power that is being sent to your motors and it can be tweaked depending on your motor and stepper driver setup. So if your max current limit on your motor is 1AMP, and you are using the standard A4988 driver, you will have a Vref of roughly 0.4. This is because 0.4 x 2.5 = 1. This 0.4 would be your target number that your multimeter will read out. If your Vref is lower than 0.4, you will not be having enough power sent to the motors, meaning they can result in layer shifts and motor skips. Going higher than 0.4 can result in an overheated motor.

To test this out, you will actually need to plug back in your power and turn the machine on, while you still have access to the board. Be careful now that everything is on. Make sure the driver you are testing has the stepper motor unplugged from the board. You would then grab your multimeter. No real way to do this without a multimeter.

Set your multimeter to 20V DC, and touch your black negative lead to a ground pin on the stepper driver (titled GND). If you are unaware which the ground pin is, you can also touch the black negative lead to the negative section of your power supply. Just make sure to only touch a ground section.

You can then clip the positive lead of your meter to the metal shaft on the screwdriver to help read everything out while you change it. If you do not have a clip to connect the lead to the screwdriver, you will need to test, tweak, and test again. You then touch the positive lead (or the screwdriver if you have it clipped) to the potentiometer on the stepper driver. This is a very tiny screw like object on the driver. You will then see a voltage number on your multimeter. This is your Vref, which you want to make sure equals your calculation above.

You can turn the screwdriver clockwise to increase the voltage, and counterclockwise to decrease (which is actually the opposite on the TMC driver, so just make sure you are testing after each small turn). A 1/8 turn of the potentiometer will make a drastic difference in your Vref – so make sure to not turn too fast.

Remember, this shouldn't really be necessary on factory made, high end machines, since everything should be set to the proper ratings stock. But if you are experiencing layer shifts from skipping X and Y motors, it is definitely worth checking out.

## Stepper still skips

If your stepper still skips, you may have a malfunctioning motor or have wiring issues. Check the connectivity for each wire going from your stepper to your board.

If there is a break somewhere you will have to replace it or cut it and rewire.

The stepper or driver itself may be malfunctioning, so try switching the connectivity to a different axis and see if the motor still skips when moving that axis. If it does, replace the stepper to fix your layer shifting and skipping issues.

It also may be worth re-flashing your firmware or going back to factory settings if this issue came out of nowhere.

## Cheap or worn-out pulleys

Pulleys for your motors need to have sharp defined teeth with the proper spacing in order to work properly moving your belt the correct amount of steps. They also need to be tight on the stepper motor shaft, since any slippage on this will cause a layer shift.

If you buy a poorly made pulley, or notice that yours have had the grooves worn down, you will want to upgrade and purchase a new set. Go for products made from aluminum or stainless steel made products, since small items such as this are not that much more expensive, and can make a huge difference.

Make sure the small inserts on this pulley are tight to the motor shaft, with one of the inserts pushing against the flat part of the shaft, making sure it can't spin freely at all.

## Bed too heavy

This normally is not an issue if you have your drivers putting out the proper current and everything is lubed, but if you have an abnormally heavy bed you may experience shifts in the Y-Axis (on Cartesian machines, this should not happen at all on a CoreXY machine.). If you are trying out an experimental bed with a lot of wiring and extras on top of a ¼" thick glass bed, this axis may have difficulty moving without experiencing some layer shifts.

## Running into the print

A less common problem with layer shifting can be when the printer head runs into the layer it just printed. This can cause a skip in the motor and will have the print continue where it left off. You are more likely to get a print knocked off the build plate in this occurrence, but sometimes it can cause a layer shift.

This is most common when you are over extruding at very low or very high layer heights with a very strong bed adhesion.

As explained in the "Parts Being Knocked Over" chapter, you will want to add a Z-hop to that of your layer height, that your hotend is assembled tight and not oozing, and you will want to make sure you have your printer head avoid printed parts in your slicer settings.

# Z-wobble

Some may consider Z-wobble in the class of layer shifts, but I have it as its own category. If you are experiencing a wobbly looking print in the Z-Axis (never ending extremely small layer shifts), please refer to the "Z- Axis Wobble" chapter

## Summary of Fixes and Precautions

- Clear the printing path of your carriages from any obstructions. – Zip tie all wires and loose cords, and maintain a clean printing area.

- Confirm end stops are in the correct spots and that the frame is built correctly so that when you home the nozzle it is in the furthest part of the corner that it can be.

- Check for errors in model or reslice if G-code is corrupted.

- Increase z-hop, turn off combing, use lines for infill to prevent nozzle from hitting the print on large layer heights.

- Make sure belts are tight enough (but not too tight).

- Do not over tighten bed corners.

- Make sure the rods are not dry or that any bearings are broken.

- Replace any bent rods.

- Reduce your acceleration and/or speed.

- Increase or decrease the current going to your stepper drivers (if you are confident the stepper is underpowered).

- Check to see if your stepper or drivers are malfunctioning or overheating.

- Make sure your pulleys are attached tight to your stepper motor shaft and cannot spin freely.

- Replace or upgrade your pulleys.

# LCD Blank or Dark

If your LCD goes out there are really only a couple of solutions available. Most of the time you can still print with a blank LCD screen, but you can no longer use an SD card to load G-code. If your LCD goes out and you cannot control your printer by using a computer, it is likely your board needs a new NANO fuse, or the screen itself has burnt out.

## Replace NANO fuse

I am not familiar with every board on the market, but Rambo boards use two small NANO fuses. Companies such as LULZBOT use Rambo boards on their TAZ machines.

These NANO fuses can become quite a nuisance because they do go out more frequently than you would expect. When one of these fuses goes out it can cause your LCD screen to go dark. You also will not be able to control any axis or activate any heaters via Octoprint or Repetier when you are have a blown NANO fuse.

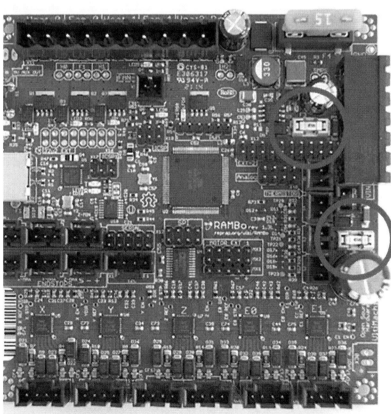

When this first happened to me about 4 years ago, I had to call the manufacturer, because I went through all of the procedures and could not get the LCD screen to work. I had not thought to replace one of these small fuses. You can buy replacements on Digikey or Mouser by searching for a 5A NANO fuse, such as ones made by Littlefuse. The specific part number is 0448005.MR for this Rambo board, and they are roughly $2 each. I highly recommend having extra on hand if you have a board that uses these NANO fuses.

Be sure your machine is off and unplugged before working with these fuses. Carefully remove one and replace it with one of these fuses you purchased. I suggest using a set of tweezers. Re-plug your machine in and see if it fixes your problem. If not, switch the second NANO fuse instead.

I believe every time my screen has gone out yet I could not control the printer it was due to one of these NANO fuses blowing.

## Check connections to LCD screen

If you can control your printer but your screen is out or dark, you will want to check all the connections to your LCD screen. Confirm that nothing has been disconnected from either the screen or the board and that there are no breaks in the cords. I have not personally experienced this since the LCD screen does not rattle around during the print, but I can only assume it to be possible. Use your multimeter if required to check continuity.

## Replace LCD screen

I understand this is not ideal, but LCD screens do burn out, especially on a machine that is over a year old with frequent usage. Luckily, LCD screens for basic RepRap machines will only be about $10, but ones for machines such as a Lulzbot TAZ will be closer to $70.

Personally, I have only had to replace three LCD screens in my roughly 5 years of printing history. So while it is not common, it is definitely possible.

If you have a brand new machine, or one only a couple of months old, your LCD screen should not be burnt out. If this is the case you may want to check with the manufacturer if it is under warranty, or if they will replace due to it being faulty.

Finally, as with many other solutions in this book, if your screen is still dark you will want to re-flash the firmware, and then replace the board if all else fails.

## Replace the LCD cable

If you still can't get the LCD to come back alive, it is very likely that the issue is with the LCD cable. If you have another printer available, swap the LCD screens and see if you can get it working. I've seen one case in which the old screen lit right up when swapping it like this. In this case, the system was back up and running with the original screen after replacing the cable.

## Summary of Fixes and Precautions

- Check to see if you can still control your printer when plugged into your computer.
- If you cannot control your machine, it is likely a Nano fuse was blown. Replace one or both.
- If you can control your machine, check to see if there are any breaks in the wire to your LCD or if any connections are dislodged.
- Replace the LCD screen if you do not see any problems with the wiring.
- Re-flash firmware, and finally, replace the board if all else fails.

# Mandatory Maintenance for your 3D Printer

The majority of the tips covered in this section are covered elsewhere for specific issues, but these are all mandatory to do frequently to achieve consistently clean prints. I will perform all of these once every couple of months as precautionary steps to not have to worry about fixing a problem after it occurs.

Most of these steps are also covered in depth in a video I made titled "Mandatory Maintenance for your 3D Printer" on my 3D Print General YouTube channel.

## Check there is no gaps or rattling from the bearings

Most machines have bearings that allow the X and Y axis to move along their rods. These bearings are attached to your carriages normally via printed parts. These are not present on a rail systems.

What you will want to do is grab your hotend when the machine is off and try to rattle it around. There should be no movement via this rattling. If there is, and you have made sure your hotend is setup properly, this rattling may be coming from gaps in your bearings.

Many machines use plastic bearings that can actually be stretched over time. Bearings should be gripping tight onto your metal rods, and if there is any free play, it can result in ugly prints. I have had to replace plastic bearings on all machines I have used with them after about 6 months of consistent printing. It is very noticeable after switching to new bearings that the rattling is entirely removed.

If you are using metal bearings, this is very unlikely to be the issue. That said, you will want to make sure these bearings themselves are harnessed tightly to your carriage. This may mean you will need to print new parts or use new zip-ties, since the bearings should be held as tightly as possible to your carriages.

This same exact process should be done for your printer bed, assuming you have a Cartesian machine. In the video I made mentioned in the introduction to this chapter, I had to replace all of the zip ties holding the bearings to my build plate, since they stretched over time.

There are many printers on the market that do not use standard bearings, but rather use rollers that move across an aluminum T-slot called in a rail type system, and these are not only beneficial due to their sturdiness, but will also not require any maintenance on bearings.

# Tighten all belts

Other than confirming all harnesses are tight and that there is zero rattling on the extruder and build plate, the next most common reason for Z-wobble is a loose belt. Minor Z-wobble will not be extremely noticeable, so it is important to do check this frequently to keep prints to their proper dimensions.

As explained elsewhere in this book, it is possible to over tighten a belt, but it is pretty difficult to do so on low end machines where the belt is just held together via zip ties. Both the X and Y axis belts should be very springy to the touch with zero droop. There is no real method to measure if your belts are properly tight, you just want to make sure there is no droop and that the belt isn't being stretched. Somewhere in between those two is the ideal range.

If there is any droop in your belt, you will need to tighten. For low end, non-upgraded machines, cut the zip tie that is holding the belt together, grab some pliers, and pull tight as you put on a new zip tie. Make sure the belt is tighter than it was and that the zip tie is pinching everything so that the belt won't slip.

Even better than doing this would be to print a manual way to tighten your belts. There is likely a file on Thingiverse for your specific machine setup, you would just need to search. I have added such a way to tighten the X-axis belt on my CR-10 by a model designed by donnyb99 on that site. I disassembled the X-axis belt and where the bearing is connected, and then added this printed part. I can now easily tighten the X-axis belt via a simple turn on the knob.

Be careful when adding one of these, since you will now be able to over tighten, which I had mentioned is difficult to do without this. Just turn the knob until the belt is very springy to the touch. There is no real scientific way to do this, you just want to make sure there is zero droop whatsoever.

# Clean up wiring

Just because you aren't experiencing an issue doesn't mean you shouldn't keep your wiring neat. Tangled wires from disorganization can lead to potential layer shifts or ripped out wires. If your barrel cooling fan's wires are ripped out mid print, you will get a nozzle clog – one that could have been prevented if you made sure your wiring was organized.

Make sure everything is tucked away and that there is no chance for any wire to get snagged mid print.

# Replace nozzle (especially if brass)

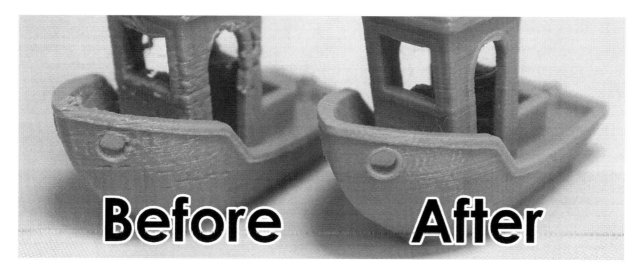

Above is a photo from a print with a worn out nozzle next to a brand new one.

As mentioned elsewhere, hardened steel nozzles do not need to be replaced nearly as often as brass ones, but replacing to a new nozzle can never hurt. I would replace brass nozzles just about every month or two to ensure that I don't run into any issues in the future, but I have since upgraded to only using hardened steel nozzles. As discussed in the "Over/Under Extrusion" chapter, even hardened steel nozzles can be worn out over time leading to very ugly prints even with all the proper slicer settings.

I can't tell you how many times I have gone crazy trying to figure out why my prints were coming out ugly only to replace the nozzle and have my problems disappear.

Refer to my video titled "The Importance of Replacing Nozzles" on my YouTube channel for further information and comparison images of before and after.

## Check E-Steps

This is the exact same process covered in the "Over/Under Extrusion" chapter, but you shouldn't wait until you see a problem before checking. Once every month or so I will check my E-steps to make sure they are on point, and will tweak if necessary. I don't wait until I see an under or over extruded part since I would rather prevent the problem before it happens.

For most under and over extrusion issues, you will want to check and calibrate your E-steps. To do this is actually quite simple.

You will want to start off by measuring out 100mm of filament. You can actually measure out even more for a more precise readout – you will just have to account for that in the calculations below. I prefer to use White PLA because it is the easiest to write on, has a low printing temperature, and is cheapest - though you could use any material you have at your disposal.

You can do this in whatever method is easiest for you. I found it easiest to measure this 100mm when the filament is already fed into the extruder. You can also do this on a desk before feeding, but 3.00mm filament, and 1.75 near the end of its spool, are quite hard to keep from rolling back up.

Be as precise as you can by using a fine tip sharpie and holding the material as straight as possible. Use calipers if you have them at your disposal. After heating your hotend, you then want to push the filament down until the lowest dot you made lines up with the top of your extruder, or somewhere else you can easily line up the starting point (because you will need to compare it to where it finishes).

The next thing you will want to do is to tell your printer to extrude 100mm. This is done with a simple G-code command in your terminal.

If you normally print via SD card you will need to hook up to a computer for this. If you print via Octoprint or a similar online program, you can send the G-code commands from their terminals.

When hooked up to Repetier Host, or whatever program you use to control your machine, and with your hotend hot, you will want to give your machine the command:

`G92 E0`

This sets your extruder to 0. Next you will want to give either the command:

For 3.00mm Filament: **G1 E100 F30**

or

For 1.75mm Filament: **G1 E100 F60**

This will tell your extruder to feed 100mm, and is why it was important you lined up your starting dot with either the top of your extruder or something else that is easy for you to compare to.

Once your extruder has finished you will want to mark your filament at the same spot you lined up your original dot (top of extruder in my examples). If your 100mm dot lines up perfectly, then your E-steps are right on - but even 1mm means that your printer is extruding incorrectly by 1%.

After marking where 100mm actually was, you will want to compare it to where you measured 100mm to be at the beginning of this process. If higher on the filament, your printer is over extruding, if lower on the filament, your printer is under extruding.

After measuring this difference you will want to write down somewhere how much your extruder actually fed. If your printer over extruded by 2.1mm, you will want to mark down 102.1mm. If it under extruded by 2.1mm, you will want to mark down 97.9mm. You will need this number later on.

The next step in this process is to determine what your current E-Steps are. You can do this by either checking the firmware for your machine, by going into the "Motion" section of your EEPROM (LCD Screen), or just by giving it the command

"M503" in your printer terminal. Non-geared extruders have E-steps of around 90, while Greg's wade and other geared extruders can have E-Steps of 500 or more. Something like the Titan has a starting point of 420. If you have an extruder from a popular manufacturer, they will list what their standard starting point for E-Steps should be.

If you are checking in the firmware that you use to flash your machine, you will want to open it up. While in Marlin you will go to the "Configuration.h" tab and scroll all the way down to where it says "DEFAULT_AXIS_STEPS_PER_UNIT", with E-steps being the 4th and final number (if using one extruder). The X, Y, and Z steps should never be changed and are a calculation based off of the parts you are using.

You could also type M503 into your terminal to be given a readout of what your current E-Steps are. You can then set the E-steps to the starting point of your new extruder. If you are using a Titan extruder, you would type "M92 E420". Then you would type M500 to save the settings. You can then run the 100mm feed out as explained above to tweak this number further.

After running your 100mm feed out test, you then take your current E-steps number and multiply it by 100 (the amount you were attempting to extrude). You will then divide this new number by the number you wrote down earlier.

If you decided to check your E-Steps by feeding out more than 100, you would multiply by that number. I actually will often feed out 200mm instead, in order to get back a more accurate number. Just remember to change the calculations accordingly.

For example, if your current E-steps are 90.5 as shown in Marlin above, you will multiply it by 100 to get 9050. We will then divide 9050 by how much you extruded earlier. So if you extruded 102.1mm, you will take 9050 and divide it by 102.1 to get 88.64.

## 90.5 x 100 = 9050

## 9050 ÷ 102.1 = 88.64

88.64 in this above example would be your new E-steps. As you can tell it is lower than it was before, because in this example you were correcting for over extrusion.

You will now set your E-steps. You can do this through your terminal, EEPROM, or by flashing your firmware. If you are going to do this through your terminal you will want to give the M92 command, by typing "M92 E88.64". You will then want to type "M500" in order to save these settings. Without typing "M500", the number will be reset when turning off your machine.

While you can set this number on LCD screens under the "Motion" section, it will only save permanently if you have the option to save your settings after doing so, just as with typing M500 in the example above. Otherwise your E-steps will reset once you turn your machine off.

Thomas Sanladerer has a great older tutorial video going over all of this on his channel which you can find by searching "calibrating your extruder" on YouTube. Thomas really knows his stuff and I suggest to everyone that they follow what he does.

## Clean your build plate

Cleaning your build plate frequently will help to prevent bed adhesion issues. Don't wait until your print won't stick before you clean your bed – proper precaution is important.

Depending on your build plate and what you were using for adhesion will determine how you clean, but I suggest to everyone that they clean their plate after every 5 prints or so. This is especially important when working with PEI beds, since they will gradually lose their adhesion as they become dirty.

## Lubricate Rods and Leadscrews

Grab a paper towel and clean off all of your metal rods. Then get some white lithium grease and rub it over both your smooth rods and threaded rods. While the bearings you use are advertised as "self-lubricating", they don't last forever.

After adding some grease, move all of your axis to all positions. This will help spread the grease out and you should notice a distinct difference in moving your carriages around.

## Tighten all screws and bolt on your machine

Frequent rattling of your machine can get screws and bolts loosened on your machine. If you haven't checked in a while, you will be surprised just how many aren't tight anymore.

When I say check every screw, I mean every single one. The ones holding your frame together, the ones holding your build plate, the ones holding your extruder – all of them. The last time I did this I had waited about 2 months. I found over 5 screws that had become entirely loose. Consider adding non-permanent thread locker to your screw threads to reduce the impact of vibrations over time.

These loose screws can lead to z-wobble or entirely failed prints. Take the precautionary steps to prevent this from ever happening.

**Note about ghost printing:**

If you have a printer that looks like it is printing, but isn't, it could be a few issues as noted in the "Diagnosing Failures" section. If you checked the other tips mentioned, and none worked, it could have to do with this need tighten all screws.

If you are able to push down filament without any issue, but the extruder just wont extrude filament (or just stops randomly), the hobbed gear on your extruder may not be tightened snug to the stepper motor. The hobbed gear which turns and feeds filament based off of your stepper motor turns is connected to your stepper motor via a tiny threaded insert. If this threaded insert becomes loose, the hobbed gear may spin freely around the stepper motor. This means that as your extruder turns, no filament is fed out.

This can result in a print that is "ghost printing", where your printer looks like it is moving just fine, but no filament is being extruded, and there is no clog to speak of.

# Material and their Settings

By this point you are well aware that different manufacturers with different printer setups will require different specific slicer settings. That said, I will review some of the settings that work best for me on both a geared direct drive and geared Bowden machine. These will be good starting points, though the speeds should be turned down a bit when working with non-geared extruders.

While Bowden machines can move faster without experiencing rattling, since the carriage is much lighter without the extruder, they are limited on specific materials due to the distance between the extruder and hotend. This also means it is more likely to print stringy and have difficulty travelling over small distances without leaving a trail, requiring an increased speed and distance for retraction.

All of the settings below are editable in Cura 4.0 and higher, and likely editable in your slicer as well. Make sure to read the PLA section entirely regardless of what material you are printing with, since there are some overall notes factored within.

Also note that speed that I mention, including retraction, can depend on what extruder you are using. I personally use a Bondtech BMG dual drive extruder, which can handle higher speeds than a non-geared extruder. These are just starting points to which you can tweak later if the quality is not to your liking.

** This chapter will go over the basics for printing with materials, but does not go into the actual science of what makes up different types of filament. For that, you should continue to the next section for the newly added "Material Science" chapter, contributed by Nicolas Tokotuu of Polymaker. I suggest everyone reads that next chapter since it will explain the "why" on everything, and how you would definitely want to tweak the settings you read below depending on your exact setup.

If you would like further information about 3D Printing materials, I would suggest you visit OptiMatter by SD3D (OptiMatter.com). OptiMatter provides a wide range of data on materials used for 3D printing and can even help to calculate the best printing configuration for you.

## NOTES ABOUT ALL MATERIALS:

This will be covered in the "Settings" section in this book, but first I will cover a few specific slicer settings that will be used regardless of the material. I almost always use Triangles or Hexagonal infill patterns, since I see no need for many of the other options, and I will always have at least 1mm of top layers. I keep acceleration and jerk lower than most other operators because I notice this is one of the most important things to keep low for a clean print, but it does increase the print time required. Both acceleration and jerk can be set higher on a Bowden machine though, due to its decreased carriage weight.

Make sure you always properly purge the filament when switching between materials in order to reduce the chance of black blobs on your print. Read the "Built up Material in Nozzle" chapter for a further explanation.

As of writing this book, Cura also has an experimental feature called "Coasting" that I use for almost every Bowden print. You will see throughout this section that Bowden machines come with an increased difficulty reducing stringy and hairy prints. Coasting replaces the last part of an extrusion path with a travel path, meaning the oozed material is used to print the last piece of the extrusion path to reduce stringing. This is great, but if you go too high, you can experience under extruded prints. For most materials I use the following Costing settings on Bowden machines:

```
Coasting Volume: 0.064 (nozzle diameter cubed)
Minimum Volume Before Coasting: 1mm3
Coasting Speed: 90%
```

Please also note that I am currently tweaking my travel speed settings due to further understanding from Polymaker and Nicolas's "Material Science" chapter contribution. Since travel speed really shouldn't affect the quality of your print, you should be able to bump this up to the highest you are able to. This not only will save on print time, but should reduce the amount of oozing debris/hair left on your prints. So while I have a travel speed of 100mm/s on all materials down below, I am now playing around with speeds around 200mm/s.

# PLA

Polylactic acid (PLA) is the most common and easiest to use 3D printing material. While PLA has a very high tensile strength, it has a very low bend-to-break ratio, making it one of the most brittle materials upon impact. The low glass transition temperature means that the printed part cannot withstand heat higher than 50°C without deforming, which means parts will deform when left on the dash of a hot car. These two factors mean that PLA is likely not going to be your choice for practical mechanical parts.

While you aren't going to be using PLA as a load bearing mechanical material, it has numerous other applications. Its ease to print, low shrinkage rate and inexpensive price makes it the perfect choice for models, prototypes for sizing, molding, cosplay, and other fun prints. Being a stiff part that holds its dimensions makes it a great choice for anyone wanting to make a negative cast for molding. For these exact reasons I personally use PLA far more than any other material. All of my fan art around my house and most of the examples used in my YouTube videos are made via PLA.

## PLA Slicer Settings:

### *Print Temperature (180° - 220°C)*

This print temperature range is huge and is only this large due to the vast variations among individual manufacturers. Most PLA manufacturers either ship their filament with a processing temperature range of 180°- 205° or 205°-220°, you just have to check with your individual spool. Even then, these ranges are larger than the average material you work with, and you will find that you may be able to achieve a successful print almost anywhere within these ranges. My personal choice is to go to the higher side of the material range. I like to print around 200°C in the materials with the lower range, and around 212°C with PLA that has the higher range on both Bowden and Direct Drive machines - though you can play around a bit and lower if you are experiencing blobs.

### *Build Plate Temperature (50 - 60°C)*

PLA is a bit unique in the fact it can actually print on a bed that is not heated, but it will stick and work best on one that is heated to its glass transition temperature of around 60°C. You can go down to 50°C if you are experiencing "elephant foot", as explained in that chapter.

While working with a 60°C build plate, you can actually just print directly onto a clean glass bed, but it is best to add additional adhesive. My favorite adhesive solution is some hair spray since it is easy to add, remove, and keeps the underside of the print clean. When working with a printer that does not have the ability to heat it's bed, you will need to go out of your way to make sure the part can stick on the initial layers beyond just hair spray. This is when you will likely want to use blue painters tape or another form mentioned in the "Bed Adhesion" chapter, along with including a brim or raft on just about every print. Having a heated bed will definitely reduce your headaches, but it is not mandatory for this material.

While working with a heated bed, I reduce the amount of times I use a brim to as minimal as possible. This is because most models should stick just fine without warping and removing a brim for PLA is not nearly as easy as it is on other materials. I have definitely regretted using a brim in the past when printing 30 small parts on a single bed – leading to an extra couple of hours of post-print manual cleanup.

### *Retraction: (Direct Drive: Distance: 3.5mm – Speed: 35mm/s – Minimum Travel 0.9mm) (Bowden: Distance: 4.8mm – Speed: 55mm/s – Minimum Travel – 0.8mm)*

Please note that retraction may need to be tweaked for individual models. Some models require retraction to be turned off entirely in order to print properly, but these are good starting points for your average model.

This is the setting that has the most difference between a direct drive and Bowden setup. Due to the pressure built up between the extruder and hotend in the Teflon tubing, Bowden has increased propensity for stringiness and so will require increased retraction settings on every material (some more than others). With a geared direct drive setup, these retraction settings work great on most PLA manufacturers that I have used, with minimal tweaking required for specific models.

Bowden machines need more tweaking than direct drives when it comes to this regard. Some models may be under extruded with these settings and need you to reduce the distance and speed. This is why I often tweak with the minimum travel. If you have a part that requires a lot of retraction to reduce stringiness, but there are a couple very small areas on your print that will be under extruded, you can bump this number up so that no retraction occurs over those small sections.

I almost always also keep the COASTING option turned on for Bowden prints, available in Cura 3.3 and newer, mentioned in the 'Notes about All Materials' section a few paragraphs earlier.

*Speed: (Direct Drive: Speed: 55mm/s - Outer Wall: 27mm/s – Top/Bottom: 30mm/s – Initial Layer: 20mm/s – Travel Speed: 100mm/s) (Bowden: Speed: 60mm/s – Outer Wall: 30mm/s – Top/Bottom: 30mm/s – Initial Layer Speed: 25mm/s – Travel Speed: 100mm/s)*

Please note that I normally suggest starting around 45mm/s on non-geared extruders, but since I am running a dual drive geared extruder, I bump this up to the 55mm/s you see above.

This section will get a lot of dispute from other experienced users, and definitely is different than the manufacturer advertised speeds. Personally, I don't mind a print taking an extra hour or two if it means that the quality is increased and the chance of failing is decreased. Reducing these numbers (as well as jerk and acceleration) from the recommended settings has done nothing but improve my print quality and reduce my failure rate.

PLA is the material I run the fastest due to its ease of printing. A light Bowden allows for fast printing, and if your setup has very little rattling with a geared extruder, you can likely go 65mm/s without any reduction in quality. Due to its rigidity, PLA is an excellent material for fast processing on a Bowden setup because it will not compress much, if at all, in the Teflon tubing.

Anyone saying they can achieve print speeds over 150mm/s is either lying, getting poor quality prints, has a very experimental machine, or does not understand how acceleration works. For any print to reach its top speed, enough distance is required and acceleration speeds set high enough to reach these speeds.

If your printer starts rattling when moving in-between parts, reduce your travel speed. If you don't see any ghosting and your parts are coming out extremely clean, you can try bumping speed and acceleration up to see if you get the same results.

These settings are also for when I am printing 0.2mm layer heights on a 0.4mm diameter nozzle. When printing with a very small nozzle at very small layer heights, these speeds will drastically need to be reduced. When I print on a 0.25mm nozzle I reduce everything by about 20%, and I drop my print speed all the way down to 25mm/s when running the extremely small 0.15mm nozzle.

While you should be able to achieve faster speeds than this when using a large nozzle diameter at large layer heights, you run into the issue of overheating your extruder stepper and getting skipped steps. You can keep speeds as they are if you have a powerful extruder, but it is also likely you will need to reduce these speeds when going over 0.6mm diameter nozzles. When I print with a 0.8mm diameter nozzle at 0.5mm layer heights I also have to decrease my speeds by about 20%.

This is one of the benefits to getting a Volcano or SuperVolcano hotend by E3D. They allow for faster printing with these large nozzles since they allow for a larger melt zone without causing heat creep in the barrel. If you want to print fast, large diameter nozzle and layer height prints, you will want to invest in one of these Volcano hotends.

I have a video titled "Taking it to the Extreme with the SUPER Volcano" in which I show how these speeds can be much higher when using this new hotend.

***Support Settings: Overhang Angle: 50-55° - Density: 12% - Z Distance: 0.2mm – X/Y Distance: 0.8mm – Enable Support Interface – Interface Thickness: 1mm – Interface Density: 90% - Interface Pattern: Concentric)***

These settings are the ones that will require the most additional tweaking for your individual printer and model. These are also for single nozzle parent support material. If you are using dissolvable support material, you will likely want to increase the density and decrease the Z distance. The 12% density may be too little for specific models, as well as the overhang angle, but since the interface density is so high, the underside of your print should hopefully still be clean. If you have support interface turned off, make sure you increase the density. Your Z distance is entirely dependent on your layer height, since it will always be a multiple of your layer height.

I have found that the support interface works great with PLA with difficult overhangs, it will just require you to be extra careful when removing the support material. Since PLA is so rigid and brittle, the part can easily break when trying to remove stubborn support that was not processed with the right settings. With the settings I provided above, it results in a very clean underside with support material that can kind of be "cracked" off in a couple of sections, with a minimal amount of razor cleanup.

There is a video on my YouTube channel titled "Detailed Cura Support Settings" in which I go over this further in depth. I can't stress enough how much support interface has helped with the quality of my prints ever since it was first introduced in Cura a little over a year ago, and I suggest everyone to check out that video so you understand exactly what is happening, along with examples of my prints.

## NOTES ABOUT PLA:

PLA is the easiest of the materials you will read about in this section to work with. You can get just as clean results with all of these settings tweaked slightly. As with almost all materials, PLA also can absorb moisture when not stored properly, though not quite as common. If you want to check if your PLA is good to work with, it should be breakable with a bend on the spool, or with a slight amount of effort. If it requires you to get scissors out to cut the material, since you cannot break it, it likely has absorbed moisture and needs to be dehumidified. If it is extremely brittle to the touch where it breaks without any effort at all, there is also an issue with the spool that will result in poor quality prints.

Since PLA is one of the least warping material, you should also always have your active cooling fan on full blast after the initial layer. This makes a drastic difference in surface quality and overhangs achievable.

# ABS

Acrylonitrile butadiene styrene (ABS) was the second most used material by myself, as it was always the go-to material for mechanical parts with a low price tag. ABS is what LEGOs are made out of, and its properties make it a great choice for mechanical parts as well as those requiring a high heat resistance, handling a heat deflection temperature up to 95°C (or 205°F). It is also soluble in acetone, allowing you to blend layers together and add an injection molded shine in an acetone vapor bath.

One thing you will hear from just about every experienced 3D printer is the difficulty to print this material without warping and delamination. Small parts may be achievable, but any large model will require a well-built enclosure with ambient air of over 50°C for any hope of success. Even with this environment, a level PEI build plate, and a model with 30 lines of brim, it is difficult to get a non-warped part weighing over 500 grams. This is why you will need an ABS Slurry for very large prints, and this added difficulty has turned ABS into a material I only use for small models. This is explained further in the next chapter.

You will want to keep your active cooling fan OFF when printing with ABS to help prevent warping.

## ABS Slicer Settings:

### Print Temperature (220° - 240°C)

ABS has a slightly higher printing temperature than PLA. I seem to prefer to print ABS at 230°C, but you may have better results tweaking within this range. Always check with your manufacturer's suggestions first.

### Build Plate Temperature (105°C)

This is one of the reasons it is so difficult to print ABS – bed adhesion. With a high glass transition temperature, you will want to run your print bed at a hot 105°C.

The issue with this will come from having drastically different ambient air temperature. Having cool air surrounding your print will cause those areas to want to shrink before the bottom of your print, leading to warping and delamination.

I have no problems printing small parts in ABS on an open printer, but it would be smart to print anything of size on an enclosed machine. I have been able to reach ambient temperature of over 55°C in an enclosed machine, which works perfectly to prevent warping and delamination. You just need to make sure the electronics used inside the machine can handle those temperatures, and that your board is located outside of this enclosure.

Even when having your print bed at 105°C, warping will still occur. I personally just use Aqua Net hairspray on a glass bed for adhesion, but this won't work on large parts. If your part absolutely needs to stick and has to be in ABS, you will need to make an ABS slurry if your printer is not entirely enclosed (explained further in the "Bed Adhesion" chapter).

I haven't used an ABS slurry in roughly 3 years because I have essentially switched to Nylon blends and PETG for parts that require a lot of strength.

### Retraction: (Direct Drive: Distance: 1.8mm – Speed: 15mm/s – Minimum Travel 1.2mm) (Bowden: Distance: 3.5mm – Speed: 35mm/s – Minimum Travel – 1.2mm)

For ABS I reduce my retraction settings a bit from PLA. It seems that ABS doesn't have as many issues with "stringiness" or "hairy" prints as other materials, so these numbers don't need to be quite as high. This is because ABS has a lower heat capacity than most of the materials we work with. PLA, PET and elastomers have much higher heat capacities. The lower the heat capacity, the faster the material can cool. This leads to less stringing but also lower interlayer adhesion. ABS is also still fairly rigid so it doesn't have to deal with extreme compression like what would be dealt with when processing a nylon or elastomer on a Bowden setup.

If you are experiencing stringing with these settings, increase accordingly, or use "Coasting" if applicable on a Bowden setup.

As with PLA, each model may require different retraction settings, with even some models having you turn retraction entirely off.

### Speed: (Direct Drive: Speed: 45mm/s - Outer Wall: 25mm/s – Top/Bottom: 40mm/s – Initial Layer: 25mm/s – Travel Speed: 100mm/s) (Bowden: Speed: 55mm/s – Outer Wall: 30mm/s – Top/Bottom: 30mm/s – Initial Layer Speed: 25mm/s – Travel Speed: 100mm/s)

As with all materials, speed is also going to be limited by the machine you are using.

Travel speed can be bumped up if you are using a strong, reliable machine, but you will always be limited based on acceleration and deceleration speeds. This is why a large printer can normally reach higher top speeds than a small one, having a longer period of time to accelerate and decelerate.

My CR-10 Bowden machine is limited to a travel speed of around 150mm/s, since the motors start making some loud noises over this. This being said, I print ABS at around the same speeds as PLA. Some machines advertise speeds much higher than this, but I always suggest starting low and increasing until failure.

These are settings for a 0.4mm nozzle and 0.2mm layer heights. These speeds will have to be decreased with smaller nozzles and layer heights, and can be increased with higher ones.

*Support Settings: Overhang Angle: 45-50° - Density: 15% - Z Distance: 0.2mm – X/YDistance: 0.8mm – Enable Support Interface – Interface Thickness: 1mm – Interface Density: 90% - Interface Pattern: Concentric)*

ABS is another material that I prefer to use the support interface on in order to improve underside quality. From my tests it seems that ABS cannot handle angles that great, so I will often set the overhang angle to 45°.

Since I keep the cooling fan OFF on ABS, it also seems to have more difficulty bridging gaps. Because of this, I bump the density up slightly to 15% just to make sure the support interface lays down cleanly. I personally see no reason to go higher than 90% support interface density on any material, so I keep that the same regardless.

## NOTES ABOUT ABS:

ABS is slowly being used less and less in 3D printing as easier, strong alternatives present themselves and their prices continue to drop. The rate of me getting a failed print while using ABS is much higher than just about every other material (with a few exceptions such as PCABS and other very high temp filaments).

One of the best parts about printing in ABS is the fact is soluble in acetone, meaning you can smooth the outer sections and make it more watertight, for a more injection molded look and feeling. You can do this via a crock pot on low for 10-20 seconds with your print lifted, you just have to be very careful doing this. For a further explanation, please read the "Post-Processing" chapter in this book.

# PETG

Polyethylene terephthalate with a glycol modification (PETG) is a plastic resin of the polyester family that is used in beverage containers, food packaging, and countless other everyday applications. While it is used for food containers, it is not recommended to use any 3D print for food parts, due to the minor gaps created in-between layer lines where bacteria can grow.

PETG has slowly become the main replacement for ABS, becoming the go to filament for strong mechanical parts at a low price tag. You can get a 1KG spool of PETG for only a couple of dollars more than PLA, and you can easily print a large piece without warping - so you will likely want to use this for the majority of your ABS applications.

Assuming you don't have a large budget, and do not need your part to withstand higher than 70°C, then PETG will likely be your choice over ABS.

PETG is very susceptible to stringiness due to its high heat capacity, and you can end up under extruding by attempting to rectify it via increasing retraction, so you may need to clean this stringing up post print on specific models.

## PETG Slicer Settings:

### Print Temperature (240° - 260°C)

Some say that you can print PETG below 240°C, but I personally have always printed at 250°C successfully (with minor tweaks for small/large nozzles and layer heights). Always check your filament manufacturers recommended settings, since some manufacturers will have a different range than I listed above.

### Build Plate Temperature (70° - 85°C)

You can actually print PETG without a heated bed, but it isn't simple. When heating to 70°C, and having a fully level bed, PETG sticks great and has no problems with warping. This, like the print temperature, can have a different range depending on the manufacturer.

I have printed parts that take up the entire 300mm x 300mm x 400mm build area of the CR-10 in PETG with absolutely zero problems with warping or delamination, though you will have to be confident on the manufacturer. I personally like Fiberlogy (sold by Wolfworks 3D in the USA) for my PETG needs, since it is the cleanest and strongest I have tested thus far.

### Retraction: (Direct Drive: Distance: 3.5mm – Speed: 35mm/s – Minimum Travel 0.7mm) (Bowden: Distance: 5mm – Speed: 55mm/s – Minimum Travel – 0.7mm)

Many of the settings for PETG are similar to PLA, but I have found a slightly increased retraction to help out immensely to reduce stringiness. As mentioned earlier, PETG seems to ooze out more than other materials, so you will want a bit of an increased retraction over PLA, and you will also want to have Coasting turned on for Bowden prints.

If you see under extrusion after increasing these numbers, reduce these settings and you will just have to clean off the string post-print with a blow dryer or a razor.

### Speed: (Direct Drive: Speed: 50mm/s - Outer Wall: 25mm/s – Top/Bottom: 40mm/s – Initial Layer: 25mm/s – Travel Speed: 100mm/s) (Bowden: Speed: 55mm/s – Outer Wall: 30mm/s – Top/Bottom: 30mm/s – Initial Layer Speed: 25mm/s – Travel Speed: 100mm/s)

This sounds a bit crazy, but I keep everything just about the same as I do when printing with PLA. These numbers worked perfectly so I saw no reason to change anything.

Keep in mind, as with all materials, these settings are for a 0.4mm nozzle and 0.2mm layer heights, with speeds needing to be tweaked if you are using something different.

*Support Settings: Overhang Angle: 60° - Density: 12% - Z Distance: 0.2mm – X/Y Distance: 0.8mm – Enable Support Interface – Interface Thickness: 1mm – Interface Density: 80% - Interface Pattern: Concentric)*

While I keep the actual support settings the same as PLA, the angle which support is required is much higher than PLA. When printing overhang tests, it seems that PETG achieves some of the cleanest overhangs of any material. This means you can go all the way up to 60° without requiring any support material, saving you a ton on material and time required to print lots of models. I have actually achieved 65° without the need of support material, which is quite high for any material.

With the support interface you may need to get your razor out, but removing support should essentially "crack" off and leave you with a very clean underside.

Every PETG I have ever tested has had a lot of difficulty bridging. So while you can achieve some great angles, you will not be able to bridge large sections without support material.

## NOTES ABOUT PETG:

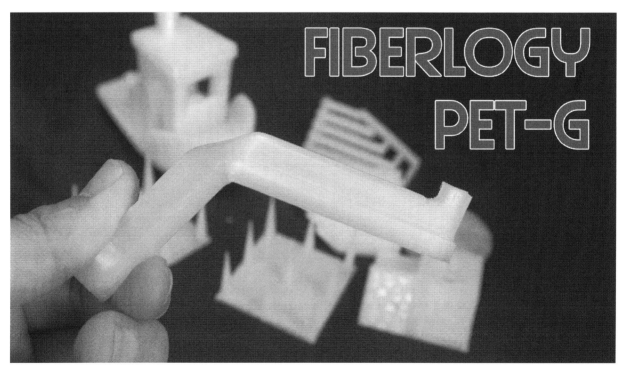

There is a video on my YouTube channel titled "PETG Cura Settings" in which I go over this more in-depth, though that was using a PETG material I do not really prefer any longer. I go over my testing of my current favorite PETG in a video titled "Fiberlogy PET-G Review".

I have always used the active cooling fan "on", but others have said to keep it off for increased layer adhesion. If you are noticing difficulty with layer adhesion, try turning the active fan off. If you are getting some ugly surface quality with the fan off, try turning it on and see if the strength of your part does not decrease.

PETG also seems to have difficulty bridging gaps (when compared to PLA), so you will require support settings turned on for small gaps

## Flexible Filaments

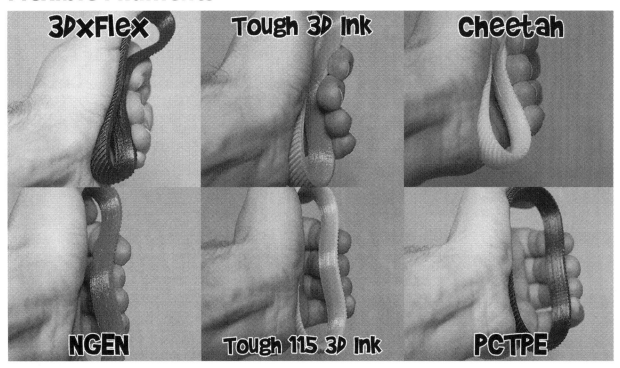

Flexible filaments come in a wide variety of properties and print settings, so it is just about impossible to give an all-inclusive profile. I have made 2 YouTube videos in which I go over 10 popular flexible titled "3D Printing Flexible Filament Comparison" part 1 and 2 to get a bit more of detailed description of options available.

While there are quite a lot of flexible options out there, my personal favorite for a lot of applications is Cheetah by NinjaTek.

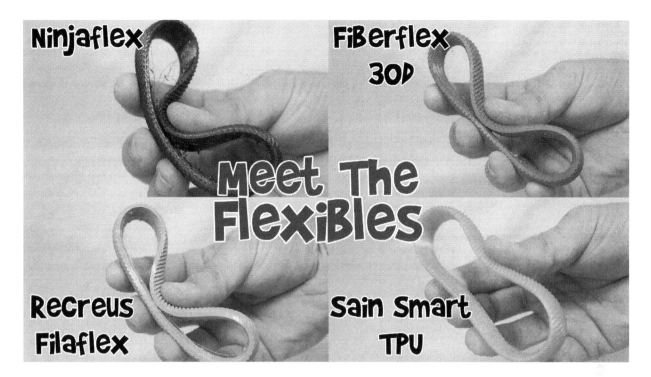

NinjaTek makes NinjaFlex, one of the most flexible options available on the market, but it is extremely difficult to print. Cheetah was created in order to fix this by allowing you to print faster, hence its name. I will be using Cheetah below as the example because of this, and because of the fact you can print this on a Bowden machine such as the CR-10 with an upgraded extruder.

Some overall notes for flexible filaments:

• All flexible filaments print better on a direct extruder vs. a Bowden machine, and some flexible materials are entirely impossible to print on a Bowden extruder.

• The general rule of thumb is – the softer and more flexible the material – the harder it is to print, and the more you need a direct geared extruder.

• You will need a geared extruder rated to print flexible filaments in order to print a wide variety of flexibles. You can print a basic Greg's Wade and purchase minimal parts, or you can purchase an upgraded extruder. My favorites are the E3D Titan, and the Bondtech BMG Extruder. The Bondtech BMG has a dual-drive, meaning there are two gears gripping onto the filament. This, along with a 3-1 ratio, makes it my favorite extruder to use when having difficulty printing flexible filaments. I have yet to find a material I can't print when using this Bondtech BMG as a direct extruder.

• Slow your print down! Print at speeds about 25% lower than recommended manufacturer settings to start with, and reduce further if needed. For some very soft materials such as 3DXFlex and NinjaFlex I have to print at 25mm/s in order to not experience a failed print.

• The harder the flexible filament, the easier it is to print. Almost any flexible filament with a shore hardness of 90A or lower is very difficult to print

• You may not be able to use smaller than a 0.4mm diameter nozzle, depending on how flexible the material is.

• Parent support material is extremely hard to remove. Flexible filaments with a large bend-to-break ratio have high layer adhesion, making parent support material very hard to remove cleanly. Because of this, I do not use support interface. You should always factor in the difficulty to remove support material when designing your flexible part.

## CHEETAH Slicer Settings:

### Print Temperature (235° - 245°C)

Flexible filaments have a wide range of printing temperature depending on the particular manufacturer. For Cheetah, I have found good results printing at 240° while something like Tough 3D Ink by M3D prints better at 250°C.

### Build Plate Temperature (45°C)

Many flexible filaments seem to prefer a print bed temperature of just 45°C, but there are of course exceptions to this. NGEN by ColorFabb requires a print bed of 80°C and PCTPE by taulman3D requires a coat of PVA be applied to prevent warping. Cheetah seems to print just fine without any warping with a 45°C glass bed and Aqua Net Hairspray.

### Retraction: (Direct Drive: Distance: 2mm – Speed: 20mm/s – Minimum Travel 1mm) (Bowden: Distance: 3mm – Speed: 40mm/s – Minimum Travel – 1mm)

I have retraction turned down from other materials due to the difficulty to print flexible filaments. Since speeds in general are reduced, retraction speeds should be reduced as well.

If you are printing a part that requires a lot of retraction and are doing it in flexible filament, even Cheetah, you are going to be left with some string you will have to clean up post print. You just need to grab a razor and scrape off the residue left on the print. There isn't much that can be done to help this.

### Speed: (Direct Drive: Speed: 40mm/s - Outer Wall: 20mm/s – Top/Bottom: 35mm/s – Initial Layer: 20mm/s – Travel Speed: 100mm/s) (Bowden: Speed: 35mm/s – Outer Wall: 17.5mm/s – Top/Bottom: 17.5mm/s – Initial Layer Speed: 20mm/s – Travel Speed: 100mm/s)

I am able to print cheetah faster than any other flexible filament, so these will be the upper bound for flexible materials. Remember you require an upgraded extruder (and likely hotend) if you want to print Cheetah on a Bowden machine such as the CR-10. I currently have a Bondtech BMG on my CR-10 and it is able to print Cheetah like a champ with the settings provided.

That being said, even with this $100 upgraded extruder and a $60 upgraded hotend, I am unable to print extremely soft materials such as 3DXFlex on my Bowden CR-10 regardless of how slow I run the print. If you plan on printing a lot of flexible filaments, it is worth your money and/or time to upgrade to a geared direct drive setup.

My CR-10 with a direct Bondtech BMG extruder has printed every flexible filament that I have tested thus far without any issues – which should show you the benefit over Bowden.

***Support Settings: Overhang Angle: 50° - Density: 15% - Z Distance: 0.2mm – X/Y Distance: 0.8mm – Disable Support Interface)***

These settings are definitely not perfected, but they work well for me while printing with Cheetah. As mentioned in the earlier notes, removing parent support material both cleanly and easily is near impossible with certain flexible filaments.

The overhang angle when support material is required will need to be found out for each material. NGEN by ColorFabb can get closer to 60°, so make sure you print an overhang test to find out when you will need support.

## NOTES ABOUT CHEETAH:

Cheetah has been the easiest to print flexible filament for me, so make sure you decrease most of these numbers when working with other materials. Some flexibles require a specific print bed since they have a nylon mixture.

Always store your flexible filaments in dry area vacuum sealed with some desiccants. This is true with all materials, but flexibles and nylons absorb water the fastest and will need to be vacuum purged if left out in a semi-humid area.

# Nylon Filaments

Nylon can also be referred to as a polyamide and are generally strong (and often semi-flexible) options for 3D printing. Almost all nylon options offered on the market are more expensive than PETG, but they are best for many applications. If you require impact resistance, you are likely going to want to with nylon due to its durability to flexibility ratio.

The strongest material I have ever tested to date is actually a Nylon. It is PolyMide CoPA by Polymaker, and I am not just saying that because they have contributed a chapter to this book. You can view my video "Nylon Comparison Part 1" on YouTube to see exactly how I have come to this conclusion. If you need strength – check this material out.

Nylons come in a wide variety of options, but almost all have a bit of difficulty sticking to build plates without extra help. As mentioned elsewhere in this book, you will likely want to grab some Elmer's glue, do a 1-1 mixture with water, and lightly brush it onto a clean glass build plate. After evaporated, nylons will stick great and pop off fairly easily with a scraper. You can also use a glue stick if that is your preferred method.

This may not be needed for all nylons, but I prefer doing this for most to prevent warping or parts being knocked off the print bed.

For the example below I will be using PolyMide CoPA by Polymaker since it is my current favorite nylon material, but every single nylon will require its own settings.

Some overall notes for nylon filaments:

• Nylon is hygroscopic and must be kept dry. This is not an option as leaving out your nylon spool can actually make it absorb too much moisture in a matter of a day or two. You should keep all nylon spools vacuum sealed, and in a dry area (45% humidity or lower).

• Many nylons have a shelf life and will not print as well after a year of being on the shelf, regardless of how well you store it.

• Nylons are very durable and have an excellent strength to flexibility ratio.

• Nylons often do not come in many color options, but most can be dyed (since it can absorb moisture). I have tried this in the past to mixed results.

• Just as with flexible filaments, removing parent support material can be very difficult with Nylons.

## PolyMide CoPA Slicer Settings:

### Print Temperature (263°C)

PolyMide is one of the few nylon mixtures that does not require PVA on a glass build plate, but I still do it as to help mitigate any bed adhesion issues.

While PolyMide requires a higher print bed, the majority of nylon materials I have worked with in the past prefer a 45°C print bed, and the vast majority require a glass bed with a PVA mixture to print. Refer to the beginning of this Nylon section to read further on how to do this properly, and refer to the next chapter to understand why.

Most nylons shouldn't give you much issue warping, but some, such as Alloy 910 by taulman3D, has warped on me in the past. You just need to make sure you evenly apply your PVA mixture and that your bed is levelled at the correct z-height.

Check with the manufacturers recommended print bed settings to be sure.

### Retraction: (Direct Drive: Distance: 3.5mm – Speed: 35mm/s – Minimum Travel 1mm) (Bowden: Distance: 4mm – Speed: 40mm/s – Minimum Travel – 1mm)

Without going too much into detail, these settings seem to work well with me and this filament. There isn't much to go over here, but you will need to tweak accordingly depending on the nylon you end up using.

### Speed: (Direct Drive: Speed: 45mm/s - Outer Wall: 22mm/s – Top/Bottom: 22mm/s – Initial Layer: 20mm/s – Travel Speed: 100mm/s) (Bowden: Speed: 40mm/s

*– Outer Wall: 20mm/s – Top/Bottom: 20mm/s – Initial Layer Speed: 20mm/s – Travel Speed: 100mm/s)*

These settings worked for me when working with PolyMide CoPA, but may not be great for other Nylons. Since the CoPA is a decent amount stiffer than many other nylon blends, you will likely need to go slower than this for other manufacturers.

I don't recall working with a specific nylon that required drastically slow print speeds, so proceed with what I have above, unless you read otherwise by the manufacturer.

*Support Settings: Overhang Angle: 50° - Density: 15% - Z Distance: 0.2mm – X/Y Distance: 0.8mm – Disable Support Interface)*

These settings stay the same as flexible filaments due to the difficulty to remove the support material cleanly. If you cannot remove the support material and it is stuck to the print, increase your Z distance.

If you notice a lot of drooping and that the particular nylon you are working with is unable to bridge gaps, increase the density. If you think you will be able to remove the filament, go ahead and test out support interface – I just personally haven't had great results in being able to easily clean it all up.

## NOTES ABOUT POLYMIDE COPA NYLON ALLOY 910:

I haven't done a ton of work with PolyMide CoPA, but what I have done has impressed me immensely. It is the only material I have ever done my strength test on that I was unable to break whatsoever. Polymaker has made me a believer when it comes to this material – especially since it is not that difficult to print.

Alloy 910 is another favorite of mine made by taulman3D and was a go to for me whenever I really need a part to have strength (until discovering PolyMide CoPA). I have used this material twice now for 3D printed planetary gear skateboard wheels, and they held up to a LOT of impact. They wouldn't break no matter how hard I jumped on my skateboard, and they eventually cracked under the pressure of a few professional skateboards (which can be seen in a couple Braille Skateboarding YouTube video). Compared to an ABS set that broke the moment I jumped on my board, it is clear nylons have their place in 3D printing.

Finding the right elasticity, shore hardness, and tensile strength for your part may be difficult, but there seems to be a wide variety of nylon options on the market today. You just need to think about what you need for your particular application.

# Carbon Fiber Reinforced and Filled Filaments

Carbon fiber reinforced materials are filled with continuous fibers or fiber particles that result in parts with improved physical properties and high stiffness. There is a variety of carbon fiber reinforced options out there for 3D printing, but they all require drastically different print settings. Because of this, I will not be going over particular slicer settings. In general, you will need similar settings to the material that Carbon Fiber is reinforcing. This means when working with Carbon Fiber Reinforced PLA, you will want to use similar settings to that of PLA. The same is true with ABS and Carbon Fiber Reinforced ABS, and so on.

Essentially, you will want to use carbon fiber reinforced materials when you require properties of the original material, but with a higher tensile strength.

Carbon Fiber Reinforced ABS has the high glass transition temperature of ABS, yet is much more stiff and strong. It is also easier to print. Carbon Fiber Reinforced Nylon is an awesome combination, one that is perfect for a wide variety of strength and heat resistant applications.

Personally, I have never found a use for Carbon Fiber Reinforced PLA, since it turns out more brittle than standard PLA (due to a lower elongation), but I am sure there applications for everything.

You will HAVE to work with hardened steel or ruby tipped nozzles when working with carbon fiber nylons, since the hardness will add abrasion and lead to your brass nozzle being worn out rapidly fast. A hardened steel or ruby tip nozzle will have a higher hardness than the carbon fiber blend and should not wear down your nozzle (or it will at least take much, much longer).

I am not going to include specific slicer settings for carbon fiber blends because they all vary drastically depending on what the carbon fiber is blended with. Just please note that as of now, all carbon fiber blends have lower layer adhesion properties.

# Material Science

## Written by Nicolas Tokotuu, Product Manager at Polymaker

I would like to express my special thanks to the Polymaker team for helping in writing this chapter. Polymaker is an innovative company where research and innovation are the core of the team and company growth. I joined Polymaker in 2016 as a 3D printing engineer and kept growing my polymer science knowledge to the point where I can start sharing with the 3D printing community.

## Polymers

In this chapter we will walk through the common issues and challenges encountered in 3D printing with a material science approach. The idea behind the chapter is to provide more scientific knowledge to common issues in order to easily overcome them.   Understanding this chapter can help to prevent the need to reference elsewhere in this book.

To begin, it is important to understand what material is being used in 3D printing: Polymers.

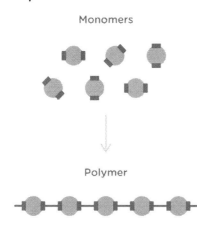

Polymers are large molecules, or "macromolecules", formed by large numbers of repeating units known as "monomers" in the polymerization process. The polymerization process bonds the monomer molecules together in a chemical reaction, forming the backbone of the polymer.

The type of polymers produced can vary depending on the chemistry and composition of monomer compounds that construct them. The links created between the monomers will be defined as covalent bonds.

Polymers can be divided into 2 families: thermosets and thermoplastics.

Thermosets are polymers that are irreversibly cured from a soft solid or viscous liquid pre-polymer into a solid polymer. The curing process is also known as cross-linking, which proceeds via a chemical reaction that connects all the monomers and pre-polymers to form a network structure. A cured thermoset can no longer be melted and usually is not thermally processable.

 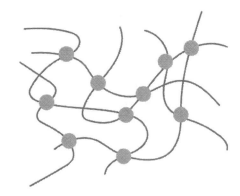

Thermoplastics are materials which become soft when heated and hard when cooled. Thermoplastics can be heated, molded and cooled multiple times with minimal change in their chemistry or mechanical properties. Unlike thermosets where each of the polymer chain is linked to others with a covalent bond, thermoplastics have their polymer chains linked with each other with weaker links which will be defined as non-covalent bonds.

Polymers can also be divided into two main categories depending on their micro-structure:

**Amorphous and Semi-Crystalline**

One of the ways that different thermoplastics can be identified is through their micro- structure, which can define the properties and behavior of the polymer.

# Amorphous

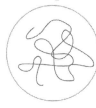

Amorphous

Amorphous polymers are identified for not having a long-range ordering. This means that the polymer chains are randomly oriented.

Generally speaking, clear plastics are often made with amorphous polymers, such as PMMA, PS and PC.

# Semi-Crystalline

Semicrystalline

Semi-crystalline polymers are identified for having an ordered structure with structural domains known as "crystals".

Crystals are an ordered and tightly packed group of polymer chains. Crystalline domains and amorphous domains co-exist in semi-crystalline polymers, thus the "semi". The proportion of crystallized areas is defined by the degree of crystallinity. A specific characteristic of semi-crystalline polymers is that this degree of crystallinity can highly affect their mechanical and thermal properties.

Now that we have a better understanding of the material structure we will dive into its thermal properties to understand its behavior as a function of the temperature.

In order to do that, we first need to define the test which will reveal the thermal properties of a polymer: DSC.

# DSC definition

Differential scanning calorimetry (DSC) is a type of thermal analysis in which a specimen is placed within a chamber and the amount of heat required to continually increase the internal temperature of the chamber is measured. This form of analysis is designed to pinpoint the temperatures at which the specimen undergoes certain state transitions e.g. Glass transition, crystallization, and melting, by documenting how a polymer reacts to the gradual heat increase via its level of energy absorption and release.

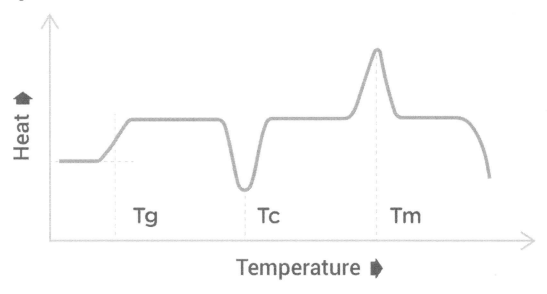

### Glass transition temperature (Tg)

The glass transition temperature can be found in all polymers, it refers to the temperature at which a polymers physical state transitions from glass (hard & brittle) to rubbery (soft & flexible). The Tg is usually used to highlight the highest working temperature of an amorphous polymer.

### Crystallization temperature (Tc)

Crystallization happens between Tg and Tm (melting temperature). It is the process of polymer molecules aligning to form crystals. The crystallization temperature is the point at which the polymers crystalize at the highest speed.

### Melting temperature (Tm)

The melting temperature is the point at which the crystalline domains of a semi-crystalline polymer starts to melt/deform. Amorphous polymers do not have a defined melting temperature.

### Decomposition temperature (Td)

The decomposition temperature is the temperature at which a material begins to deteriorate, meaning that the backbone of the polymer begins to break down.

### Notes about the above graph and definitions

A simple way to understand it is that the heat(energy) injected in the chamber will be used to increase the internal temperature, however if the sample (polymer) inside the chamber absorbs some thermal energy for structural realignment, more heat will be needed to be injected to continuously increase the temperature at a constant rate.

Referring to the graph above, at the beginning a constant amount of heat is applied to the system to increase the temperature at a certain rate. At Tg (glass transition temperature), we can notice that more heat is required to increase the temperature at this same rate, this is because the sample will absorb some thermal energy to break its non-covalent bonds and make the polymers move more freely (resulting in the material becoming soft).

After this phase transition, the sample will have a higher heat capacity, so the system will still require a constant amount of heat to be injected to increase the system temperature at the same rate, but this amount will be higher than before Tg. The energy continuously absorbed by the sample will make the polymer microstructure move more and more freely (excite them). At Tc (crystallization temperature), the polymer chain of the sample will have enough free movement to form crystals. The sample will then release energy (heat) which means that we need to inject less heat to the system to increase its temperature.

The reason is that the crystals structure (a more ordered structure) is coming from a more disordered structure, which will require less energy, thus the release of the extra energy. Once the crystals are formed, no more energy will be released from the sample to the system. However, soon after creating the crystals, at Tm (melting temperature), the polymer chains will continue gaining energy(movement) which will excite them too much and make them break the crystal structure, thus absorbing energy from the system, thus needing to inject more energy in the system to continue increasing the temperature at a constant rate. After breaking all the crystals, the sample will not require any additional energy from the system. This explains the two opposite spikes at Tc and Tm. At Td (decomposition temperature), the sample will start to decompose, meaning that covalent bonds will start to be broken, the sample will lose its heat capacity and thus less heat will be needed to increase the system temperature.

# Warping, Oozing and Overhangs

Now that the thermal transitions and behavior of polymers in function of the temperature are better understood, we can use this knowledge to explain some of the 3D printing phenomena:

**Warping, Oozing and Overhangs.**

Before jumping into these phenomena, we need to clarify an important point regarding printing speed and printing temperature:

Usually printing temperature is defined as the heat block temperature (in °C) and the printing speed will always define the print head speed when printing (in mm/s).

In this chapter we will refer to more useful factors for us such as the extrusion temperature and the extrusion rate:

**Extrusion Temperature:** The temperature at which the plastic exits the nozzle (in °C)

**Extrusion Rate:** The rate at which the plastic is extruded from the nozzle (in mm3/s)

Same printing temperature/speed          Different extrusion temperature/speed

Printing Temperature = 200°C          Printing Temperature = 200°C
Printing Speed = 50mm/s          Printing Speed = 50mm/s
Layer height = 0.1mm          Layer height = 0.2mm

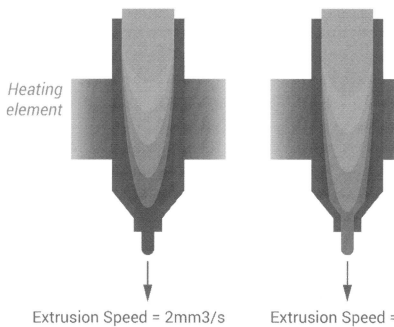
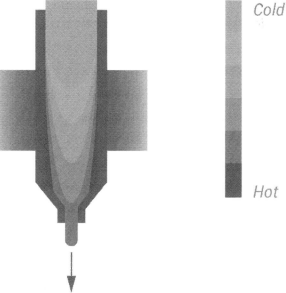

Heating element

Cold

Hot

Extrusion Speed = 2mm3/s          Extrusion Speed = 4mm3/s
Extrusion Temperature = 200°C          Extrusion Temperature = 195°C

The extrusion temperature can be increased using different factors:

Increase the printing temperature, reduce the printing speed, reduce the layer height, or increase the nozzle heated chamber length.

**The extrusion rate can be decreased using different factors:**

Reduce the printing speed, reduce the layer height, or reduce extrusion thickness.

# Warping

In 3D printing, occasionally we will encounter a part that deforms on the printer, curls or lifts up from the bed because of what is known as warping. This is caused by the accumulation of stress created by the 3d printing process.

The origin of the internal stress is still under debate, and depending on your 3D printer configuration, many factors may be contributing to the as-built internal stress. Here is one hypothesis which should be considered for all FDM machines:

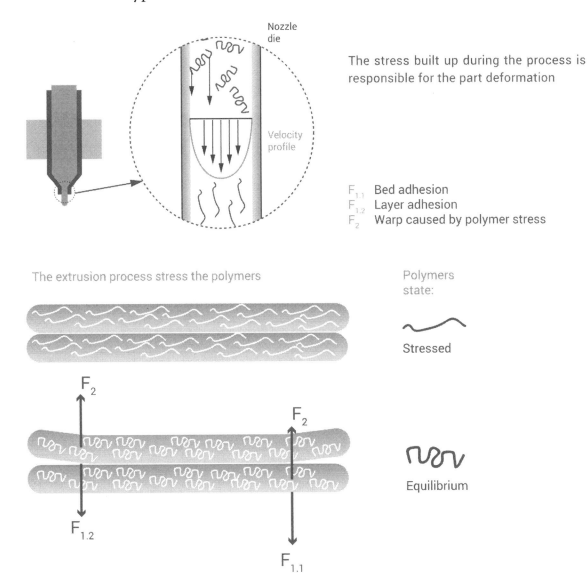

Nozzle die

Velocity profile

The stress built up during the process is responsible for the part deformation

$F_{1.1}$   Bed adhesion
$F_{1.2}$   Layer adhesion
$F_2$   Warp caused by polymer stress

The extrusion process stress the polymers

Polymers state:

Stressed

Equilibrium

$F_2$

$F_2$

$F_{1.2}$

$F_{1.1}$

During the extrusion process the polymer is forced through a die (small hole/nozzle), and during this step the polymer chains will be stretched to a stress state, then stuck to the build plate or a previous layer of plastic. This stress will slowly be released over time, however if the temperature does not allow the polymer to freely move enough to release the stress, or if the layer is not well stuck to the bed or the build plate, the accumulation of this stress throughout the layers will force the part to macroscopically deform.

Warping and cracking is always representative of this accumulation of stress exceeding the bond between the bed or layer adhesion.

As a result, we have three ways to prevent warping/cracking:

## 1. Give polymers enough energy to move freely and release their internal stress.

Most of the stress release happens right after the extrusion, indeed the material will be extruded at a high temperature then cooled down below Tg. It is during this time above Tg that the polymer will release most of its internal stress, however if this time is too short, it will not have time to reach equilibrium. Increasing this time period is a way to reduce warping.

This time period can be increased with the following ways:

**Increasing the extrusion temperature (PT):**

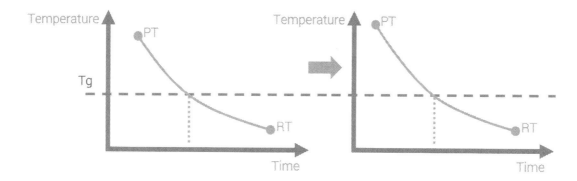

**Increasing the room or chamber temperature (RT):**

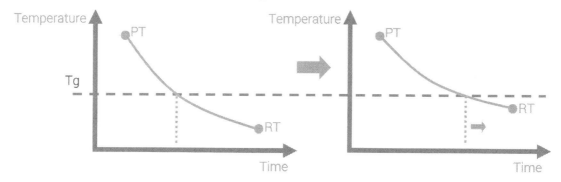

**Decreasing the cooling rate:**

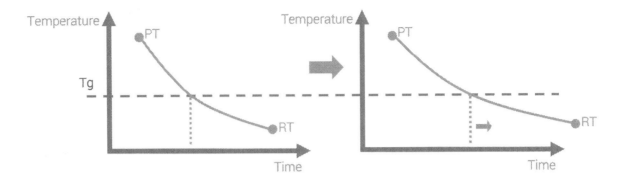

## 2. Improve bed or layer adhesion

The accumulation of stress will tend to lift up the layer from another layer (delamination) or the bed (warping). However, if the bed/layer adhesion is strong enough to resist the deformation, the polymer will be able to release its stress without deforming the part. The bed adhesion can be improved by using adequate bed surfaces and coating (refer to the "Bed Adhesion" chapter).

Before talking about how to improve layer adhesion, let us have a look at what layer adhesion is:

Layer adhesion is possible thanks to the entanglement between polymer chains from one layer to another.

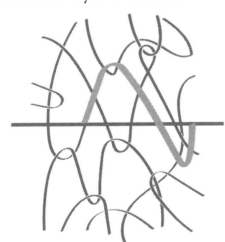

This entanglement is possible when both layers are heated up above Tg and both layers have their polymer chains moving freely, and through this movement the chains entangle with each other.

To improve the layer adhesion, we have to increase the number of entanglements between the polymer chains at the layer interface. The number of entanglements can be increased by increasing the time where both layers are in contact with each other with a temperature above Tg. As we can see this is the same solution as number 1. However, an extra factor which can improve the layer adhesion is increasing the contact surface between the layers by increasing the extrusion width.

## 3. Reduce stress creation

This third solution to solve warping relies on reducing the root cause of warping: internal stress.

As mentioned earlier, the stress is created by forcing the material through a die which will create a velocity curve which will stretch and align the polymer chains. Reducing the stress creation relies on flattening this velocity profile. This velocity profile can be flattened by increasing the nozzle size, reducing the extrusion rate, decreasing material viscosity (by increasing the printing temperature) or coating the internal nozzle surface with low flow resistant surface.

The above explanation of warping can be applied to amorphous and semi-crystalline polymers. However, semi-crystalline polymers face an additional source of stress: crystallization.

Indeed, when printing, the part will undergo crystallization when cooling down creating small crystals which, as ordered structure, take less space and will force the part to shrink. This is why Nylon materials will warp even though the build plate may only be 45 degrees. If the crystals are formed too quickly, each layer will have small crystals creating a lot of stress per layers and the accumulation of this stress will macroscopically deform the part.

# Oozing

In this part we will differentiate two kind of oozing depending on the root cause.

The first root cause is oozing created by the extruded filament being linked with the material inside the nozzle. The extruded filament will then force the material inside the nozzle to stretch out of the nozzle as the nozzle is moving to another location. We will rename this phenomenon as stringing (because of this string created).

Polymers with a high molecular interaction, or polymers which have absorbed moisture tend to have this issue.

A simple way to solve this stringing issue is to cut the extruded filament from the material in the nozzle by performing a wiping movement with the nozzle before moving the nozzle to another location.

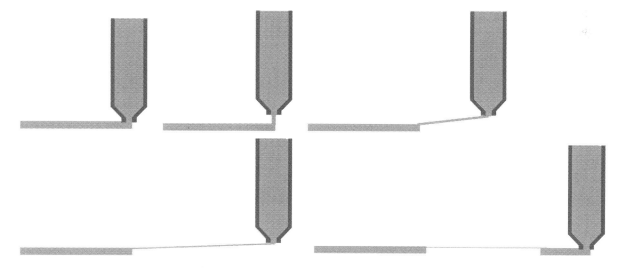

The second root cause is the actual material oozing created by the residual pressure and gravity which will force the material out of the nozzle over time.

As mentioned, the above 3 factors will define the amount of material oozing out of the nozzle:

**Residual pressure, gravity and time.**

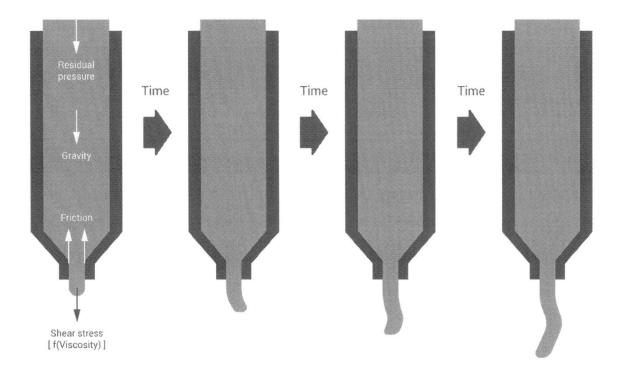

In order to reduce oozing, we will need to decrease or counter each of them:

**Residual pressure:**

Residual pressure is a result of the printer building up pressure within the nozzle to extrude at a certain volumetric speed. This pressure can never be completely discharged from the nozzle over a very short period of time and therefore the material will keep extruding slightly. To decrease the residual pressure, we can increase the retraction settings (distance, speed), increase coasting (using the residual pressure to finish the layer), decrease the extrusion rate (need less pressure to extrude) or increase the printing temperature (need less pressure to extrude).

**Gravity:**

Gravity will always pull the filament out of the nozzle, and if the gravitational force is stronger than the flow resistance of the plastic against the nozzle's internal surface and shear within the plastic, it will ooze out. Note that the flow resistance between the internal surface of the nozzle and the plastic can be increased by increasing the die L/D ratio (L: length of the die capillary, D: diameter of the nozzle hole). The shear within the plastic can be increased by lowering the temperature of the nozzle (thus the stand-by temperature in several dual extrusion 3D printers).

**Time:**

The amount of material oozing from the nozzle also depends on the amount of time the nozzle is inactive. The greater the duration, the larger amount of material there is. This time can be significantly reduced by having high travel speed, acceleration and reasonably high jerk settings. The material will not have time to ooze out before reaching the other part of the model. Having a high travel speed and acceleration should not affect ghosting as it would with increasing the print speed and acceleration. However, for dual extrusion printing, this factor cannot really be changed.

# Overhangs

Although it is recommended to use support for overhang angle, it usually saves time and material to being able to print high quality overhang surfaces.

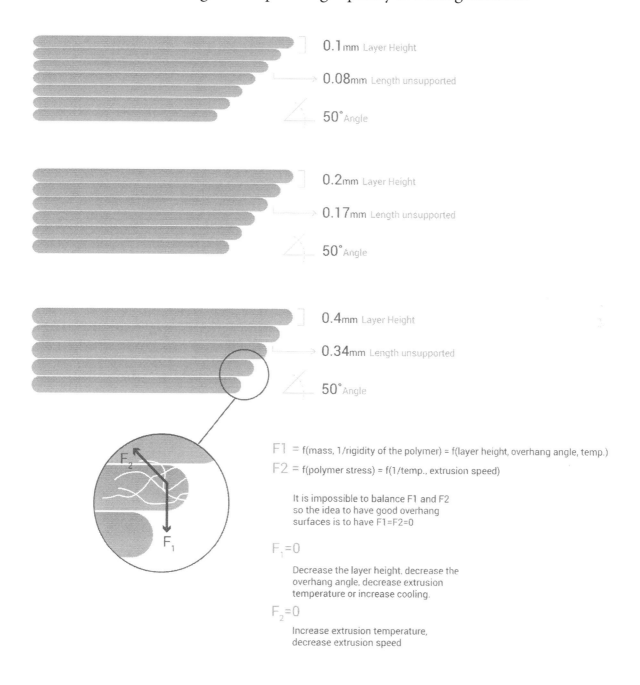

0.1mm Layer Height

0.08mm Length unsupported

50° Angle

0.2mm Layer Height

0.17mm Length unsupported

50° Angle

0.4mm Layer Height

0.34mm Length unsupported

50° Angle

F1 = f(mass, 1/rigidity of the polymer) = f(layer height, overhang angle, temp.)

F2 = f(polymer stress) = f(1/temp., extrusion speed)

It is impossible to balance F1 and F2 so the idea to have good overhang surfaces is to have F1=F2=0

$F_1=0$

Decrease the layer height, decrease the overhang angle, decrease extrusion temperature or increase cooling.

$F_2=0$

Increase extrusion temperature, decrease extrusion speed

The challenge when printing overhang surfaces is the amount of actual unsupported area. As you can see above, the same angle can give different unsupported area depending on the layer height. It can appear that the smaller the unsupported area the better, however the smaller the layer height the less rigid the unsupported area will be. It will always be a balance between rigidity and amount of unsupported area. You can visualize this relationship through one of Sean's videos titled "How to Avoid Needing Support Material" on YouTube.

Different factor can affect the overhang surfaces. As represented on the graphic below two main forces will be applied on the unsupported area: its weight (F1) and the polymer stress (F2).

The main factors affecting theses forces is summarized below, however generally speaking the best overhang surfaces will be given with a high layer height (more rigidity), low printing speed (more consistent extrusion) and high extrusion rate (more consistent extrusion).

## Mechanical Tests

Before closing this chapter, it can be useful to also learn about the different mechanical and thermal properties which can define a polymer. These 3 tests can determine how "strong" a material is depending on the application you require from your print. CNC Kitchen on YouTube has some great tests of 3D printed parts with the below methods.

Let us first review the 3 main mechanical tests:

### Tensile testing

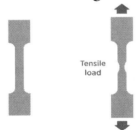

Tensile load

The tensile testing is where a polymer specimen is subjected to tension until it breaks. The test can be used to determine a specimen's tensile strength, Young's modulus, and elongation at break.

### Charpy impact test

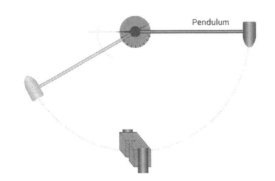

Pendulum

The Charpy impact test is the process of measuring the amount of energy upon impact that is required to fracture a test specimen. For plastics, the IZOD impact test is more commonly used, but they are similar. This test is conducted by fixing an appropriate polymer specimen in place and releasing a pendulum with a set mass at a set height to collide with the test specimen.

## Three-point flexural test

Three-point flexural test is the measurement of a specimen's resistance to deformation under a gradual load. The test samples are subjected to significant tensile and compressive stresses in their plane in addition to shear stresses. This test can be used to determine the bending strength and bending modulus.

Each of these tests will give important data which will define the material performance:

The tensile strength will give a graph similar to the below one:

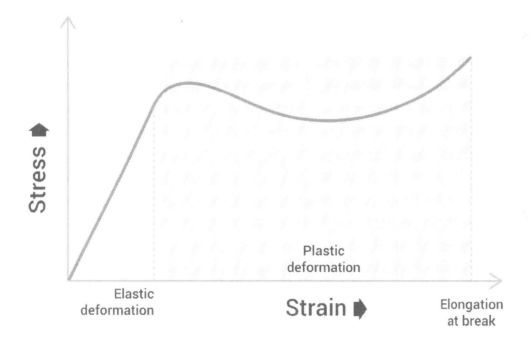

## Tensile strength:

Tensile strength characterizes the maximum stress required to pull the specimen to the point where it yields or breaks. Tensile strength at yield measures the stress at which a test specimen can withstand without permanent deformation, tensile strength at break measures the stress at which a test specimen breaks, and the ultimate tensile strength is the maximum between both. This allows us to understand the limit of a materials strength and its behavior when under stress. Tensile strength at break is not that common to use since the part has already started necking, usually only yield strength and ultimate tensile strength are of interest.

**Elongation at break:**

Elongation at break measures the deformation ratio between initial length and increased length right before breakage. This allows us the see the amount of stretching a material can endure before breaking.

**Young's modulus:**

Young's modulus measures the resistance of polymers to deformation under stress along a single axis. The Young's Modulus is a material property that is used to calculate the stiffness of a structure.

The bending strength will give a graph similar to the below one:

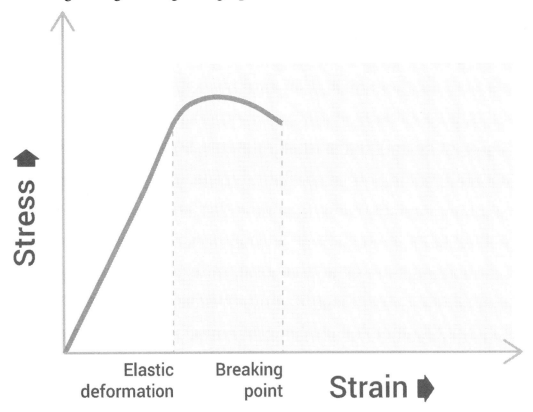

**Bending modulus**

Bending modulus is a local physical property that is computed as the ratio of stress to strain in flexural deformation. The Bending modulus has similarities to Young's modulus as it tests the polymers ability to resist deformation.

**Bending strength**

Bending strength represents the highest stress experienced within the material at its point of yield or break.

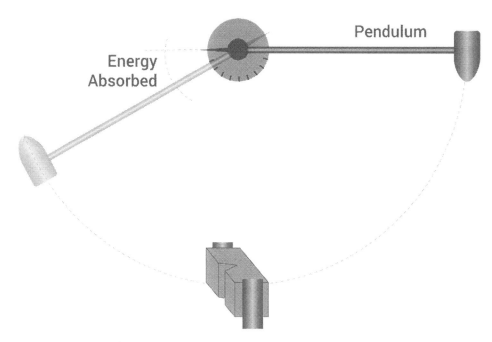

## Charpy impact strength

The charpy/IZOD impact tests measures the amount of energy that is required to fracture a material sample under a sudden load/impact. During the test the potential energy of the impact hammer is converted to kinetic energy. A part of this kinetic energy is absorbed by the sample during impact, so the hammer will not swing as further up as in the beginning. The difference between the initial potential energy and the potential energy of the hammer after the impact is the impact energy. This value is put into relation to the reference area of the sample that broke to calculate the impact strength ($kg/m^2$).

# Thermal Properties

## Heat deflection temperature:

Heat deflection temperature is the measure of the temperature at which a polymer undergoes a certain amount of deformation. The test is conducted using a specific load, while steadily increasing the temperature by 2 °C/min and measuring the temperature once the displacement of the contact sensor of the specimen reaches 10mm.

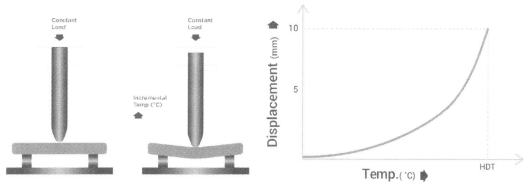

### Vicat softening temperature:

Whilst comparable to HDT, the Vicat softening temperature differs by providing a testing method that simulates the point at which temperature softens the material's physical properties enough for an external object under a set pressure to penetrate the outside surface of the specimen by 1mm.

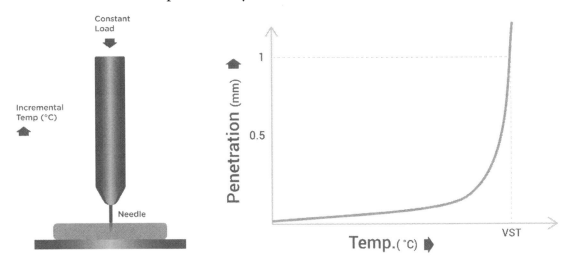

### Melt index:

Melt index characterizes the flow behavior of a polymer under a set pressure and temperature. This is achieved by extruding the polymer and measuring the total weight of the extrudate in a set time-period. The more material that extrudes, the increased weight and therefore the lower viscosity.

## Polymaker Technologies

Now that we have more material science knowledge it will be easier to understand the different technologies that Polymaker is using in their products to help combat some of these material limitations:

### Jam-Free™ Technology:

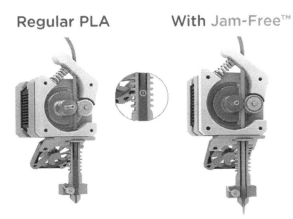

To understand this technology, let us understand the main root cause of jamming issues:

The print head is divided in two main parts: the hot end and the cold end. The hot end is where the heat block will heat up and melt the filament, the cold end will prevent the heat from the hot end to disperse and damage other components or soften/melt the filament before it needs to be.

However during long prints, dual extrusion prints and simply with a badly design heat sink the heat will climb up to the cold end and soften the filament which can lead to filament expansion thus jam, or the extruder chewing the filament (which we call "heat creep" in the "Nozzle Clogs" chapter).

PLA is the most concerned by this issue because it has a very low Tg (~60°C) so if the temperature raised a little bit over 50°C, it can already create a risk of jam. 2.85mm filament is less concerned by this issue because they are thick enough to stay more rigid than 1.75mm.

To solve this issue, Polymaker increases the heat resistance temperature of their 1.75mm PLA based product to 140°C.

Since PLA is a semi-crystalline polymer, Polymaker is able to do this by annealing the filament first, which will increase the crystallinity degree of the filament. As we explained earlier, the crystal will start to break at Tm (~150°C for Polymaker PLA) so it provides more heat resistance to the material.

**Warp-Free™ Technology:**

This technology is used by Polymaker in their PolyMide™ family (Nylon based material). We already learned a lot about warping issues and potential root cause earlier in this chapter. This technology solves one of the root cause of warping issues: Crystalization.

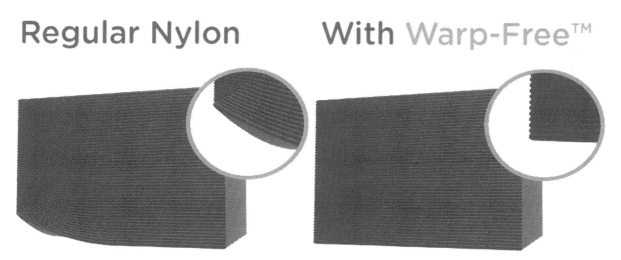

Indeed, Nylon is known as challenging to print because of its warping behavior, because when printing, the quick formation of crystals within each layers will create a lot of internal stress - resulting in part deformation.

Polymaker's technology is not only reducing this stress, but it is increasing the mechanical properties of the part. The technology slows down the crystallization rate of the polymer, which prevents it from quickly forming small crystals within each layer as they are printed. Instead, it allows the polymer to slowly build big crystal across layers, since multiple layers have time to be printed before the formation of crystals. These crystals across the layers will also significantly increase the inter layer adhesion. This is also the reason why Polymaker will recommend to anneal the part after the printing process. Annealing ensures the part has reached its highest degree of crystallinity, providing the best thermal and mechanical properties.

You can see how strong this nylon can be by watching Sean's video titled "Nylon Comparison Part 1" on YouTube.

## Layer-Free™ Technology:

This technology involves less of polymer science but more a perfect combination of the right material with the right solvent. Polymaker was interested in the smooth results that an acetone bath could give to an ABS print, however they thought that the ABS was too difficult to print, and the acetone could be a dangerous chemical and not safe to use. And there were no actual devices which were designed for the purpose of using this solvent to polish an ABS part (as you can tell in Sean's "Post-Processing" chapter, he used to use a crock pot).

The first challenge for Polymaker was to find a polymer which could be easy to print and also react with a solvent which could be sourced easily and less dangerous than acetone.

Polymaker finally found PVB as the perfect candidate. From there they started to develop specific material formulas PVB based and PolySmooth™ was the results of this development.

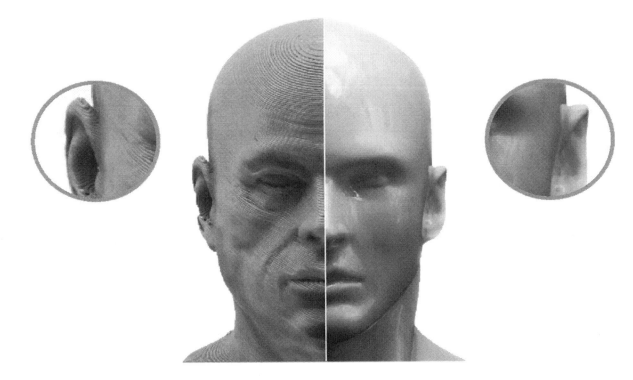

PolySmooth™ could be printed with the same settings as PLA and could then be smoothed with alcohol.

The second challenge was to design a device which could safely and reliably polish a PolySmooth™ model using alcohol. The Polysher™ was the result of this device development. The core of the Polysher™ being the nebulizer, the carefully chosen membrane and the specific algorithm developed to find the right frequency for the nebulizer.

Sean has a few videos on the PolySmooth™ going over its possibilities titled "Polysher by Polymaker Review – Smooth your 3D Print", "Transparent 3D Prints", and "More Transparent 3D Print Tests".

**Ash-Free™ Technology:**

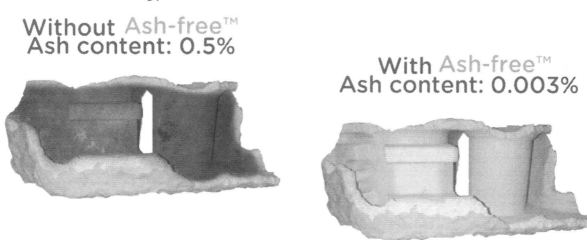

This technology is used in Polymaker Polycast™. It uses a specific combination of different precisely chosen components to create a material for casting. These components are carefully chosen to burnout without any residues.

**Fiber Adhesion™ Technology:**

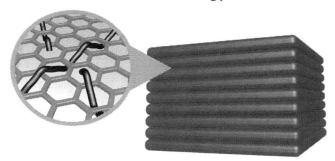

Fiber reinforced materials provide excellent thermal and mechanical properties, however in extrusion based 3D printing, it can negatively affect the layer adhesion. Polymaker believes that the layer adhesion issues come from the fibers not bonding/matching well with the matrix polymer.

After months of development, they successfully optimized the surface chemistry of the fibers to achieve better dispersion and bonding to the matrix.

When implementing this technology to PolyMide™ PA6-CF and PolyMide™ PA6-GF, the layer adhesion was not negatively affected, but actually stronger (+27% for CF, +15% for GF).

**Nano-reinforcement Technology:**

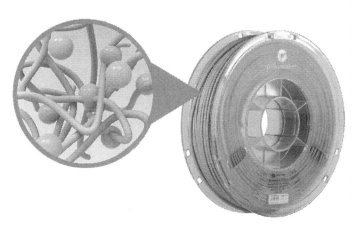

This technology is used in Polymaker's PolyMax™ family of products. It reinforces the polymer with nano-particles that make it much tougher, while simultaneously keeping similar printing conditions. PolyMax™ PLA, PolyMax™ PETG and PolyMax™ PC are the 3 products from the PolyMax™ family. They all print with the same settings as their regular counterpart: PolyLite™ PLA, PolyLite™ PETG and PolyLite™ PC, however they can achieve up to 5 times the toughness, making them more durable.

As reviewed earlier in this chapter, the fracture toughness can be well represented by the impact resistance of the material.

**Stabilized Foaming™ Technology:**

This last technology is one of the earliest developments by Polymaker. After several bad experiences clogging nozzles with printing wood filled filament, they thought about ways which could make a filament look like wood without actual wood powder in it, since wood powder in the filament could negatively affect the printing process.

Wood          Stabilized Foaming™

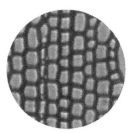 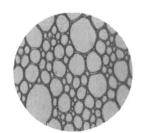

Polymaker realized that the main reason for the appearance of wood was its plant cell structure and color. It was easy to copy the color of a certain wood, and the plant cell structure was copied using a foaming agent, creating a similar cell network.

The main challenge was to design and formulate a foam structure which would not be negatively affected by the extrusion process of the 3D printer, thus the "stabilized" in "Stabilized Foaming", meaning that the foam will remain stable after the printing process. They have finally developed PolyWood™ from this technology.

# Missing Layers

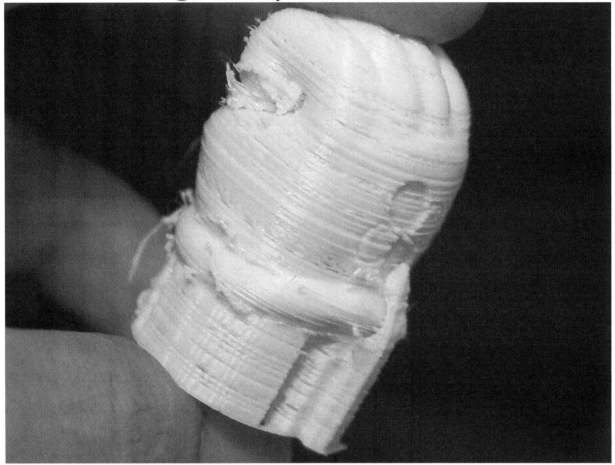

This is an issue that occurred for me randomly and I had a lot of trouble diagnosing it. I actually have a video on this titled: "Diagnosing and Fixing an Unknown 3D Printing Failure" on my YouTube Channel. This problem can also be known as "temporary under extrusion".

## Replace poorly made extruder

If you were to watch my video listed above, you would find out that replacing my extruder is what finally fixed this issue for me. This is not an ideal solution, but I was using a home-made Greg's Wade extruder, which likely had tolerance issues and may have worn down over hundreds of hours of printing.

If you are using an extruder that you personally made, or one that is made with lack luster tolerances, I would suggest changing it. As mentioned elsewhere I have standardized to the Bondtech BMG extruder, which I think is well-worth the $100 investment if you plan on 3D printing a lot.

At the minimum you should replace any home-made or plastic extruder with a metal one made by a reputable manufacturer if this problem is occurring (which can be found for under $20 for non-geared). TH3D sells a great metal upgrade extruder for Creality style printers for only $14, which should drastically help with this missing layer problem if you do not wish to buy a geared extruder. You can always reprint your home-made extruder parts after fixing this problem if you wish.

## Check for extruder skipping

One of the main reasons this will occur is if your extruder motor is skipping. I have a chapter on this topic, so you will need to read that if your extruder is skipping and making a "clicking" noise.

## Extruder Idler tension

The idler on your extruder is what is creating the tension on your filament. Some basic extruders may not have one, but all extruders will have some form of spring that puts tension so that your filament is held tightly between the threaded bolt and the bearing (or both threaded bolts for dual drive extruders).

Confirm that the filament is held tight so that no slipping can occur. One reason for missing layers is that the filament is not held tightly enough.

## Turn up your extrusion temperature

This can happen on a print when your hotend isn't hot enough for the particular material you are printing. The PLA I normally use has a temperature range of 205-220 degrees Celsius, and I almost always print at the higher range, right around 215 degrees. I experienced this issue once on my main printer with upgraded parts since I was printing at 205 degrees. Right when I bumped this back up to 215, the issue went away.

Printing at too low of a temperature for your material can cause too little of filament to extrude. And this can happen at random times during your print rather than throughout, since the hotend doesn't have enough time to heat the material when going at its top speeds. This would result in temporary under extrusion and missing layers.

## Slow your print down

Just as with running to low of a temperature, you can be feeding your filament too fast for either your extruder or your hotend.

When working with a stock non-geared extruder, along with a stock hotend, I wouldn't run my printer any faster than 45mm/s, no matter the material. With my upgrades I can easily print 60mm/s or higher, but whenever I run prints on a stock lower end machine, I decrease this to 45mm/s or less. If I am experiencing any issues, I go closer to 35mm/s.

This is a common solution to many problems in this book. Slowing your printer down can not only help you to diagnose particular problems, your printer may actually require you to slow down. Don't always believe manufacturers advertised printing speeds.

## Make sure your fan isn't dropping your printing temperature

If your active cooling fan is blowing onto the heaterblock and nozzle, rather than right below the nozzle, you can experience your extrusion temperature dropping in the middle of your print. Since we said that having your printing temperature too low can lead to this problem, your active cooling fan dropping the temperature can be the culprit as well.

Always use a silicone sock if possible on your heaterblock, since they will help to prevent any fluctuation. I use them on every one of my E3D hotend prints. If possible, re-print your active cooling fan to one that blows downward and wraps around the nozzle. Search on thingiverse and elsewhere for a file if you are unable to design one yourself.

Be sure to read the "Hotend Can't Reach or Maintain a Temperature" chapter if this is occurring for you, since there are a few solutions including running a PID auto-tune.

## Filament diameter problems

You should always confirm that your filament diameter in your slicer settings match what you have on your spool. This should always be set to either 1.75mm or 2.85mm, since those are the only two standards used in 3D printing.

That said, your particular manufacturer of filament may not have very tight tolerances. The tolerances of materials can be anywhere from .01mm to 0.1mm.

You can use calipers to confirm the average diameter of your material, but in all honesty, I would just suggest going with a more reputable manufacturer with tighter tolerances. Most reputable manufacturers produce filament with tolerances between .03mm and .05mm these days which is adequate for most prints.

## Potential under extrusion

For this particular issue, I would assume under-extrusion isn't the main problem, but it could be adding to your problems. Since having a missing layer is temporary under extrusion, the rest of your print should be extruding properly.

Check your E-steps, just as explained in the "Over and Under Extrusion" chapter. This likely wouldn't fix the problem by itself, but the symptoms may be reduced.

## Re-slice your part

If this is happening across multiple prints, then obviously re-slicing won't fix your problem. But if you are only using the same G-code, and the problems keep occurring at the same layer, it is worth your time to re-slice and export new G-code.

Before exporting, go into the layer mode of your slicer and analyze. I have actually had in the past where you can see the missing layer right in the slicer. This was due to a model error, and after fixing it, the slicer then showed that layer being printed.

## Check your rods/rails, bearings/rollers, and lubricate

Be sure to look up and down your printer to see if there are any issues, and perform a full maintenance check as explained in the "Mandatory Maintenance for 3D Printers" chapter.

One thing that chapter details is for you to lubricate your rods. This obviously isn't needed on rail systems, but all rods should be lubricated for bearings to move easily.

With your stepper motors disabled, move your hotend and build plate around its axis and check for any rough spots or where there is more friction than others. If there are rough spots, then you will need to lubricate, check your frame for any bends or misalignments, confirm your build plate corners are tightened too tight, and make sure your bearings/rollers aren't broken.

You may need to replace your bearings and/or re-align your frame to make sure everything moves freely.

## Extruder motor overheating

While this has never personally happened to me, I can only assume that your extruder motor, or stepper driver, overheating can lead to temporary under extrusion.

When stepper motors or stepper drivers overheat, they will not turn or work until cooled down to a working temperature. If this happens on your stepper motor, then it won't turn properly, under extrude, and then kick back on.

Your extruder stepper is working harder than any other axis, since it is under very high loads when forcing filament through the nozzle. You always want to make sure that you have a heatsink attached to the motor, and a small one attached to your driver on your board.

Refer to the "Stepper Motors Overheating or Malfunctioning" chapter if this is happening to you for a full fix.

## Old filament

As explained elsewhere in this book, old filament, especially those that have absorbed moisture, can lead to some confusing issues. If you have tried everything else, it might be worth just trying a different spool to see if your problems are alleviated.

## Summary of Fixes and Precautions

- Replace a cheap or poorly made extruder.

- Check for extruder motor skips, and refer to that chapter if occurring.

- Turn up your extrusion temperature to closer to the top of the recommended range.

- Slow your print down, especially when using a stock non-geared extruder.

- Confirm that the printer isn't dropping temperature mid print due to the active cooling fan.

- Confirm you are using the correct filament diameter, and that you are using from a reputable manufacturer tight tolerances.

- Check your e-steps as to not exasperate the problem.

- If occurring on one model, make sure to re-slice and examine the layers mode to see if the slicer is showing the problem.

- Do a physical mechanical check of your printer and perform all important mandatory maintenance.

- Make sure your extruder stepper or stepper driver isn't overheating. If so, refer to the "Stepper Motors Overheating or Malfunctioning" chapter.

- Try again with new filament that hasn't absorbed moisture.

# Model Errors

I am personally not a designer, nor am I extremely familiar with all the designing software out there, so I am not the best for giving advice when it comes to combining parts and properly exporting them in your preferred program. That said, there are some common issues that come into play with models exported for 3D printing.

## Holes, one sided walls, and other model errors

Other than the problems described below, there can actually just be errors within your model itself. This is extremely common if you used SketchUp to do your designing. I do not have the exact reasoning for this, but it seems to happen with .STL's exported from SketchUp more so than any other program.

Someone who takes all of the proper steps to design a model for 3D printing, including combining and exporting properly, should never experience a model with errors. But there are some free and paid programs out there that can help you diagnose and fix model errors.

I personally use the free version of Netfabb Basic. This actually isn't available any longer (at least without some hunting on GitHub), but there is the ability to fix models via Cura. Below is an example of a model missing a face and being too thin to print since it is not solid.

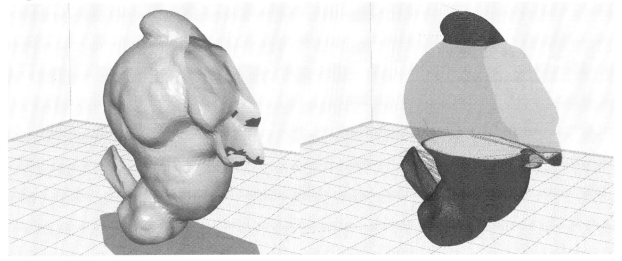

When you open up your settings you are given "Mesh Fixes" as a settings option. You can play around here and go back and forth from layers view to see if your problem was corrected.

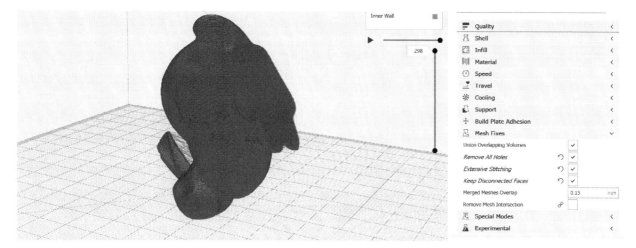

If you are able to download a previous version of Netfabb, this is also very easy. I was able to download this old version via some hunting online and finding a version of Netfabb Basic on GitHub. When you bring an .STL into Netfabb, you will see a red exclamation mark telling when there is a model error. You would then click on the "Repair" button up on the top toolbar

Choose "Automatic Repair", execute the default repair, and then click "Apply Repair". This fixes the vast majority of model errors so that it can be 3D printed.

If you still see the exclamation mark after attempting this repair, or you can't figure out how to download Netfabb Basic, you can also try out Microsoft's free online model repair tool at tools3d.azurewebsites.net. There are likely other free methods to fix models, such as using MeshMixer, but I personally do not use those.

If you are still experiencing issues, you may need to redesign or re-export the part.

## Parts that are not actually 3 dimensional

A common practice for those who do not have much designing for 3D printing experience will be to take a 2D object and fold it around itself.

If you were to take a 2 dimensional rectangle and then fold it around itself so that it is a cylinder with an open top and bottom, the object will look 3 dimensional to the human eye, but will not be recognized as such by the 3D printer or slicing software.

This is because the object you are looking at has walls that are infinitely thin – they do not have any actual depth to them.

You will need to close off these objects and make them solid, or do some other designing practices that allow them to become actual 3 dimensional objects with solid walls.

## Wall thickness

These next few may not be considered a technical error in the model, but essentially result in the same problems. You will always need to consider the thickness of the nozzle diameter you are using when designing the thinnest part of your print.

An FDM 3D printer can only print walls that are at least as thick as the nozzle diameter (or rather, the line width). I personally almost always print with the same line width as the nozzle diameter, though I have been experimenting with increasing it by 10% lately.

I normally suggest walls be at least 2-3x as thick as the nozzle diameter/line width, but the absolute minimum requirement is the diameter/line width itself. So, if you were using a 0.4mm nozzle (with 0.4mm line width), but some of the walls on your print are 0.3mm thick, those walls will not be recognized, and therefore will not print.

Along with increased detail, a smaller nozzle will allow you to print walls that were not visible on nozzles with larger diameters. You can always see if your walls are recognized by your printer by checking the "layer mode" in your slicing program.

In the example above, the tips of Old Man Logan's claws (designed by Exequiel Devoto on MyMiniFactory) are thinner than 0.4mm – the diameter of the nozzle I was using. Increasing the size of this part will allow you to print more, since the diameter of the blades will increase. If you are unable to print larger, you will need to use a smaller diameter nozzle.

If something is thinner than the thinnest diameter nozzle available, you have a part that cannot currently be FDM 3D printed. I have further information on the pros and cons with printing in small diameter nozzles in a video titled, "3D Printing with Extremely Fine Nozzles".

## Unprintable models

A model can be considered unprintable for many reasons, one of which being it requires support material that is impossible to remove. This is also explored in the "Limitations Involved with 3D Printing" chapter at the end of this book.

If you were to design a hollow cube with a single small hole giving you access to the inside, you will likely never be able to print this model.

This is because a cube of any decent size will require either infill (not hollow), or removable support material. If your hollow cube does not give you access to the inside, you will not be able to get that parent support material out. The other option would be to attempt to bridge the large gap, but no printer or material will be able to bridge 100mm+. This is why this hollow cube may be possible if small, but just about impossible if large.

You can see this a bit better with the above example. It would be just about impossible to remove that support through the hole, but you wouldn't be able to bridge this large gap without support material.

While this basic model may have no actual errors, you will not be able to print it successfully.

You can see my video titled "Cura Tricks for 3D Printing" where I am able to print one of these unprintable models, but it was quite difficult and may not work for all models.

## Summary of Fixes and Precautions

- Try to avoid designing on SketchUp.

- Always combine parts and export them using the proper methods of the program you are using. Do not cut corners.

- Use Cura, Netfabb, MeshMixer, or a similar program to diagnose and fix printing failures due to poor models.

- Make sure the walls of your print are at least as thick as the diameter of the nozzle/line width you are using.

- Inspect your print in your slicing programs "layer mode" to see what toolpath the printer will actually follow.

- Always take note if you have the ability to remove the support material that is being laid down.

# Not Finding Home and Inverted Prints

When you start a print your extruder and bed will go to its "home" position. It does this by moving the carriages until hitting their respective endstops. If there are any obstructions in the way of this process, or if there are any malfunctioning endstops, you can run into some serious structural issues.

The other way this can happen is via your firmware being set up improperly. If your printer is going to the incorrect location for home, you may also be experiencing inverted prints. This should not be an issue on a printer that you have not done any tweaks to.

Remember to refer to the "Diagram of a 3D Printer" near the beginning of this book in order to know what and where endstops are.

## Clear axis's of any obstructions

Each axis and machine setup will come with different obstructions that can prevent your printer from finding home. When this happens, your stepper motor for that axis will continue to turn and skip even though it cannot move any further. If this is on the X or Y axis, you may not experience any long term damage to your printer, but when on the Z axis you can have a nozzle that continues to dig into your build plate, resulting in issues to your frame, nozzle, and possibly even cracking your bed.

The most common obstruction I have experienced when dealing with a printer's X axis is when I leave the extruder idler open and start a print (which isn't possible with all extruders). This particular idler is just long enough to run into the printer's frame before engaging the endstop, causing quite a lot of noise when starting a print. You can also get an obstruction in the X axis from tangled filament or an extruder setup that is unable to engage the endstop.

For the Y axis, the most common obstruction seems to be wires and power cords. Since the build plate remains at ground level during a print on a Cartesian printer, and since it requires thick cords to power its heating, they can get in the way during and after a print. Throughout a previous print these cords may have gotten in the way of the build plate hitting its endstop, and you wouldn't know until you try to home or start a new print. You can also get a Y-axis obstruction if the endstop is unable to be engaged due to it being in a slightly improper position.

The Z axis really does differ on every machine and setup, but if you are using a mechanical screw to check your Z-height, there is a possibility it has been dislodged and not engaging the endstop. Confirm that the screw lines up properly with its endstop and that it is able to engage it to the point that the endstop clicks. This isn't as much as a problem today as the past, since auto bed levelers have become more common.

Clear any obstructions and confirm all endstops can be engaged when homing before moving on to the next solution.

# Malfunctioning endstop

A malfunctioning endstop is one that does not send a signal to the controller (i.e. light up) when engaged (pushed down until it clicks). This could be due to a broken endstop, or due to the wiring being disconnected.

First confirm that all wires are plugged into the end stop and board, and that none have been pulled out from their connectors. Then check for any easy to see visual issues such as frayed or burnt out wires. If you do not see any, pull out your multimeter and check each wire for continuity, as explained in the "Stepper Motors Overheating or Malfunctioning" chapter. If one wire does not read out any noise or continuity, attempt to find where the break is, cut and solder, or replace the wire entirely.

If all wires show connectivity, your endstop itself may need to be replaced. Luckily, these are very cheap and I recommend having a spare on hand to test and fix this issue fast.

# Homing to wrong side or endstop on wrong side

These next steps should only really be an issue on a machine you are building yourself. If this is occurring on a machine that was sent to you from the manufacturer, it was likely their fault, and worth contacting the manufacturer.

Bed Moves in Y Axis

Extruder Moves in X Axis

"Home"
Nozzle at X0, Y0

3D printers can have very different understanding of where "home" is depending on the manufacturer. For some - home is when the X carriage is all the way to the left and the bed is all the way back, others it can be the exact opposite. CoreXY printers will have the bed homing by either moving it up to the nozzle, or down to a specific set point. Though this can vary, the standard for the majority of Cartesian (non CoreXY or Delta) machines is having the nozzle home to the front left side of your build plate (as pictured).

If you have your endstop on the incorrect side for where your machine is homing, it will clearly never be able to find it. You will hear a lot of noise as the extruder or build plate continues to try and move and cause your stepper motor to skip.

If you are unaware of where "home" should be on your printer, it is a good bet that it is where your printer moves to when starting a new print. If you are sure that home should be on one side, yet your printer always moves to the other, you may have your settings incorrect in either the firmware or when slicing your G-code. You will definitely be able to tell if this is the case if your prints are coming out inverted.

If your prints are not coming out inverted, it is likely easiest for you to just physically change the location of your endstop. If you would rather go the firmware route, open up Marlin when re-flashing your machine, and go to the Configuration.h tab. Scroll down until you see "ENDSTOP SETTINGS:" followed by each axis's home direction being defined by either 1 or -1. If the axis that is homing on the incorrect side for you, and it says 1, change it to -1. If the axis's that is homing on the incorrect side for you says -1, change it to 1.

```
// ENDSTOP SETTINGS:
// Sets direction of endstops when homing; 1=MAX, -1=MIN
#define X_HOME_DIR -1
#define Y_HOME_DIR -1
#define Z_HOME_DIR -1
```

# Inverted prints

If your prints are coming out inverted, it is normally when one of your axes is inverted via firmware, slicing program, or your motor is wired/setup improperly. You would really only need to change one of these regardless of which was causing you this issue. If you setup your stepper motor on the wrong side, so that it is turning your belt the incorrect direction, it will likely be easier to just invert this axis in your firmware rather than rebuilding that part of your machine.

To do this open up marlin to flash your machine. While in Configuration.h, scroll down to where it says "#define INVERT_X_DIR" followed by either true or false, and the other axis's below it. Whichever axis is inverting for you, switch the language (turn "false" to "true", or vice versa).

```
#define INVERT_X_DIR false    // for Mendel set to false, for Orca set to true
#define INVERT_Y_DIR false    // for Mendel set to true, for Orca set to false
#define INVERT_Z_DIR true     // for Mendel set to false, for Orca set to true
```

If you are currently homing properly, but your axis is inverted, you will want to change the language on both sections of the Configuration.h tab mentioned above. This will correct the inverted axis but still allow home to be in the same location, meaning you do not need to relocate any endstops. If you only change the invert, but not the endstop settings, you will be homing in the incorrect spot.

When finished, plug in your machine, choose the correct board and port, and upload.

Another option is to literally invert the wires going to your stepper motor in question. If your wires are in the reverse order, the stepper will turn in the opposite direction. This will of course change where "home" is, so you should only do this method if you are homing in the wrong spot AND have inverted prints.

## Summary of Fixes and Precautions

- Confirm that there are no obstructions from any axis hitting its respective endstop.

- Confirm that the endstop lights up when engaged.

- If the endstop does not light up, check that all wires are showing continuity. Replace any that are not.

- If all wires show continuity, replace the endstop in question.

- If homing to opposite side of your machine but parts are not inverted, you can either physically move your endstop to the other side or you can change the proper language in Marlin.

- If homing to opposite side of your machine but parts are inverted, change the proper language in Marlin.

- If parts are inverted but you are homing to the correct side of your machine, change both the language in both sections of Marlin mentioned above.

# Nozzle Clogs

Nozzle clogs are just what they sound like and are a fairly consistent problem with FDM machines. They can take a very long time to fix and can normally not be diagnosed until the print has been going for a while. Most of the time these nozzle clogs will actually be clogs in the barrel, but we will still refer to this issue as a nozzle clog. We can think of these as more "filament clogs" where the filament is clogged somewhere in the hotend.

If the nozzle clog is frequently happening, even after doing these fixes, you will need to review the "Settings Issues", "Hotend Can't Reach or Maintain Temperature", and "Hotend Not Reading Correct Temperature" chapters.

One way to help prevent nozzle clogs is to use an all metal hotend. Many inexpensive machines do not come with an all metal hotend, and have PTFE tube go all the way to the heat break. This can cause unwanted issues and further nozzle clogs. An upgrade to an all metal hotend is not only needed for printing at higher temperatures, but recommended to just avoid nozzle clogs.

***IMPORTANT NOTE:*** Anytime you switch filament you will ALWAYS want to push the material down around 1 cm before removing. Some minor heat creep can occur when the printer is cooling down after a print and is only noticeable when you attempt to remove it. This practice can save you from an untold amount of barrel clogs. I never change filament without pushing some out before removing it.

## Heat Creep (Ghost Printing Where You Cannot Easily Remove the Filament):

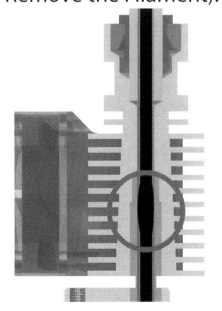

Heat creep refers to when heat creeps up the filament and causes unwanted expansion. If filament within the barrel gets too hot, it causes the plastic inside the barrel to heat beyond its glass transition temperature, and will often create a little bubble. This bubble will cause a ghost print where the printer continues to try and print, grinding filament, skipping your stepper, and result in filament that you cannot remove.

Please keep in mind that this used to be a common issue for me, but over the past year or two it has only happened a handful of times. If you take all of the proper precautions outlined in this book, it should not become too much of an issue.

Heat creep is far more common on materials with a low glass transition temperature, since it allows the material to deform at a lower temperature. Be sure to refer to the "Material Science" chapter in this new 2020 edition for a further explanation on this, and how Polymaker has been able to work out a PLA that doesn't run into this issue.

If the heat creep is minor, you may be able to use a small Allen wrench to push the filament through while the hotend is hot until it makes it past this bubble, but you do not want to put too much pressure on your machine or else you will cause extra problems for yourself.

When the heat creep is more excessive, you will want to disassemble your hotend. If your filament hasn't already grinded to the point where it has snapped, you can break it off now. Disassemble as far as you can until you are left with the section that will not allow you to move the filament. This is normally in the barrel, but can be in the hotend itself.

If in the barrel, you will want to remove all plastic parts that may be connected (fan, printed adaptors for your machine, Teflon tubing), and any wiring that you can. There shouldn't be any direct wiring to the barrel, but you will need to remove any Teflon tubing from inside if using 1.75mm filament. If you have an all metal hotend, you will then want to get a lighter or a propane fueled torch. Be sure to not use a high temperature torch due to the possibility of it melting your barrel. You can use a standard Bic lighter if in a pinch.

Before proceeding I must warn that this is dangerous and should only done at your caution. You will want to be in a very well-ventilated area and wear a mask for your protection. Do not attempt this procedure if you do not feel comfortable handling the following equipment. Use gloves and take proper precaution.

Hold the barrel with a wrench or pliers that have rubber grips up to the flame (while wearing the proper gloves). Doing this with a wrench that does not have metal grips will cause the handles to get far too hot.

If possible, pinch the filament in-between another set of pliers with your other hand. You can then carefully pull until the barrel gets hot enough that the filament will melt and the material will be easily pulled or pushed through. Clean out the barrel from remaining debris if you see any by pushing a small Allen wrench through.

If the clog is in the unlikely section of your hotend, you will want to do this same process, only you must make sure all wiring is out of the way or removed. This type of clog is rarer because the hotend can normally heat itself hot enough to push filament through without the need of a torch.

Be sure to allow the barrel to cool all the way down to room temperature before reassembling. Once reassembled you can now move forward with future prints, but be sure to read on to prevent this from happening in the future.

# How to prevent heat creep:

Since heat creep means that the temperature from the hotend is creeping up the material, there are a few prevention tips that can be tried.

## Confirm your barrel cooling fan is on and not obstructed:

The majority of hotends will have a fan that blows on the barrel of your hotend. I wire my barrel cooling fan directly to the power output on my board so that it is always on, something you may want to consider (and most manufacturers have built-in). If this fan is not blowing or is obstructed by debris when your hotend is heating, you will need to fix it in order to prevent heat creep. The same is true if the fan itself has broken blades. Some of these fans do not have shields over them, and I have accidentally bumped one or two in the past with an Allen wrench. This caused a blade to break off and not have as good of airflow – meaning a replacement fan was required.

First turn off and unplug your machine. Make sure your fan is of the proper voltage for your machine (12v/24v) and that all the blades are intact. If you have an extra fan of the proper voltage available, connect that fan instead and turn back on your machine. If it works, you can skip the next section since the issue was a burnt out fan.

If the above solution does not work, unplug and turn your machine off once again. Inspect the wiring of your fan. You may easily see that a wire has come loose or been disconnected. If you do not see a problem, you will have to use a multimeter tool to check the continuity of the wiring from your board to the fan. If one of the wires does not show continuity, you will either need to re-solder the unconnected section, or rewire entirely.

This is simple on many machines, but can be quite a headache on others. Having the proper connectors and ability to solder will make this process exponentially easier. Be sure you see connectivity on the wire all the way from your board to the fan, there are no exposed wires, and turn your machine back on.

If the fan still does not turn on, there may be a problem with the section of the board that that fan is wired to. With the machine unplugged and off, wire the barrel fan directly to the power input section on your power supply (red to + and black to -). Turn your machine back on, and if you are using a new fan and new wiring, everything should be working again. If not, reconfigure marlin and re-flash your machine for one final attempt before possibly needing a new board (which shouldn't be needed when wiring directly to the power supply).

If you are using a stock Creality hotend, or something similar which has a small barrel section, you will want to make sure the fan has enough airflow to keep it all cool. Even though they are quiet, try to avoid Noctua fans. Where you can purchase fans and other accessories are explained in the "Important Accessories and Replacements" chapter, and links for which are always at my website 3DPrintGeneral.com

## Confirm you have a heat break in your hotend

A heatbreak is a small metal tube that connects your heaterblock to your barrel. This small part helps to have a break between the two as to disperse heat and prevent your barrel from getting too hot. By itself without a barrel cooling fan will not be enough, but it will definitely help in preventing heat creep. The vast majority of hotends, including the common E3D variety that I use, have these built in, but I have had an inexpensive machine not have one. This inexpensive machine has a lot of problems with heat creep, even though it has a barrel cooling fan.

## Make sure you are not printing too slow or too hot:

This will involve you checking the settings on your slicing program. If you run your machine too hot, too slow, or a combination of the two, it will allow heat to move up the filament easier. Try lowering the heat a bit or speeding the print up to see if this helps with the problem. Normally lowering the print speed will help to diagnose and fix issues, but when combined with a very hot nozzle can create a bit of heat creep.

Reference the "Settings Issues" chapter of this book for further help with tweaking your slicer settings for a more accurate print.

## Swap materials

This really shouldn't be needed if you are doing everything correctly, but some manufacturers or old filament may be more susceptible to heat creep. Check out Polymaker's PLA where they have been able to make heat creep impossible by annealing their PLA first.

## Lubricate filament for all metal hotends

This one is a bit odd and new to me, but I have learned that the one issue with all metal hotends is the fact that PLA is starch based filament, meaning it will stick to the steel heat breaks when hot. This can add to friction and potential clogging.

It would be smart to add a bit of lubrication for your filament if you are experiencing hard to diagnose clogs on an all metal hotend. To do this would just involve adding a small sponge to where your filament runs through before going into your hotend. You would then add a drop or two of Canola oil, or another similar oil.

This oil will then slightly rub onto the filament as it feeds into your hotend, lubricating the heat break. The heat break will eventually get seasoned like a cast iron skillet and not require further lubrication.

If you do not lubricate, you can have more frequent clogs, or just under extruded parts.

## Final attempts to fix:

If you have done everything above and are still experiencing heat creep, you may want to invest in a new barrel or an entire new hotend. I have personally used E3D hotends for a while, and while they do have an occasional heat creep, it is not a consistent issue. Your barrel may have been degraded over time causing the diameter of the hole to be inconsistent. Or the company you may have purchased it from may not have the tolerances and quality that other products guarantee. I have seen other makers cut an E3D hotend in half and compare it to off brand Chinese cheaper products, and you can easily tell the tolerances are much more precise on the name brand E3D version. Sometimes you get what you pay for.

Finally, your thermistor may be reading the incorrect temperature. Though very uncommon, your hotend may think it is 230°C, when it is actually running at 250°C. To fix this issue, please refer to the "Hotend not Reading Correct Temperature" chapter of this book.

# Clog in the Actual Nozzle (ghost printing, can't push filament through but may be able to remove the filament):

A clog in the nozzle and not your hotend or barrel is normally caused by one of two issues: settings issues with the diameter of your nozzle, or improper purging of the previous filament. You will want to treat a clogged nozzle in the same way you would with a clogged barrel that I go into further detail above: Remove the nozzle and carefully apply a torch in a well-ventilated area until you can push the clogged filament through. Remember to always remove and replace nozzles with the hotend set to 240°C due to the expansion of metal.

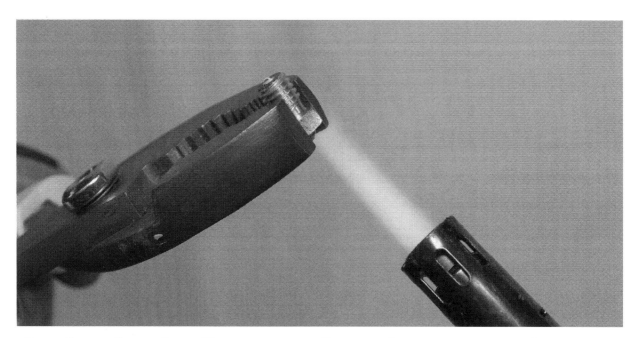

## Too fast for the diameter of nozzle you are using:

It's easy to understand that the larger diameter of nozzle you are using, the easier it is to print without any clogs. E3D makes nozzles from as large as 0.8mm in diameter (up to 1.4mm in their SuperVolcano nozzles) all the way down to 0.15mm. I have personally used every diameter of nozzle they offer and can personally attest to the increase in nozzle clogs the lower you go. It took me roughly two dozen failed prints on their 0.25mm nozzle before I honed in the proper speed and retraction settings for this nozzle diameter without any clogs or issues (mind you, since upgrading to the Bondtech BMG extruder, the issues have plummeted) .

This meant that I torched out the nozzle quite a few times before I got everything right, each time having to wait hours into the print before the issue showed itself. I repeated this process with the 0.15mm nozzle, and with each type of material. Once honed in, you should only use the same manufacturer, since each company you purchase filament from may require slightly tweaked settings, and these minor differences in settings become more apparent the smaller in nozzle diameter you go.

There is no one step solution for this - you will need to manually tweak your settings until you achieve a print without any clogging (though upgrading your extruder may help). Refer to the "Settings Issues" chapter of this book for further detail on how you may be able to fix this yourself. You can always move up in nozzle diameter if you can't seem to get things to print properly. I have found that a 0.4mm diameter nozzle achieves very accurate prints with very minimal issues of clogs, and a 0.6mm nozzle is extremely easy to use and fast to print, but not the greatest when it comes to X/Y accuracy of text and other detail.

If you want to print really fast with large nozzle diameters – you will need a hotend that allows for this, such as the Volcano setup by E3D. This is because the standard hotend does not allow enough time for the material to heat up when extruding so fast – something the Volcano compensates for.

# Filament Grinding (ghost printing and you can remove the filament and push it through again):

The filament will often grind to the point of snapping with the two possibilities above, the difference here being there is no heat creep requiring you to disassemble your machine. You can just use some pliers to remove the filament, reload the material, and push everything through without any clogs.

When this failure gets extreme, it can lead to you needing to read the "Stripped Filament" chapter. This is likely due to having too much moisture in the material.

If you are using flexible material, you may see the filament curled up before it grinds. Make sure you slow the print down if this happens, and confirm you have an extruder with enough torque for flexible material. Also confirm that there is a straight, clear path through the hotend. Bowden machines cannot print many flexible materials, even when using a strong geared extruder. The longer the tubing run between your extruder and hotend, the more difficult it will be to print with flexible materials.

While the cleanup is easy, you are still left with a failed print. If you just click "re-print", you will likely end up with the exact same results.

## How to prevent filament grinding:

Loose or tight idler tensioner, blockage, wrong hot end temperature, and too fast of retraction and print speeds are all common causes, yet easy to correct. The one that is the most annoying is from having too much moisture in your filament. Make sure you also read the "Stripped Filament" chapter in this book.

If you were to speed up your machine 10x what it normally prints at, you can imagine how your extruder gear would be turning far faster than material can be pushed out the nozzle. This would cause the filament to grind until the point of snapping (if not just causing your extruder motor to skip).

Before clicking re-print, try slicing your part with both your print speed and retraction speeds slower. Watch the print and see if there are any sections where the extruder is moving too fast, and attempt to fix in your slicing program or by turning the knob on your LCD screen. The general rule of thumb is to limit the maximum print speed to 100x the nozzle diameter, printing at no greater layer heights than 75% of the nozzle diameter. The print speed maximum is a starting point, and with a good geared extruder on a well-built frame you can get closer to 175% print speed compared to the nozzle diameter.

Next, adjust your idler tension. Start by loosening the idler and then feed filament through and tighten until you no longer experience slipping, but not so tight you experience grinding or stepper motor skipping. Filaments vary in diameter, so although the idler will absorb some variations, some material will require fine adjustments. I have my idler extremely tight on my Bondtech BMG since the grip and torque on that are good enough where I do not experience extruder motor skips, but you will have to find a happy medium with a less powered extruder.

You should also check the temperature you are running your hotend at and make sure it is not running too cold. If you try to print ABS at 200°C, you might be able to get some filament to extrude at first, but it will eventually get stuck. If slowing your printer down didn't help, try increasing the hotend temperature a bit (which is the opposite advice given for heat creep).

## Summary of Fixes and Precautions:

- Push filament down before pulling it out.
- Don't keep material heated for long periods of time without printing.
- Make sure the barrel cooling fan is working and that all the blades are intact.
- Confirm wiring from the board to the barrel cooling fan is connected properly.
- Clean your barrel cooling fan and remove all dust.
- Make sure your hotend has a heatbreak.
- Check your settings that you are using the proper extrusion temperature for the material you are printing.
- In a well-ventilated area, torch metal parts when required.
- Make sure your thermistor is reading the correct temperature.
- Adjust the idler tension.
- Tweak the print speed.
- Confirm you understand what is said in the "Settings Issues", "Hotend Can't Reach or Maintain Temperature", and "Hotend Not Reading Correct Temperature" chapters.
- Read the "Stripped Filament" chapter if experiencing this issue frequently.
- It is smart to have replacement heater blocks, heaters, and thermistors so you do not need to wait for delivery to fix your machine when required.

# Over/Under Extrusion

Over and under extrusion is normally caused when your stepper motor is not turning the proper amount of steps, and results in either too much, or too little plastic being extruded. This will lead to ugly and/or brittle parts.

Keep in mind that a minor amount of under or over extrusion can be unnoticeable to the human eye, so it is smart to check this intermittently regardless if you are experiencing issues (as mentioned in the "Mandatory Maintenance" chapter). Unnoticed under or over extrusion can cause issue with parts that need to fit together or are used under significant loads.

**NOTE: For most of your issues, you will want to skip down to the Check and Fix your E-steps section of this chapter.**

## Confirm the proper filament diameter is set

This sounds silly – but it has happened to me. Without thinking, I have had my filament diameter set to 2.85mm on Cura, but I was actually using 1.75mm. This will 100% result in a print that looks far under extruded.

The opposite is true if you are using 2.85mm filament but have your slicer set to 1.75mm – your part will look massively over extruded.

Check this before doing any further solution explained, since you will just be wasting your time. This is an easy fix – just make sure you have this set correctly in your slicing software.

# Over Extrusion

Drastically over extruded parts will be fairly easy to tell either to the naked eye, or easy to tell because parts are not fitting together. If you factored in your machine tolerances (which I go over in the "Parts not to Proper Dimensions or Not Mating Together" chapter) and parts are still not mating together, you likely are experiencing a bit of over extrusion.

## Check to see if nozzle is degraded

Nozzles can become degraded over time from material constantly running through them, as well as from times you started a print too close to the build plate. Some materials, such as the Carbon Fiber Reinforced blends, require a hardened steel nozzle to prevent rapid degradation.

When your nozzle degrades, the diameter will get slightly larger than it was when factory shipped to you. This can lead to some parts of your print looking as though there was over extrusion (or may just look generally ugly). You won't really be able to tell if you have this issue, unless your nozzle looks like the one on the left below. The nozzle on the right has been used, but it clearly has not been as degraded as the one on the left. Worn out nozzles will lead to ugly prints far before they get as bad as the one pictured below:

Normally a nozzle won't be this noticeably degraded, so you will want to keep track of how much printing you are doing on a machine. If you have gone 6 months of daily printing on a brass nozzle, it is definitely time for a replacement. It is smart to always keep 1-2 spares on hand to test if this solves your issues of over extrusion.

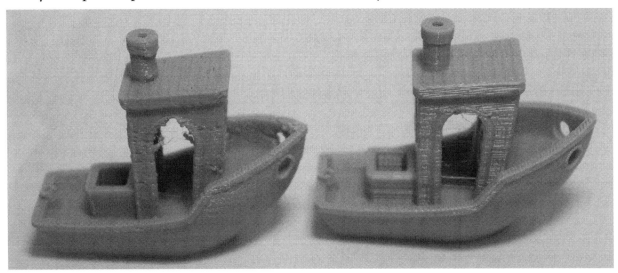

Above the two parts have the exact same G-code, but the one on the right is with a new nozzle. The part on the left was printed with a hardened steel nozzle, so even these wear out after hundreds of hours of printing with abrasive materials. While the print on the right is not perfect, you can see just how much a nozzle with the proper tolerances will help to achieve clean prints.

Before replacing your nozzle though, you should check your E-steps, as explained further in this chapter. It is also well worth the investment to get a hardened steel nozzle so you do not have to worry about this issue for a long time. I personally have not used one due to the price, but you can even go with a ruby tipped nozzle to never have to worry about this issue again (they cost roughly $100 though). I have standardized to using the NozzleX by E3D.

# Under Extrusion

Unless extreme, under extrusion is much more difficult to diagnose with the naked eye. This is because parts will bridge gaps just fine, the surface quality will look good, and parts will mate together with ease. The biggest issue comes with the integrity of your parts. They will delaminate easier and will break under far less pressure than the part should be able to handle.

## Check tension on extruder idler

Make sure there is enough tension on your filament by the idler that pinches the filament to your hobbed bolt/gear. When this idler is too loose, you may experience less filament feeding through the hotend than there should be. Too tight and you will experience further skipped steps in your extruder motor, or even stripped filament.

## Are you experiencing extruder motor skips?

If you notice that your extruder is making a "clicking" noise, then the stepper is skipping. Please refer to the "Extruder Stepper Skipping" chapter to fix this issue – since an extruder that skips will cause under extrusion.

## Not enough torque to extruder for nozzle diameter

When using a direct drive non-geared extruder on a 0.25mm diameter nozzle, I was experiencing what looked like massive under extrusion. I checked my E-steps and tweaked my slicer settings multiple times but could not fix the problem. What was occurring was minor skips in the extruder motor, and minor grinding of the filament.

As explained in the "Extruder Motor Skipping" chapter, I did not hear the normal clicking noise you hear from extruder motors skipping, but I was essentially experiencing the same issue. This is because a non-geared extruder does not have enough torque to push through such a small nozzle.

You will even see on E3D's website that they say a geared extruder is required to print using their extremely fine diameter nozzles. After upgrading to a Greg's Wade setup, I was able to print through a 0.25mm and 0.15mm nozzle without this under extrusion issue, and then after upgrading further to a Bondtech BMG, I never experienced the issue again.

## Reduce retraction and/or coasting

Having retraction set too low will result in stringy prints, but too high and you may experience under extrusion.

## Lubricate filament for all metal hotends

This one is a bit odd and new to me, but I have learned that the one issue with all metal hotends is the fact that PLA is starch based filament, meaning it will stick to the steel heat breaks when hot. This can add to friction and potential under extrusion.

It would be smart to add a bit of lubrication for your filament if you are experiencing hard to diagnose clogs on an all metal hotend. To do this would just involve adding a small sponge to where your filament runs through before going into your hotend. You would then add a drop or two of Canola oil, or another similar oil.

This oil will then slightly rub onto the filament as it feeds into your hotend, lubricating the heat break. The heat break will eventually get seasoned like a cast iron skillet and not require further lubrication.

If you do not lubricate, you can have more frequent clogs, or just under extruded parts.

## Confirm you aren't set to "Volumetric Extrusion"

Another way that you can be under extruding can be if you have "volumetric extrusion" turned on in your firmware. This can accidentally be turned on if you scroll through your LCD screen as well, or it may have just been turned on for a reason you weren't aware of. Volumetric extrusion will make it so you vastly under extrude if you didn't set your slicer up to be volumetric extrusion as well.

You can turn this off in Marlin, but an easy G-code command is "M200 D0". Just make sure to type "M500" after to save.

# Check and Fix your E-steps

For most under and over extrusion issues, you will want to check and calibrate your

E-steps. To do this is actually quite simple.

You will want to start off by measuring out 100mm of filament. You can actually measure out even more for a more precise readout – you will just have to account for that in the calculations below. I prefer to use White PLA because it is the easiest to write on, has a low printing temperature, and is cheapest - though you could use any material you have at your disposal (my example below is actually with purple AIO Robotics PLA).

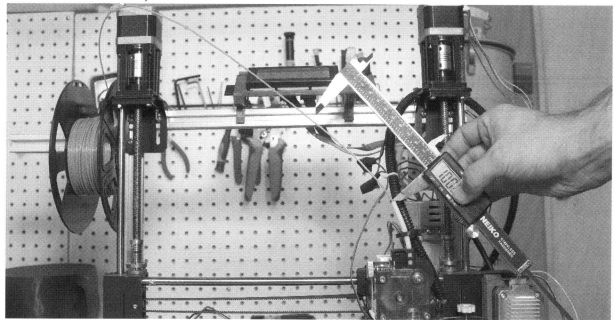

You can do this in whatever method is easiest for you. I found it easiest to measure this 100mm when the filament is already fed into the extruder. You can also do this on a desk before feeding, but 3.00mm filament, and 1.75 near the end of its spool, are quite hard to keep from rolling back up.

Be as precise as you can by using a fine tip sharpie and holding the material as straight as possible. Use calipers if you have them at your disposal. After heating your hotend, you then want to push the filament down until the lowest dot you made lines up with the top of your extruder, or somewhere else you can easily line up the starting point (because you will need to compare it to where it finishes).

The next thing you will want to do is to tell your printer to extrude 100mm. This is done with a simple G-code command in your terminal.

If you normally print via SD card you will need to hook up to a computer for this. If you print via Octoprint or a similar online program, you can send the G-code commands from their terminals.

When hooked up to Repetier Host, or whatever program you use to control your machine, and your hotend hot, you will want to give your machine the command:

**G92 E0**

This sets your extruder to 0. Next you will want to give either the command:

For 3.00mm Filament: **G1 E100 F30**

or

For 1.75mm Filament: **G1 E100 F60**

This will tell your extruder to feed 100mm, and is why it was important you lined up your starting dot with either the top of your extruder or something else that is easy for you to compare to.

Once your extruder has finished you will want to mark your filament at the same spot you lined up your original dot (top of extruder in my examples). If your 100mm dot lines up perfectly, then your E-steps are right on - but even 1mm means that your printer is extruding incorrectly by 1%.

After marking where 100mm actually was, you will want to compare it to where you measured 100mm to be at the beginning of this process. If higher on the filament, your printer is over extruding, if lower on the filament, your printer is under extruding.

After measuring this difference you will want to write down somewhere how much your extruder actually fed. If your printer over extruded by 2.1mm, you will want to mark down 102.1mm. If it under extruded by 2.1mm, you will want to mark down 97.9mm. You will need this number later on.

The next step in this process is to determine what your current E-steps are. You can do this by either checking the firmware for your machine, by going into the "Motion" section of your EEPROM (LCD Screen), or just by giving it the command "M503" in your printer terminal. Direct drive non-geared extruders have E-steps of around 90, while Greg's wade and other geared extruders have E-steps of 500 or more. If you have an extruder from a popular manufacturer, they will list what their standard starting point for E-steps should be (such as 420 being the starting point for the Titan extruder).

If you are checking in the firmware that you use to flash your machine, you will want to open it up. While in Marlin you will go to the "Configuration.h" tab and scroll all the way down to where it says "DEFAULT_AXIS_STEPS_PER_UNIT", with E-steps being the 4th and final number (if using one extruder). The X, Y, and Z steps should never be changed and are a calculation based off of the parts you are using. This is only if you plan on working in Marlin, rather than using your printer terminal.

Over/Under Extrusion

You could also type M503 into your terminal to be given a readout of what your current E-steps are. You then take this number and multiply it by 100 (the amount you were attempting to extrude). You will then divide this new number by the number you wrote down earlier.

If you decided to check your E-steps by feeding out more than 100, you would multiply by that number. I actually will often feed out 200mm instead, in order to get back a more accurate number. Just remember to change the calculations accordingly.

For example, if your current E-steps are 90.5 as shown above, you will multiply it by 100 to get 9050. We will then divide 9050 by how much you extruded earlier. So if you extruded 102.1mm, you will take 9050 and divide it by 102.1 to get 88.64.

*90.5 x 100 = 9050*

*9050 / 102.1 = **88.64***

88.64 in this above example would be your new E-steps. As you can tell it is lower than it was before, because in this example you were correcting for over extrusion.

You will now set your E-steps. You can do this through your terminal, EEPROM, or by flashing your firmware. If you are going to do this through your terminal you will want to give the M92 command, by typing M92 E88.64. You will then want to type M500 in order to save these settings. Without typing M500, the number will be reset when turning off your machine.

While you can set this number on many LCD screens under the "Motion" section, it will only save permanently if you have the option to save your settings after doing so, just as with typing M500 in the example above. Otherwise your E-steps will reset once you turn your machine off.

You can then of course change it in the firmware by changing the E-steps number, and flashing your machine.

Thomas Sanladerer has a great older tutorial video going over all of this on his channel which you can find by searching "calibrating your extruder" on YouTube. Thomas really knows his stuff and I suggest to everyone that they follow what he does. He has personally taught me many of the things I now know about 3D printing.

## Flash your firmware

Finally, you can reflash your firmware with your new E-steps. As mentioned in the "Tips if Still Not Working" chapter, you will want to reflash your firmware regardless periodically if experiencing non-stop issues. This is something I do not need to do quite as frequently as I have in the past, but it definitely does not hurt.

You will do this by downloading the proper firmware for your machine if you haven't already. You can normally find this firmware by searching for your machine online, but you likely already have it from when you first set up your printer.

Some printers, such as the CR-10 series, do not come with the ability to flash your firmware via Marlin. If you would like to do this on such a machine, you will want to bootload via an Arduino Uno. TH3D Studios has a great tutorial on this and ability to purchase all parts required (TH3DStudio.com). If you have a machine such as this, you can still change your E-steps via a terminal, or as a last case scenario, edit the "flow %" settings on Cura, as explained in the section below.

Double click the Arduino file to open up Marlin. If you are not changing your E-steps, you can just proceed below to the next paragraph. If you are changing your E-Steps, go to the "Configuration.h" tab and scroll down to where it says "DEFAULT_AXIS_STEPS_PER_UNIT" as explained earlier. You will then change the fourth number to your newly determined E-steps. Some firmware are a bit different than what I am showing, so be sure to do some research on your particular firmware.

Flashing your firmware is quite simple after this. Hook up your printer to your computer and then choose the proper port in Marlin by clicking "Tools", scrolling over "Port" and choosing the port to which your machine is hooked up, normally the highest number.

You will then choose the board you are using. If you are using a RAMPS board, you will choose "Arduino/Genuino Mega or Mega 2560". If not – you will need to check with what board you are using and what the manufacturer says. Once ready, you will want to click on the arrow "upload" button:

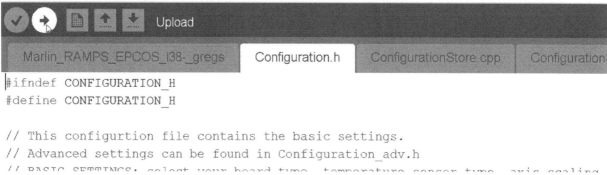

The code will then compile and upload to your machine. If you experience errors while compiling, read the specific error you are fed out. If could be something very simple to understand and fix, or it could be something much more complex.

If confused, copy and paste the error message that is read out to you into a Google search. There is likely someone who has experienced and fixed the same problem. This is exactly how I fixed my issues with compiling when I was fed out an error that did not make sense to me.

Assuming you have the proper firmware for your machine, you shouldn't have these issues.

Please keep in mind I have had to restart my computer a few times in the past when the file would just not upload. It may be worth restarting yours if you are experiencing an issue you are unable to diagnose.

Many people now prefer TH3D's firmware since it is so user friendly to setup rather than standard Marlin.

You can also reset your printer to factory settings, which is similar to flashing it, by giving the command "M502". Remember that this will reset your numbers, so if you need to change your E-steps, you will then need to give a new M92 command with M500 saving the settings.

## Changing Flow % in slicing software

If you have a machine that will not allow you to use Marlin and cannot save the settings using the M500 command, you could literally just change the Flow % in Cura.

This is not ideal, but can get the job done if needed. Essentially, you will not need to know any E-steps, you will just need to know the percentage that you over or under extruded in your test you performed earlier. If your extruder fed out 102.1mm, then you would divide 100 by 102.1 to be read out .9794. You can then set your flow percentage to 97.94%.

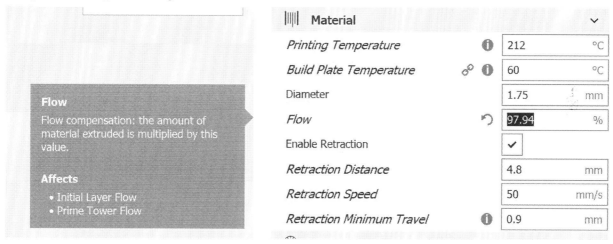

## Summary of Fixes and Precautions

- Step one should be to see if you have your slicer set to the correct filament diameter.

- Step two is to check your E-steps.

- Read the guide above on checking your E-steps or watch Thomas Sanladerer's YouTube video on "Calibrating your extruder".

- Correct your E-steps via your terminal, EEPROM, or by re-flashing your firmware.

- If you cannot change your E-steps via one of the three methods above, you can also change your flow %.

- Replace nozzle if degraded or if you have done countless prints on a standard brass nozzle.

- Check the tension on extruder idler.

- If under extruding on an all metal hotend, try lubricating the filament.

- Confirm you are giving enough torque for the nozzle diameter you are using.

- Understand the possibility that your hotend is not reading the proper temperature as mentioned in that corresponding chapter.

# Parts Being Knocked Over

Your part being knocked off the build plate can happen quite frequently, especially when dealing with tall, skinny prints on Cartesian machines.

## Proper bed adhesion

Goal number 1 when it comes to having parts not being knocked over is having the proper bed adhesion. This includes knowing the right mixture or bed sheet for the material you are using, the correct bed temperature and brim/raft application, as well as having the proper z-height with a level build plate.

To review this further, make sure you check the "Bed Adhesion", "Unlevelled Build Plate", and "Z-Height" chapters. If any part of your print is too far from the build plate, you will be very susceptible to your part being knocked over.

## Adding a Z-hop

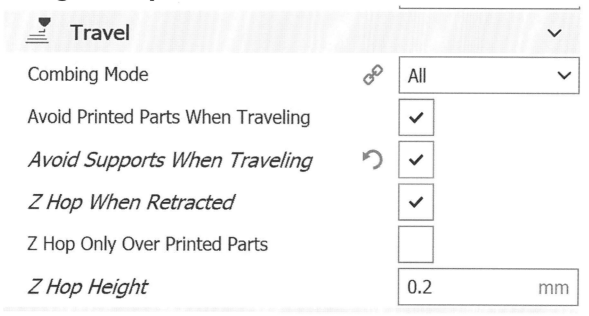

As mentioned elsewhere in the book, a Z-hop refers to the printer head moving up while travelling. The printer head (or build plate when working with a CoreXY machine) will have the nozzle move away from the print by the determined amount in your slicer settings. This will mean that the nozzle will not be running into your print when travelling, reducing the odds of it being knocked over.

I always have my Z-hop height set to the layer height of my print. As you can see from the photo, it is currently set to 0.2mm on this profile, meaning my layer height for this print is 0.2mm. I have just found this to work best, because if you have a Z-hop set lower than the layer height, you run the risk of still bumping into the top of your print. I increase the Z-hop larger than my layer height when printing at large layer heights (over 0.4mm).

## Avoid parts when traveling

As you can see in the photo above, I also have both the avoid supports and avoid printed parts when travelling checked. This is a fairly new feature offered in Cura, in which the path of your printer head will avoid both printed parts and supports while moving. This can increase print time, but I find it best to use to avoid any parts being knocked over.

To be honest – I am not quite sure if both Z-hop and this feature are required, or if one cancels out the need for the other. I figure I have had so many parts get knocked over in the past that it would just be best to take all precautions to prevent this, but you can play around at your own discretion.

## Turn combing off

When combing is on, you get the option to avoid printed parts when traveling. This isn't always the best option though, since it will depend on just how large your layer heights are. It seems that when I use large layer heights, even with avoid printed parts when travelling checked, my nozzle will still run into the infill. For this you will want to turn combing off. It may add to your retraction headaches, but the printer will always perform a z-hop when travelling and will avoid your printed part.

I have combing on for any print that is 0.3mm layer heights or lower, but anything higher I will have it turned off.

When combing is off and you are printing with large layer lines, it should also be accompanied with an infill pattern that only goes in one direction per layer (such as "lines). That is something I learned when printing with the E3D SuperVolcano at 1mm layer heights.

## Working with very thin tall prints

This is also covered in the "Z-Wobble" chapter, but essentially a very tall skinny part is far more likely to wobble and get knocked over during a long print. This should not be an issue on CoreXY machines where the build plate only moves downward, but on Cartesian machines where the build plate rattles back and forth, the very top of a tall skinny print will start to sway back and forth.

This swaying will not only cause ugly Z-wobble prints, but it can cause a print to be knocked over. This is because the nozzle may try and start the print slightly to the side of where the top of the print swayed to. Get this happening a couple of times and this part will easily fall over.

This is especially noticeable when working with some support material. Often a part will require a very tall support structure, but may not need to cover a large surface area. These thin towers can fall over before they get to where you need them to be.

Unfortunately, when working with a Cartesian machine, there isn't much that can be done to prevent this. Of course you need to have a proper brim for great bed adhesion, but if a part is extremely thin and tall, there will be swaying. There are essentially two things you can do in this scenario – cut the part into two sections or add further scaffolding to help anchor.

There have been some thin parts I have printed in the past that I was just forced to slice in half and glue together post printing. This is clearly not ideal for mechanical parts, but anything this thin will be flimsy regardless.

You can also add manual support structures to the model, anchoring the part to the build plate every so often, to make sure no swaying occurs. If you are just building a thin tower, you will need support structures attaching to the side. This can be done in programs such as Cura.

## Anchoring Prints

I am sure there are better ways to do this, but the easiest way I know of would be to anchor your print in Cura. I have rarely done this, but it definitely helps with a tall, skinny print wobbling back and forth. This is also explained in the "Z-Wobble" chapter.

Below is an example of two skinny swords from a Deadpool print that I made for my YouTube channel. When not adding any anchors, my Cartesian machine would wobble the build plate back and forth and cause the top half of these swords to look extremely ugly (if they didn't just get knocked off).

Cura now allows you to bring in a second model that intersects with your main print. They also allow you to print a part entirely as support. This means you can drag in a second object that acts only as support for your main structure.

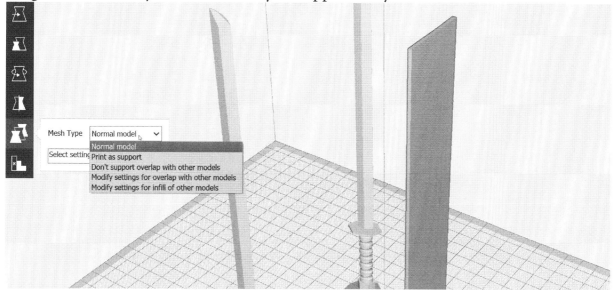

This rectangle in the example above is thin, so that it won't take up too much material, yet will extend the anchoring for the sword (I added a second sword to compare how it will slice). After bringing in a shape that will work for your model, you can choose the model and click "Print as support".

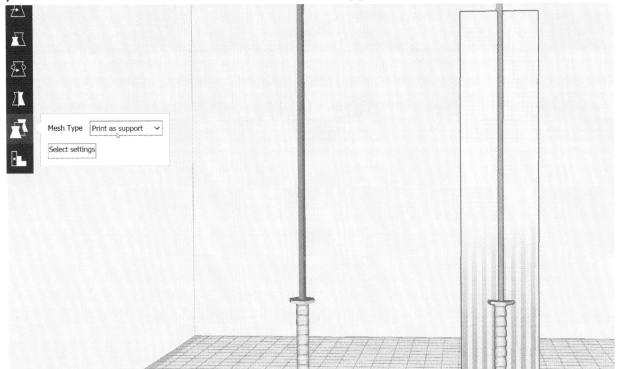

After turning the shape into "Print as support", you can then drag it over your tall, skinny print.

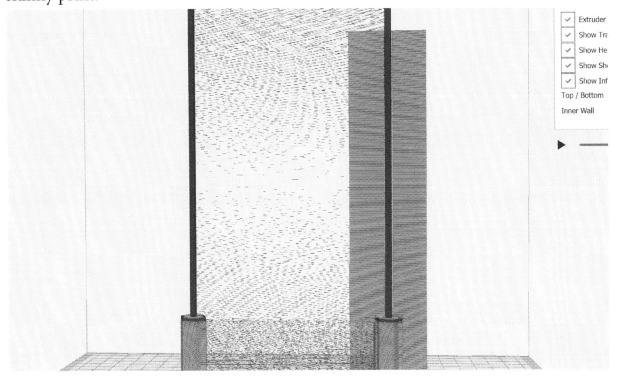

Parts Being Knocked Over

As you can see in "Layer Mode", this entire shape is now support structure that can help to anchor your tall skinny print to help prevent this wobbling back and forth.

As mentioned – there are many other ways to do this, this is just the simplest way I know of since it allows you to do this right in your slicing software.

This process is explained in detail as well on my video titled "Combining Parts on Cura" if you would like to see it in action.

## Summary of Fixes and Precautions

- Ensure you have the proper bed adhesion – including having a level build plate with the proper starting Z-height.

- Add a Z-hop (normally the same distance as your layer heights).

- Utilize the ability to avoid parts and support when printing in Cura's slicing software.

- Turn off combing and use "lines" as pattern infill when printing with very large layer heights.

- Plan ahead when working with a tall and skinny print. You may need to cut the part in half or add anchoring to make sure the part doesn't wobble back and forth.

# Parts Not Mating Together

This issue can be as minor as when you print two parts that are meant to fit together and they don't without some sanding, to as far as one or multiple axis's being off by over 100% in scaling.

You will have to diagnose how bad this problem is. If it is minor, proceed with the next couple of steps.

## Confirm you factored in the appropriate tolerances

There are clearly tolerances involved with 3D printing, and they can vary drastically on the nozzle diameter and layer heights of your particular print. While there may be sources that say the tolerances are tighter than the numbers I am saying, these are what I use and what has worked for me throughout all of my prints.

The tolerance of the print that I will use is the layer heights you are using in the Z-direction, and roughly half the diameter of your nozzle in the X/Y direction. So, as an example, if you were printing 0.1mm layer heights on a 0.4mm nozzle, your tolerances will be roughly 0.1mm in the Z-direction and 0.2mm in the XY direction.

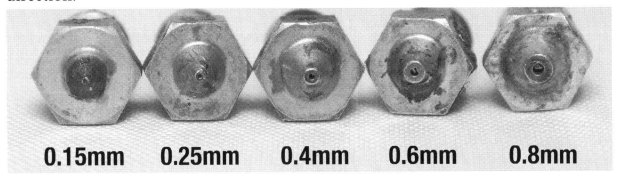

0.15mm     0.25mm     0.4mm     0.6mm     0.8mm

While that is a general rule of thumb, you may actually be able to achieve tolerances tighter than this on your particular machine depending on how everything is set up. You should find out your exact tolerances by printing a tolerance test – like the one below designed by A_Str8 on Thingiverse (though there are many out there that should accomplish the same idea).

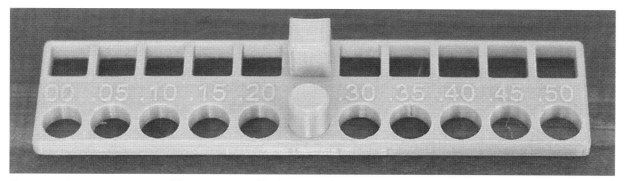

Since 3D printing is additive, it will almost always err on the side of adding more material than less material. This means that parts will be slightly larger and holes will be slightly tighter.

So, if you were to design two parts that mate perfectly together without any clearance, no matter how good your settings are, you will likely not be able to fit the printed pieces together without a lot of sanding.

I always suggest parts that need to be perfect to their dimensions, or ones that need to mate together, have the size of their holes increased, and the overall size of the part decreased. The amount you should factor in should be based off of the tolerance test I suggest you print a couple paragraphs earlier.

For instance, using the same example as above, if you are printing at 0.1mm layer heights on a 0.4mm nozzle, you will want to increase the diameter of holes being printed in the XY direction by 0.2mm, and decrease the size of the part in the XY direction by 0.2mm (and 0.1mm in the Z direction).

With this tolerance, parts will mate tightly together. If you would like the fit to be a little loose, you will want to increase this to 0.3mm in the above example.

Based off of the photo I show above, I am able to achieve tolerances of 0.25mm for a really tight fit, but 0.35mm for a looser fit. So you need to factor in the corresponding clearances in your part depending if you want a tight or loose fit.

This is another reason printing in a high resolution on a fine nozzle is beneficial for printing a part with accurate dimensions, but will of course result in a much longer print.

## Replace your nozzle

Your nozzle will be degraded over time, especially when using one made of brass. Abrasive materials at hot temperatures will slowly make the diameter larger than what you think it is.

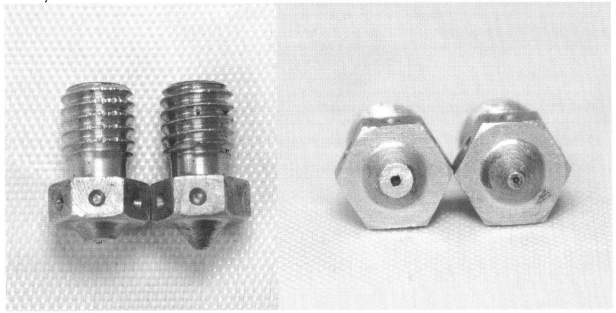

The example above is an extreme version of what I am talking about. The nozzle on the left had been worn out from being used when too close to the print bed, and from being used for a couple of months (not from my machine). Not only is the tip extremely worn down, the hole itself is clearly larger and not as precise.

You can see some example prints and more explanation in my YouTube video, "The Importance of Replacing Nozzles".

While you are trying to lay down 0.4mm layer lines, your nozzle may actually be closer to 0.6mm in diameter, and not be a perfect circle. This can lead to ugly parts, and can definitely lead to your parts not mating together. If you are using a brass nozzle, make sure you replace it every couple hundred hours of printing. I definitely suggest upgrading to a hardened steel nozzle so this does not become an issue nearly as quickly.

## Check to see if you are over extruding

You will definitely want to visit the "Over and Under Extrusion" chapter in this book if you factored in tolerances but parts are still coming out slightly too large.

Be sure you are as accurate as possible when checking your E-Steps because even a slight over extrusion can cause problems when you are trying to print two parts that are meant fit together accurately.

Many people suggest setting your e-steps to 98% of the number you are fed out, since a very minor amount of under extrusion should help with mating parts together.

## Make sure your material hasn't absorbed moisture

Materials left out not vacuum sealed or with a dehumidifier will undoubtedly absorb moisture. When this occurs, you will experience a myriad of printing issues, one of which being having trouble mating parts together.

You can read more about this issue in the "Stripped Filament" chapter.

# Tighten belts

As mentioned elsewhere in this book, it is possible to over tighten your belts, but you will really have to be trying to do that. If you are experiencing parts that are not to the correct dimensions, your belts may be too loose.

You do not want a lot of slack in your belts because not only will quality of your parts decrease, you can experience actual dimensional issues. This happened slowly over time on just about every machine I have used. A part printed on one machine over time would not mate with a part printed on another.

It turned out that tightening the belts fixed the issue immediately. This is another reason having a way to easily tighten your belts will be extremely useful and necessary for practical preventative maintenance.

# Confirm stepper pulley has proper amount of teeth

This is a strange one and should only occur if you recently changed the pulley attached to your stepper motor. This happened to me once, and it took me about 3 prints of confusion to realize what was going on.

If your stepper pulley has the incorrect amount of teeth for your machine, your scaling for that dimension will be very far off. From what I can tell, the vast majority of FDM machines use 20 teeth pulleys for their stepper motors.

# Read the *"Settings Issues"* chapter

If you have confirmed everything above, and parts are not mating together, make sure you read the "Settings Issues" chapter. You would be amazed just how much tweaking your settings can affect the quality of your print. Along with making sure you don't have your flow rate over 100%, minor fluctuations in temperature for specific materials can affect the viscosity which can cause a print to ooze more than it should. This will result in a part that is not to the proper dimensions.

# Print a large calibration cube and check XYZ steps/mm

This really should not be needed if everything is built properly and you are using the correct firmware for your machine - but it may be smart to do on very large machines that you built yourself.

Find a calibration cube on Thingiverse, or create your own that is large and uses the least amount of filament as possible. This can be a hollowed out cube that is only shells and has not top or bottom, or whatever you can think of that has specific dimensions of at least 100mm. If you have the filament, space, and time, you should go even larger.

This is because the tolerances involved with your machine will effect these numbers the smaller the part you print. This process would then be the same as when you checked your e-steps.

I cannot stress enough how important it is to check your e-steps and to check everything else described above before printing your calibration part. There is no point changing the X, Y, or Z steps/mm if a belt is loose or if you are over extruding. Your X, Y, and Z-steps should be a calculation based off of the parts you are using – and there is no reason to tweak this UNLESS you built the machine yourself and you were wrong with your calculations in flashing firmware.

Find your X, Y and Z steps per mm in your firmware – they are located directly to the left of the E-Steps/mm (as explained in the "Over and Under Extrusion" chapter). Take that number and multiply it by the number of mm your calibration print should be in that dimension (if printing a 100mm cube, multiply by 100). Pull out your calipers and measure your print in that direction for what it actually printed.

Make sure you do not scrape off your print before marking or remembering which direction is which. Divide that newly found number by the actual number read out by the calipers. This is your new steps per mm for that dimension.

As mentioned, if you have a printer that is using the proper firmware and parts, with settings that are correct for the material you are using, this should generally not be needed. I never will do this on my machines because everything is just based off of calculations.

## Summary of Fixes and Precautions

- Make sure you factored in clearances for parts that need to be mated together or precise. These tolerances have to do with your layer heights and nozzle diameter.

- Print a tolerance test to know what your clearances should be.

- Replace any worn out nozzle.

- Make sure you are not over extruding by checking the e-steps.

- Tighten all loose belts.

- For parts that are far off in their accuracy, confirm you have the proper amount of teeth for your stepper motor pulley for your machine/firmware.

- Read the "Settings Issues" chapter since many issues in minor dimensional accuracy have to do with having the proper settings for the material you are using.

- For large machines, or machines you do not have the firmware for, you may want to check the X, Y and Z steps/mm by printing a very large calibration cube. Only do so after confirming all of the above.

# Poor Layer Adhesion

Having strong layer adhesion is not only mandatory for watertight parts, but it is needed for clean, strong prints. If your individual layers do not stick together well, you are bound for a part that will break and peel apart.

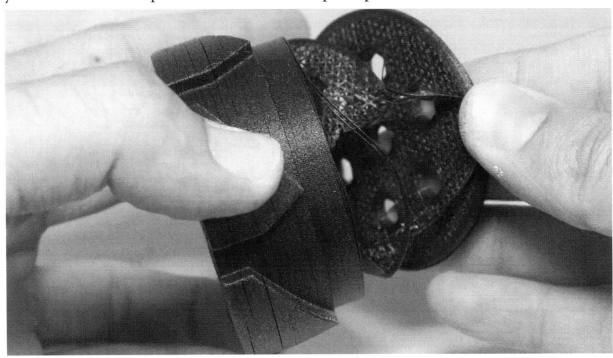

## Understand the material being used

Each material requires its own settings, including temperatures and speed. You need to make sure that you are using the proper settings for the type of material you are using.

Carbon fiber reinforced blends are more likely to have poor layer adhesion due to their properties. Polymaker is currently working on carbon fiber reinforced blends that increase this layer adhesion, but it is going to be a problem with most of these types of materials.

Refer to the "Materials Science", as well as the manufacturers print settings, before moving forward in trying to fix this problem.

## Increase the extrusion temperature

One of the most common reasons this happens is because you are printing at too low of an extrusion temperature.

Following the manufacturer guidelines is normally a surefire way to prevent this, but a few times I have had to go above these recommended settings to make sure I had a strong enough layer adhesion.

The photo above was a failed print I had when printing in NylonX by MatterHackers. They recommend 250 – 265 degrees Celsius for printing, so I went ahead and tried 250 degrees. I was left with the part you see above, something with far too weak of layer adhesion. After upping this to 265 degrees the part printed just fine.

This problem was also increased because NylonX is a carbon fiber reinforced nylon, and as mentioned earlier in this chapter, carbon fiber reinforced materials are more likely to experience poor layer adhesion.

Try slightly increasing your extrusion temperature to see if it helps with this problem.

# Under extrusion

Another reason for poor layer adhesion is under extrusion itself. If your extruder is depositing less filament than it thinks it is, you are bound to have weak layer adhesion.

Confirm you have the proper E-Steps set by referring to the "Over and Under Extrusion" chapter in this book.

# Not enough torque

As with the "Extruder Stepper Skipping" chapter, you could be working with a stepper motor/extruder setup that does not have enough torque. If your extruder motor skips, you will essentially be left with an under extruder or poor layer adhesion print.

The best way to remedy this is to upgrade to a geared extruder, if you haven't already. You can do this via printing a Greg's Wade extruder or by purchasing one. The two that I use are the Titan extruder by E3D, and my current favorite is the Bondtech BMG dual drive extruder.

# Turn off active cooling fan

While having your active cooling fan turned on will benefit the majority of prints and materials with their surface quality, many filaments require you keep this active cooling fan off for proper strength and layer adhesion. Another reason the print from the photo in the beginning of this chapter failed was that I kept my active cooling fan on. It seems that MatterHackers states their NylonX should be printed without any active cooling fan.

This not only helps to prevent warping, but will also help to achieve strong layer adhesion. Generally, the higher the heat capacity and density of the polymer, the more beneficial a cooling fan will be. For lower density polymers such as ABS, HIPS, etc. that are below 1.2g/cc, the fan is typically recommended to be turned off.

## Make sure material is stored properly

As with many other problems, make sure your material is stored properly. Old, wet material, or poorly made, off-tolerance filament can lead to issues that are very difficult to diagnose. If you consistently get poor layer adhesion from one spool regardless of what you do, try using a different spool. If the issue does not continue, it is likely problems with that particular material.

## Delamination

I personally consider delamination a different problem than just poor layer adhesion. You can have extremely strong layer adhesion but still experience delamination when working with high warping parts.

Because of this – I cover this specific issue in the "Warping" chapter, since delamination is far more a symptom of high warping materials rather than poor layer adhesion.

## Summary of Fixes and Precautions

- Read the "Material Sciences" chapter.
- Check the manufacturer recommended print settings. Do not go faster or change the temperature outside their ranges to start your tests.
- Switch from using a carbon fiber reinforced material if continually experiencing issues, since carbon fiber reinforced materials are going to have more issues with layer adhesion than other types of filaments.
- If experiencing poor layer adhesion while staying within the recommended settings, try increasing the extrusion temperature slightly.

- Confirm you have enough torque and that your extruder motor is not skipping.
- Turn off active cooling fan if the particular material does not call for it.
- Make sure there is no issues with the material you are using.
- If experiencing delamination – check the "Warping" chapter.

# Post-Processing

This is not going to be classified as a failure, but rather tips to help you combine smooth, sand, and paint your 3D printed object. There will be no tips on how to print your part in this section, just how to post-process it.

I have had a decent amount of experience with post-processing, and will let you all know my results below.

## Loctite Super Glue Gel

Combining 3D printed parts can be a difficult task, which is why Loctite Super Glue Gel has become the preferred favorite of many 3D printing enthusiasts. This stuff is quite strong and can dry in under a minute. When you have a part that can't easily be clamped together for drying, or a small part that can easily break, you will likely want to go with using Loctite. Remember that this stuff dries fast so you can accidentally glue your finger to the part if you are not careful.

After you have used everything you can get out, make sure you remove the tube from the hard plastic bottle. There is still about 30% of the glue in there that you can't get out until removed from the casing.

This works great on PLA and ABS, as well as many other plastics, but it doesn't work great on everything. Nylon materials are very hard to find the correct adhesive.

## Devcon Plastic Welder

This is a two part welder that you mix together and apply for parts you want to have a very strong hold. Devcon is just one manufacturer of Plastic Welders, I haven't tried them all. This is my go-to for any part I want to be as strong as possible. In fact, I have found that Devcon Plastic Welder is stronger than the actual layer adhesion, since on all of my tests the part would break before the bond did. The issue comes with the fact that it takes about 10 minutes to get a decent hold, and close to 24 hours before you get a fully cured weld.

Because of this, I use Loctite Super Glue Gel for those hard to hold and small spots, and Devcon Plastic Welder for just about everything else.

The only issue I have found is that every so often I get a bottle where one part will come out at a different flow rate than the other. This has led me to wasting a decent amount of the product. I believe this is due to me being shipped old product, but it is hard to say exactly why.

## Notes about Super Glue and Plastic Welding

These two products work great with PLA and many other hard plastics, but they do NOT work well with Nylons. I have only done a minimal amount of testing on bonding nylon parts together and I have yet to find something that I find acceptable. If you are designing a cosplay or fan art piece, use PLA or other hard plastics. If you are designing a mechanical piece to be printed in two parts in nylon, you should design those two parts screw or clamp together. Do not trust a super glue or plastic welding hold for parts that will be used in mechanical applications.

# Starbond Adhesives

Starbond has a wide variety of options and have recently sent me samples to test out. I will have a video out (hopefully by the time this book is released) that will go over testing different adhesive products and how they work with different types of materials. Please refer to my YouTube channel by the time of purchasing this book to find out those results.

My minimal testing with Starbond so far has me very happy. They seem to work amazingly well and come in thin, medium, and thick viscosities. The thin is similar to water, and can get into any crevice you need. The thick is similar to the Loctite Super Glue Gel. They also offer an accelerator spray that can make it so you only have to hold parts together for about 10 seconds.

So far – I definitely recommend you checking them out.

# Sanding

Sanding is key regardless of the methods you choose to go with below, and will help you to clean up any print. For the majority of materials (including PLA) I start with 220 grit sandpaper. This is just about the right roughness to help smooth your print out without deforming the look. You can go slightly lower than this for very hard plastics, just be careful.

From 220 you can move to 800 and even 2000 grit sandpaper. If you start with these high grit sandpapers, you won't get much progress, so it is smart to start with 220 and work your way up. You will likely want to wet the sandpaper as well since it helps in the process.

I use a circular power sander for many flat prints – especially those that I combine two parts, but you need to be very careful to not keep the sander in one spot for too long. This is because it will heat up your part past the glass transition temperature (especially with PLA), and can deform your print.

# Bondo

This stuff is very hard to sand without damaging your part, so make sure you are only using it to seal large seams that need to be strong. I have used this a few times in the past and you can really get a smooth seal, it just comes with quite a lot of work.

When Bondo hardens it cannot be easily hand sanded. This means you will want to have an electrical sander (or a Dremel sander for small areas). This issue with this is that you will have to be very careful to not accidentally damage the printed part. Not only can you accidentally dent the printed part, sanding gets hot, so hot it can deform a PLA part.

But when it comes to having a strong seal where no one can see the seam, you will want to use Bondo. Otherwise you might want to try out Spackle.

## Spackle

This is really for display pieces only, since it can accidentally be dented or scratched off with abrasion, even when fully dried. For very small seams, or even small gaps in layers, I will rub on some spackle using my fingers. I am able to get a very small amount of this stuff into areas, and then after a half hour use some 800 grit sandpaper to clean it all up.

The problem with spackle is that even after it dries it won't be that hard. This means you can accidentally dig a finger nail into it. This is why this is best for very small gaps on display pieces and should never be used on anything that needs to be used mechanically.

## Model Putty

Personally, I have yet to use model putty. I know I should, I just haven't yet. But from what I see from other makers, model putty can work as a great alternative to both Bondo and Spackle.

## Acetone vapor bath for ABS and carbon fiber reinforced ABS parts

One of the best parts of printing in ABS is the ability to acetone vapor finish your parts. PLA and other materials are not soluble in acetone, making them unable to be post processed this way. Not only can it make a print stronger and more water tight, it also gives a great finishing shine to parts that resemble an injection mold quality. Prints are smoother to the touch and overall easier to work with after acetone vapor finishing.

Please note that I have not actually done an acetone vapor in a couple of years, so there are likely other methods out there.

Along with a high glass transition temperature, this is another reason you would still use ABS in 3D printing today.

You do have to keep in mind though that this can definitely be overdone and lead to a destroyed print, so use caution when proceeding with these steps.

***CAUTION*** Acetone is EXTREMELY flammable, and this process should only be done in a well-ventilated area with absolutely no open flames. If you are not sure of your setup, DO NOT proceed.

**Step 1:** Prepare your slow cooker in such a way that you are using a metal grate (often comes with the slow cooker). This metal grate needs to be entirely taped off on the bottom with packaging tape and elevated slightly off the surface of the cooker. Make sure to use clear packaging tape as ABS parts will not stick to it unless overexposed to acetone vapor. This will help prevent the acetone from bubbling up and accidentally directly splashing your part during the heating stage.

Before turning anything on or putting in the metal grate with your part, be sure to add a few tablespoons of acetone.

**Step 2:** Place your part on the newly taped off metal grate and put into your slow cooker. You will then close your slow cooker and put it at the LOWEST settings. This is a VERY fast process, so do not try this without reading all of the steps and researching further.

Leave your part on the metal grate in the warm cooker for no more than 45 seconds. I had a method down where I would leave it on for 30 seconds, off for 15, and then on for 10 final seconds. This process will vary with each slow cooker you use.

I actually used to use a big broiler with a similar setup that I would put onto a hot plate for larger ABS prints. This process requires roughly 10 minutes though, due to the large volume of the broiler.

I recommend that you always error on the side of less time. You can always do another round of acetone vapor if you determine that the print requires it.

**Step 3:** After your quick acetone vapor bath is complete, remove the grate that is holding your part and put the two off to the side (onto a countertop that you do not care about). After allowing for 30 minutes or more for drying, you can remove the part to be vacuum purged.

This step is not needed but definitely helps with the strength of the part as well as the time required to dry. Doing the process above without a vacuum purge will require 24 – 48 hours before the part is to full strength.

**Note:** Now that I have parts which were acetone vapor finished over two years ago, I am noticing some issues with this process. While those parts looked great for a long time, they are now showing some cracks. I can't explain exactly why this happens, but feel it necessary to let you know that it has happened to my acetone vapor prints.

## XTC 3D for PLA and PETG

I like to be entirely honest with my reviews, and while other's have seen some amazing results from this stuff, I just personally have not. I am not sure if I am doing something wrong with the mixing or what, but my results are never quite what I see other's getting.

The idea behind this is XTC is that it is a protective and smoothing coat for finishing 3D parts that does not melt plastic. XTC-3D should fill in gaps and retain a smooth, shiny finish.

I have definitely had some semi-successful results in the past, it just often becomes more work than it is worth. First, you have to make sure the part is sanded as best as you can with standard 220 grit sandpaper. You then need to wear gloves and be in a well-ventilated area as you mix the two part goop. You then paint on an even coat, wait for it to entirely dry, and give it a further couple passes of sanding. After a decent amount of elbow grease, you should be left with a very smooth outer surface.

With some practice I am sure this can be perfected, I just personally prefer other methods at this point.

## Polysher and PolySmooth

Polymaker has also made a product called the Polysher which works exactly as an acetone vapor bath, but is made specifically for 3D prints utilizing isopropyl alcohol. Rather than being soluble in acetone, their proprietary PolySmooth filament is soluble in alcohol, making a vapor bath work perfectly to remove layer lines.

I was given a Polysher for review a year or so ago (which is up on my YouTube channel) and was very happy with the results. It is much safer than going with an acetone vapor bath, but you are limited to only using their PolySmooth material (or another alcohol soluble filament), and you are also limited on size to their Polysher. This means this is far safer than going the acetone vapor path.

This is great if you plan on doing a lot of display pieces such as miniatures or action figures, since it works perfectly to result in an injection mold look - but I would be cautious when working with mechanical parts due to the lack of detailed information on PolySmooth, though I believe it to be a form of PVB.

For further information, search for "Polysher by Polymaker Review" on YouTube for my 3D Print General review.

I have actually found that after a lot of further testing you do not even really need the Polysher to smooth out PolySmooth prints. If you have a spray bottle, or preferably a spray mister, you can spray this alcohol directly onto your print. You will instantly start to see the layer lines disappear.

This does make it so the underside of your print will stick and deform if you are not extremely careful. You can do multiple passes of sprays to get even smoother results, you just really need to wait a good 24 hours in-between sprays, with a good fan focused on your part during that dry time. If you have a way to heat the part up a bit and perform a vacuum purge, this time will be decreased a lot.

What is pretty amazing is their PolySmooth clear material. With a few coats of sprays, I am able to get this material just about entirely transparent. I have never been able to get something quite as clear as this stuff. You can see how it is done by watching my two videos on the topic called "Transparent 3D Prints" and "More Transparent 3D Print Tests".

# Primer

If you plan on painting your part, you will want to spray a coat of flat grey primer (or primer filler) before moving forward. Make sure you have combined your parts, sanded them smooth, and cleaned them entirely off of debris before going to this step. It would be smart to use a powerful air blower if you have a compressor on hand as to make sure all dust is blown off.

In a well-ventilated or outside area, with a tarp laid down, spray a light, even coat of primer about 6 inches from your part. This will allow for acrylics and other paints to stick to your part properly.

After waiting a couple of hours to fully dry, you can go ahead with spray painting or hand painting. If you went ahead and used primer filler, you can actually further sand smooth your print, which is why I prefer it over standard primer. When I want a really smooth print I actually do a coat of primer filler, wait to dry, sand, clean off, spray another coat of primer filler, and then sand once more.

# Painting

Over the past year I have done some testing with using an airbrush on 3D prints, and have slowly gotten better at it. You can see my first attempts at learning how to do this in the video titled "Learning to Airbrush 3D Prints", but many of my videos after this I use air brushing as well.

I have found it very difficult to paint within lines using an airbrush, but it works amazingly to get an even spread of paint, as well as for shading. If I want to cover an area in paint but want it as smooth as possible, I go with airbrushing. If I want to get into shading, I also use airbrushing. You can see how you can improve prints by watching the video titled "3D Printed Stan Lee" on my YouTube channel, though I may have better examples by the time you purchase this book.

If I need to paint within a small area, I will always go with hand painting. Since I was hand painting my prints for a couple of years before purchasing an airbrush kit, I have a bit more experience in this regard.

You can get a 24 color set of acrylic paints online for pretty cheap, it just requires some practice to get details down. You can also use model paint, it is just a tad more expensive. I have a few tutorial videos in this regard on my YouTube channel if interested in learning further. Remember to always allow time to dry and finish with either a clear satin or glossy spray coat to make sure everything sets as it should.

I suggest getting a thin set of good paint brushes to make sure you can stay within the lines. I always go with hand painting for features such as eyes due to the fine detail required.

Keep in mind that not all materials are great to paint. I have attempted to paint flexible filaments in the past, and it seems that acrylic paints will crack when being flexed.

I have also learned how to paint eyes properly from a great tutorial video titled "GalactiCustoms: 1/6 Paint Tutorial: Obi-Wan Kenobi- Pt 3 Eyes". The title is a bit long, but his description on how to paint eyes have transformed the look of my painted parts.

## Using shoe polish for shading

This is something I will often use watered down black acrylic for, but shoe polish can also add a great shading effect to parts that call for it. You need to make sure your part is as smooth as possible, the thicker the gaps in the layer lines, the worse this effect will be. You also need to make sure the previous painting is entirely dry with a clear coat on top, as to reduce any chance of paint chipping.

Essentially, if you get some black shoe polish and spread it out on a paper plate, you can then brush it onto your print with a paintbrush into the crevices and indents that should show shading. This works great for detailed figurines in which you want muscles or folds in shirts to show through better.

The black shoe polish will naturally go into these indents, and all you have left is to clean off the excess. Grab a sponge and get it wet. I used to suggest doing this after the shoe polish had dried, but I have found it easier to just wipe off sections as you go. Attempting to brush off dried shoe polish will require enough pressure that you may chip off paint.

For a far more detailed explanation, you should check out Cosplay Chris on YouTube, as he has perfected this approach with his "Custom Collectables" playlist.

# Print Pauses Mid-Print

This is when your printer thinks it is either still printing or the print is complete, while in reality it looks as though the machine is frozen. This is different than when you are "ghost printing" (Nozzle Clogs/Running Out of Filament) because the printer never actually completes, or attempts to complete, the full tool path it was given in the G-code.

This issue is not very common but can be another one of those frustrating failures that can be extremely difficult to properly diagnose.

## Corrupted G-code

As mentioned in some other chapters, there is a possibility that your G-code could be corrupted. I have had the experience of exporting a large G-code and then preemptively dragging the incomplete file over to my printer/SD card. You have to make sure to wait until the file is fully exported before dragging to be printed on your machine.

Since I didn't realize the G-code wasn't done saving, the print stopped right at the point I dragged it over. This caused the remainder of the tool path to not be followed, and for the end G-code to never be triggered - meaning I had a hot nozzle and build plate with a half-finished print paused just like the photo you see above.

I had assumed that it was a connectivity issue, so I just reprinted, only to experience the exact same issue at the exact same spot on the print. Re-slicing and exporting the G-code fixed this on the third try.

You will notice some larger G-codes can take 5-10 minutes to slice, so you do not want to get over zealous when trying to get your print started. An easy way to tell if your machine was sliced at the incorrect time is to just open the G-code in a notepad to see if the ending script is there.

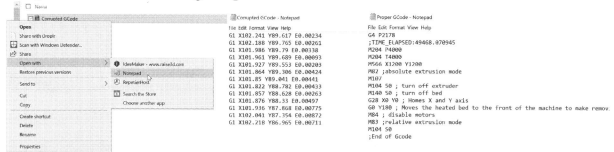

## Malfunctioning SD card

A malfunctioning SD card can lead to prints pausing mid-print. SD cards should be formatted as FAT or FAT32, and the max size should be 32GB. Try formatting your SD card, or just purchase a new one, if this is a consistent issue.

## Connectivity issues

If you are running your printer via a Raspberry Pi, this is something you may experience. A connectivity issue could be a problem with your USB cable accessing the internet, or with your Raspberry Pi itself (disconnects from internet or local network do not cause failures, but you won't be able to reach the Octoprint UI from another device to do anything with the printer if the pi disconnects from the network).

There is even the chance that your Raspberry Pi's power cable has been disconnected or bent to the point where it is not producing power. If your Raspberry Pi loses power mid print, the print will just pause exactly where it last left off.

I have experienced some very confusing situations in which I could not properly diagnose why the connectivity problem occurred. I would start a print overnight only to see it paused in place the next morning. A simple reboot of the machine and of Octoprint would fix this just about every time.

A good precaution for this is to always make sure you are using the most up to date raspberry pi and Octoprint firmware. Make sure you are using a strong, USB, power cord, and Ethernet cable (if hardwired), and that they have a good clasp (so that they stay in their ports).

I cannot stress enough how important it is to only use high quality USB cables with ferrite cores (cylindrical objects on the cord near the connectors) and make sure to have spares on hand. These cables degrade and go out more often than you would expect. High quality cables can typically be sourced locally for less than $10 and are well worth the extra $1-$2 premium over generic lower quality cables.

Don't use a phone charger, make sure you use a power adapter. Phone chargers can scale down their output, so you want to make sure it is a full power adapter. The red light on your Pi should always be on, it shouldn't be flickering.

If your pi is in a place where it can be rattled or moved repeatedly, you will experience this issue more often.

This is also true if you were to remove an SD card mid print or were to disconnect your printer from the computer when printing via Repetier.

# Power malfunction

Power malfunctions can relate to either your power supply malfunctioning, overloading a circuit breaker, or having an entire power outage - with an outage being one of the hardest to diagnose if you didn't see it happen live.

3D printers are energy hogs, especially when heating a large build platform. You will not want more than two power hungry printers on one standard circuit, otherwise you are prone to blowing it.

When I would run 12 printers simultaneously at SD3D, even though we had upgraded our electrical, I would never start the bed heating process for more than 3 machines at one time. That is because the initial amount of power that is required is more than the energy required to maintain the temperature.

Next, the power supply on your machine may actually be malfunctioning. If you are running an inexpensive machine, you are likely running a very inexpensive power supply. These blow out all the time and have issues with their fans dying. I have had a power supply whose fan died without me noticing, which would cause the power supply to overheat and shut off periodically. This will leave you confused coming back to a power supply that is working and a print that is paused in place.

If your breaker were to blow mid print, or your power supply were to give out entirely, you will be left with a similar looking problem (power off on machine, print failed mid print). Flip your printer switch off and go to your breaker to see if any switches are flipped. If so, you know that it is an issue with overloading the circuit.

And then the worst of all scenario is an actual blackout. This is not your fault and can happen periodically in any city. Two times in the past couple of years I had started extremely long prints when I experienced a blackout that affected multiple city blocks. Every company and house was without electricity for a short period of time, so the machines were powerless as well.

One of these times it happened in the middle of the night when I was not near the facility. When I came in the next morning everything powered up just fine, yet every single print was frozen in place. The only reason I was able to tell there was a blackout was by checking a time-lapse video that I had been running.

If your printer is extremely important and cannot be shut off in a blackout, it would be smart to invest in a backup power supply generator that can run the printer for an hour while power hopefully returns.

## NANO fuse issues

Finally, you may see similar issues, but some parts of the printer will still power on when it is a NANO fuse issue. If your printer turns on, yet either the LCD screen doesn't work or some other strange part is not working – preventing parts to complete – there is a chance you have a blown NANO fuse on your board.

I go over this in full detail in the "LCD Blank or Dark" chapter. I have only had this problem on Lulzbot TAZ machines with a Rambo board, so make sure you know if your board requires NANO fuses.

## Summary of Fixes and Precautions

- Make sure your G-code was exported properly and re-slice if needed.
- Check connectivity of printer to raspberry pi to the internet. Any disconnections in that chain will cause this type of failed print.

    Or

- Check to make sure your SD card is not freely moving and remains connected throughout the print.
- Check to see if power supply is working and fans turn on when hot.
- Make sure you are not overloading any circuits.
- Check with neighbors if experiencing a blackout.
- Have extra NANO fuses on hand if your board requires them.

# Quality Options

The quality, and amount of time to print, will vary based off of two factors – your nozzle diameter (line width) and the layer heights you are printing at. Below we will take a look at a few of these options.

## Nozzle diameter

0.15mm    0.25mm    0.4mm    0.6mm    0.8mm

The nozzle diameter will determine the line width of your print segments, which will affect the tolerances in the X/Y direction. While many people prefer to slightly tweak their line width from their nozzle diameter – I normally keep it the same. I have been experimenting with increasing by 10% to good results (as in printing 0.44mm line width with a 0.4mm nozzle). Any part of your print that is thinner than your line width will not be printed, so you can imagine how a thinner nozzle diameter can lead to a higher quality print.

The biggest issue with this comes with the print time required. The fact that you have to slow your print down to prevent nozzle clogs, that you have to print at lower layer heights, all along with the actual lines being thinner, your print can be exponentially longer.

The general rule of thumb is to allow for a clearance of ½ the nozzle diameter for parts that mate together, though as you see in the "Parts Not Mating Together" chapter, it is smart to print your own tolerance test to see what your clearances should be. You should be able to print with tighter clearances though when using a thinner nozzle diameter.

When printing with a very small nozzle you will need to be using a geared extruder. You need the proper amount of torque to push through 0.15mm or 0.25mm diameter nozzles. It is also smart to do this on a direct extruder vs. a Bowden, since most Bowden setups will have a rough time pushing through an extremely fine diameter nozzle.

Personally, I have standardized to using 0.25mm, 0.4mm, and 0.6mm nozzles. It seems that the 0.15mm nozzle is very hard to dial in and takes an extraordinarily long amount of time to print with, and the 0.8mm nozzle is just too low of tolerances for what I am looking for. The only time I have used a 0.8mm nozzle is when printing in vase mode, including when I try to print transparent prints with PolySmooth. I have printed with a 1.4mm nozzle on an E3D SuperVolcano, but that was only to test for a video, and I have no real applications for it.

I have a couple of videos going over printing in different nozzle diameters at my YouTube channel – The 3D Print General – if you would like further information. The most recent one is titled "3D Printing with Extremely Fine Nozzles" and it covers a ton of information on quality options and limitations in FDM 3D printing.

## How the nozzle diameter effects layer heights

As stated elsewhere in the book, you have a range of layer heights that will result in reliable prints based off of your nozzle diameter. Essentially, you want your layer heights to stay within 25-75% of your nozzle diameter. This means a 0.15mm nozzle should print roughly within 0.04mm – 0.11mm layer heights, and a 0.8mm nozzle should print within 0.2mm – 0.6mm layer heights.

When you go outside this range, the extrusion reliability and quality will often go down. When you try to print with a small nozzle with too large of layer heights, you will surely clog and grind filament more frequently, and when you try to print too low of layer heights on a large nozzle, you won't be printing at quite the tolerances and quality that you could with a proper nozzle diameter.

## Layer heights

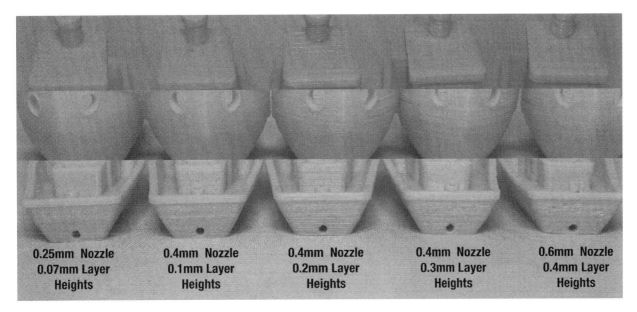

| 0.25mm Nozzle 0.07mm Layer Heights | 0.4mm Nozzle 0.1mm Layer Heights | 0.4mm Nozzle 0.2mm Layer Heights | 0.4mm Nozzle 0.3mm Layer Heights | 0.6mm Nozzle 0.4mm Layer Heights |

(Remember you can email me at Sean@3DPrintGeneral.com with proof of purchase for high def photos and color PDF)

Layer heights refer to how thick each individual layer is in the Z-direction. Large layer heights reduce the quality in the Z-direction, but allow for a much faster print. When printing at the same speeds with same nozzle diameter, a print that is 0.2mm layer heights will take half as long to complete as the same print with 0.1mm layer heights.

It seems that the speeds you can print at with a standard extruder/hotend setup works on a bell curve. You need to slow down your print as you go to very low layer heights and when using a small diameter nozzle in order to prevent bottlenecking and nozzle clogs. You also need to slow down your print speeds when going with a very large nozzle with large layer heights in order to get the proper viscosity. If you print too fast with large layer heights and nozzle diameters, the particular material may not have enough time to melt.

For example, the standard E3D V6 hotend is advertised at printing up to 15mm3/s. This can be remedied with a hotend meant for this - such as the E3D Volcano. The E3D volcano advertises printing up to around 40mm3/s – meaning you can print much faster with larger nozzles and layer heights.

It seems I can print with the fastest linear speed on my standard V6 setup with a 0.6mm nozzle at around 0.25mm layer heights. Once I bump up to the 0.8mm nozzle I need to slow down my print speeds, and the same is true when moving to a 0.4mm or 0.25mm nozzle. The larger nozzle will likely still allow the print to finish faster even with the lower print speed due to the additional volume of material that is being deposited with each move.

For over 90% of my prints I have standardized to a 0.4mm nozzle. I have this nozzle in hardened steel and will print the vast majority of my prints at 0.1mm –

0.25mm layer heights with this 0.4mm nozzle. This will work for the majority of 3D printing applications.

# Running Out of Filament

This problem is by far the easiest to diagnose but also one of the most frustrating when it occurs. You can think you have enough filament for that 400 gram print, when 20 hours in, with only 10 layers left, you run out of material.

You can avoid this by taking these precautions:

## Weigh an empty spool

It is always good to have the weight in grams of an empty spool for the filament manufacturer you are using. These do have tolerances, but it is a good starting point.

After you have the weight of an empty spool you can then weigh the spool you are about to use for your next print. Subtract the weight of the empty spool and you should have a rough estimate of how many grams of the material are left. Make sure to provide a buffer of at least 20 grams to account for tolerances in the spool itself.

## Pause at layer height if you know you will run out

If you are going to start a print with a spool that you know does not have enough filament to complete, you can add a "Pause at Layer Height" to the slice of your model. There is a plugin available for Cura and similar features on Simplify 3D that will allow you to have the print pause at a specific layer height and raise in the

Z-axis, allowing you to switch the filament out to another spool that can complete the remainder of the print.

This is especially useful for very large prints and you don't have a full spool available.

You can also use this feature if you would like the top portion of your print to be a different color than the bottom.

# Understand the density of the material you will be printing with

When you use a slicing program it will give you an estimate of the amount of material it will be using. If it gives you this number in grams, it will not be accurate if you are using a material that is different than is in your machine settings. If you are given this estimation without having to set anything up, it is likely based on the density of PLA.

If you are given the estimation in meters and not grams, you will have to do a minor calculation to find out the estimation in grams for your material.

PLA is 1.25 grams per cubic cm. If you were using 1.75mm diameter filament, one meter of filament would be 2.41 cubic cm in volume.

1 meter of PLA 1.75mm filament would then be equal to 2.41 x 1.25, or 3.0125 grams. A 1,000 gram spool should be roughly 331 meters.

Using that 2.41 cubic cm in volume for 1.75 filament, you can use the data below to figure out how many grams your material expects to use.

## Density of material

**PLA:** 1.25 g/ccm        -   3.0125 grams per meter of 1.75mm filament

**ABS:** 1.04 g/ccm    -   2.5064 grams per meter of 1.75mm filament

**PET:** 1.38 g/ccm    -    3.3258 grams per meter of 1.75mm filament

**Most Nylons:** 1.13 g/ccm -  2.7233 grams per meter of 1.75mm filament

The same is true for 2.85mm filament, you would just use 6.38 cubic centimeters as the volume per one meter of filament.

If you are using Octoprint, you can also try installing the Filtracker plugin which uses unique QR codes to monitor remaining filament length and provides alerts when attempting to print an object without enough filament remaining.

## Use a filament runout sensor

Many printers now feature a filament runout sensor. You can purchase one as well, it would just require you to do some tweaks to your firmware. These sensors are very inexpensive and work in a way that they pause your print when filament is no longer running through it. This means if your print runs out of filament while you are away from the machine, you will come back to a print that is paused with the hotend off of the print. You can then change the material to a new spool, and click "resume".

If you are consistently running large prints, where running out of filament is a frequent occurrence, it would definitely be smart for you to invest in one of these. TH3D has an inexpensive filament sensor called the EZOUT which can be retrofitted to most machines very easily.

## Summary of Fixes and Precautions

• Weigh your spool before starting print.

• Add settings to pause at a layer height to allow you to switch filament if you know your spool does not have enough.

• Know the density of the material you are using to calculate the estimated amount of grams for your print.

• Use a filament runout sensor.

• If you are running Octoprint, try out the Filtracker plugin.

# Settings Issues

This is a very vague chapter since it can deal with a variety of issues related to having a clean print with the proper dimensional accuracy. Every single material by every single manufacturer on every single machine will have slightly different slicer settings in order to achieve the highest quality print. That being said, I go over my personal settings for each material in "Material and Their Settings" chapter in this book, and Nicolas from Polymaker goes over in detail the idea behind material science in his chapter. I sincerely suggest everyone reads that "Material Science" chapter, since fully understanding it will help you to dial in your slicer settings without even reading this chapter.

When covering this chapter in my first edition, I went over the old Cura – Version 15.04.6 to be specific. Since that first book, Cura has entirely redone their interface, along with including the ability to tweak just about anything you can think of. I originally only covered Cura settings because it was the best free slicer in my opinion, but as of their continual updates, I find it better than almost any paid option as well.

Many makers prefer Simplify3D, but over the past two years I personally feel Cura offers just as many options as Simplify does, and they seem to update it even more frequently than S3D.

It may take a little while to get used to everything, but just about anything you want to tweak is now available. That is why this chapter is such a long and all-encompassing one.

Printers such as Zortrax, MakerBot, and others will require their own slicer and not have these options, but you really should not be experiencing any settings issues on those machines when using their proprietary material.

I will specifically be using Cura 4.0, but they are frequently releasing updates with increased options.

The following examples will be with printing in PLA on a direct drive machine with a gear ratio, though you can get more specific settings in the "Material and Their Settings" chapter. If you would like some further detail you can always visit my 3D Print General YouTube channel which goes more in-depth on a couple of these options.

## About Using Cura 4.0 and Newer

In order to see expanded options, make sure you are in the "Custom" print setup, and not "Recommended". You can save profiles for specific materials and qualities, but we will just be going over what each option does.

You can then click on the gear icon next to any section to option the expanded settings. When in the custom selection you can choose exactly what options you want to tweak. For anything you are not sure what it does, you can always scroll over it to be given a definition. I will personally only be going over the options I tweak, because there are literally hundreds of settings available.

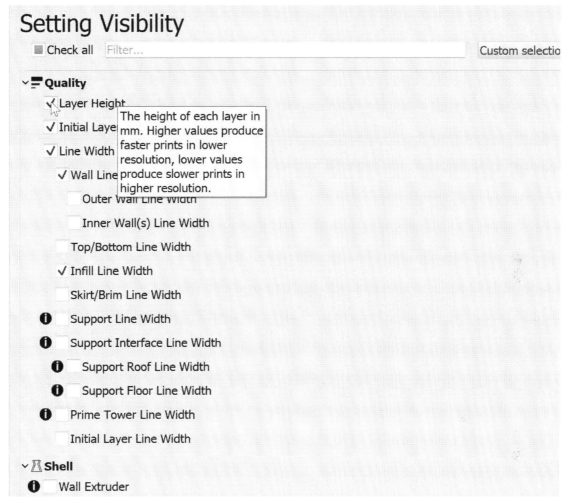

# Quality

All of the factors I will be going over in this Quality section are the same for both a Bowden and Direct drive printer.

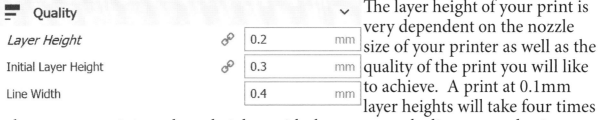

The layer height of your print is very dependent on the nozzle size of your printer as well as the quality of the print you will like to achieve. A print at 0.1mm layer heights will take four times as long as one at 0.4mm layer heights, with the same nozzle diameter and printer speeds. You can get up to roughly 75% your nozzle diameter in layer height, but remember that you sacrifice quality for time the higher you go with the layer heights. You can also achieve as low as roughly 25% the nozzle diameter without lowering your results.

Changing your layer height should not affect the amount of material you are using, just the time involved to print. The longer the print though, the higher the chance of experiencing a failure at some point. Not only will the print be longer due to the smaller layer height, you will actually have to run your extrusion speeds slower as well for a clean print.

The layer height is also affected by your Z-Axis leadscrews/threaded rods. The diameter and pitch can affect the quality due to where your carriage is on its rotation. There is a handy calculator over at www.PrusaPrinters.org/calculator if you don't want to do any math. You just choose your Motor step angle (labeled on your Z axis motors), your desired layer height, and your leadscrew pitch. Most of my machines are 1.8° step angle and a leadscrew pitch of 2mm/revolution on an M8 leadscrew. This means I can tweak my layer heights on a 0.01mm basis without any issues. But if you have an M5 threaded rod with a pitch of 0.8mm/revolution, you will have to tweak on a 0.014mm basis for best results. This means instead of 0.25mm layer heights, you should actually go for 0.248mm or 0.252mm.

This is a bit technical and will definitely lead to cleaner results, but I have printed outside of these suggested ranges in the past without much of a difference. This is for when you want to make sure everything is as tuned in as possible.

The Initial Layer Height is actually for bed adhesion more so than quality. This allows you to have a thicker first layer in order to make sure everything sticks properly. This number should always be at least as thick as your normal layer height, and should only be increased up to 75% of the nozzle diameter. I always take advantage of this because getting the first layer to stick is easiest with a thick first layer.

This is a big reason dealing with small nozzles is so difficult to get the first layer to stick properly. I have used a 0.15mm diameter nozzle before and it took me over a half hour of restarting the print to get that first layer Z-height distance correct. This is because the thickest I could print my initial layer height at is 0.11mm after factoring in the RepRap Calculator limitations. You can imagine that you have to be much more precise on that first layer when printing at a 0.11mm layer height vs. 0.3mm.

The Line Width is just your nozzle diameter. Many makers suggest slightly tweaking this, so you can play around with what others suggest, but I personally always use the nozzle diameter for the line width I want to achieve. If you want thin 0.25mm line widths, I would highly recommend using a 0.25mm diameter nozzle instead of just tweaking this for a 0.4mm nozzle.

There are roughly a dozen other settings you can tweak in Cura under Quality, but I personally do not change any of them, since they all deal with changing the line width of specific sections of the print. There may be particular applications in which you want to do this, but I always stick to the line width of the nozzle diameter I am using.

The 3D printing community is always learning and growing when it comes to how you can change your slicer settings to improve your print, so playing around is encouraged. Whenever I see improved results, I make sure to factor them into my future prints.

# Shell

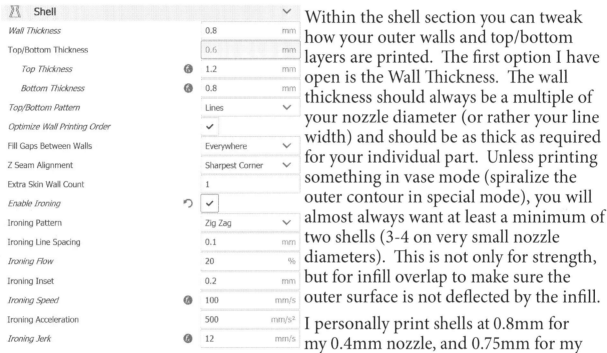

Within the shell section you can tweak how your outer walls and top/bottom layers are printed. The first option I have open is the Wall Thickness. The wall thickness should always be a multiple of your nozzle diameter (or rather your line width) and should be as thick as required for your individual part. Unless printing something in vase mode (spiralize the outer contour in special mode), you will almost always want at least a minimum of two shells (3-4 on very small nozzle diameters). This is not only for strength, but for infill overlap to make sure the outer surface is not deflected by the infill.

I personally print shells at 0.8mm for my 0.4mm nozzle, and 0.75mm for my 0.15mm nozzle. Anything less than this and the part will be too brittle.

If your particular part requires strength from the outer direction, such as when I print skateboard wheels, you can increase the shell thickness rather than increasing the infill percentage, since it needs strength in that direction. On the many skateboard wheels I have tested and worked with, I increased the wall thickness until it was 100% filled via shells. This is why it is important to understand which direction your part requires strength in before choosing to increase infill percentage, wall thickness, or both. For an average part I will keep this to a multiple of 2-3x the nozzle diameter, with a minimum of 0.75mm.

Many people prefer a minimum of 1.2mm thickness for shells, so it is up to you to determine what you think will work best here. Just do not go too thin or your part will be weak.

The Top/Bottom Thickness is how many layers of 100% fill will be left before and after the infill is printed, and is a multiple of your layer height. This number will have to be tweaked depending on how much infill you use and how thick your model is, but I always suggest having a minimum of 1mm in top layers. This is to make sure you do not have a "pitted" top in which you can see the infill below.

While this is very important to keep the top layers at a minimum of 1mm, if you are still seeing a pitted effect, it is probably better to just increase the infill percentage. The bottom layers are not as important since they do not have to cover an overhang. I still will do at least 4x the layer height, with a minimum of 0.6mm being laid down for bottom layers.

Remember that the top/bottom thickness is going to be working off a multiple of your layer height. So if you are printing 0.3mm layer heights, you will need to round to the nearest thickness in relation to that. Rather than having 0.8mm thickness for the bottom, you would want to go up to 0.9mm.

The Top/Bottom pattern is as it is described, and I almost never tweak this from "Lines". "Zig-Zag" may have some applications, but I don't know when you would want to use "Concentric".

Optimize Wall Printing Order reduces the number of retractions and the distances travelled and will benefit most parts. It should improve speed and quality on most prints, but if you are starting to see defects going up in the z-direction of your print or an increased slice time – turn it off.

The Z Seam Alignment is where the printer will decide to go up to the next layer. If you have ever seen a seam going up your print, it is because your printer was moving up in the Z-direction to start a new layer right at that spot, for every layer. These seams are just about impossible to avoid entirely, but you can determine where they are placed. If you are printing a part with corners or lots of curves, you will likely want to choose "Sharpest Corner" for the highest quality. For a smooth or cylinder shape, you may want to choose "Random" for the best quality, so there isn't a giant seam, considering there is no sharpest corner. "Shortest" will choose the fastest printing method, which will likely lead to a seam on one part of your print, but it will definitely print a bit faster.

Ironing is a very unique setting that you definitely will not always want turned on, but I am showing my settings above for when you do want to use it. It is also the only option in this section that will need to be tweaked whether you are using a Direct Drive or a Bowden (Bowden will need to run closer to the Cura recommended settings, while Direct Drive has to be bumped up to what is shown in the previous photo). Ironing was originally a Cura Experimental feature that was moved to the "Shell" section.

Ironing is a very cool feature in which I cover in-depth on a video on my 3D Print General YouTube channel. It has your nozzle go over the top surfaces an additional time, but without extruding any material in order to melt the plastic on top further, creating an extremely smooth top surface. This will ONLY work on parts that have flat tops and is not needed on parts that are entirely curved, but if you ever wanted to remove those pesky layer lines on top surfaces, you can now do so.

This will definitely need honing in for your particular machine, as it took me a couple dozen prints to get everything you see dialed in for my direct drive printer.

Personally, I do not use this setting very often, since the results can often vary depending on how much surface area has to be covered. Use this setting at your own discretion and play around before printing a part you need to come out clean.

# Infill

This section is what you will want to change if you need to increase the strength of your part in the top/bottom direction, reduce the "pitted" effect on your print, or decrease the time required for your part to print. Everything explained below will be the same on both a direct drive and Bowden extruder.

You will have to recognize how thick your part is before realizing how much infill you require. If your whole part is made up of thin walls, it is likely the infill percentage will not make any difference at all, since the majority of the print will be filled via shell walls. But if you are dealing with a large block, it will be a deciding factor in a successful or unsuccessful print.

Most models can print successfully at 10% or lower, but not for large/thick models. Think about the top surface contour of your print. If it is a flat top that needs to bridge a large gap, you are likely going to need to increase this infill to a minimum of 20%.

Personally, most parts that I print that do not need to be mechanically strong, I print at about 8%. So make sure you know your geometry and application since you can save a lot of time and material printing by reducing this number.

To be honest, most parts you print will not require higher infill than 50%, and you will get diminishing results when you go much higher than that. You will use a ton of material to print at 100% infill and your printer will take a lot longer to complete, when you will likely get a lower quality print without much increased strength. I will rarely print something at 75% infill and almost never at 100% (other than just for testing materials). The majority of my decorative or prototype pieces are at 8-15% infill, parts I mechanically use are 20-40% infill, and very strong parts I go around 50%. There are many parts that can actually be printed below 10%, even 0%, if the geometry calls for it and you put enough top layers in your Top/Bottom Thickness.

The Infill Pattern refers to the structure shape of the infill. While you are given plenty of options, I almost always keep this on "Triangles". Hexagons are one of the strongest shapes in this regard, but your printer nozzle has to go over the same line twice in order to actually make the shape. Because of this (and because Cura does not offer the Hexagonal option), I go with the second best shape being a triangle. Triangle infill can be printed extremely fast and still has a lot of strength properties.

Others online say they get great results from some of the other options, I just stick with "Triangles". Feel free to play around with these and see if you prefer one over the other.

Infill Overlap Percentage is the percent that your infill overlaps onto the shell walls. When this number is set too high, along with not having enough shell walls, you can get what I called a "Veiny" print in the diagnostic section, and too low of a percentage can result in infill that rattles around detached from the walls, decreasing the strength of your part. I almost always reduce the standard set by the slicer and prefer a number around 8% or 9%. This, in combination with 2-3 shell walls, will result in a strong print without any infill veins showing throw the outside.

Please note this is for opaque materials. If you are dealing with a translucent material you are going to need to increase the shell walls drastically if you do not want to be able to see the infill. That is not a veiny print, but rather a print you can see through.

Another way to reduce this "veiny" look is to check off the "Infill Before Walls". This makes sure your infill prints before your shell walls, reducing the likelihood you will get a "veiny" print.

Finally, the infill layer thickness is just what it sounds like. For well over 95% of prints I just keep this the same as the rest of my layer heights. But let's say we are printing a large detailed print in which the strength does not really matter. We may set our layer heights to be 0.1mm, but the quality only matters on the outside walls. You can set your infill layer thickness to be 0.2mm, meaning that it only prints the infill every two layers – drastically speeding up the time required to print. This could save you hours of print time.

here are at least a dozen other options available in which I personally do not tweak in this section.

# Material

| IIIII Material | | | ⌄ |
|---|---|---|---|
| *Printing Temperature* | 🎯 | 212 | °C |
| *Build Plate Temperature* | 🔗 ↺ | 55 | °C |
| *Flow* | | 100 | % |
| Enable Retraction | | ✓ | |
| *Retraction Distance* | | 3.5 | mm |
| *Retraction Speed* | | 35 | mm/s |
| *Retraction Minimum Travel* | 🎯 | 0.9 | mm |

Printing Temperature is very straightforward and will be the temperature in which your hotend is set to. This is entirely dependent on the material you are using and the printing temperature will be tweaked depending on the nozzle diameter and layer height.

As covered thoroughly in the "Nozzle Clogs" chapter, if you have the hotend set to the wrong temperature, you can have quite an annoying cleanup on your hands. Be sure to refer to the "Material Science" chapter to understand a bit more about melting points and what may work for different filaments. Below are generic print temperature ranges for different materials.

**PLA:** *180°C – 220°C*

**ABS:** *225°C – 235°C*

**PETG:** *245°C – 2552°C*

**CFR – ABS:** *245°C – 253°C*

**Cheetah by Ninjatek:** *223°C - 235°C*

**Ninjaflex:** *223°C – 235°C*

**PCTPE:** *232° - 235°C*

**Nylon 910:** *245°C – 252°C*

**Polycarbonate ABS:** *267°C – 275°C*

As mentioned elsewhere, you may need to tweak these settings depending on the manufacturer you purchase from, and the machine you are using.

Bed temperatures for specific materials are covered in the "Bed Adhesion" chapter, so below you will find the generic temperature ranges I like to use for extruding different materials. The range is in reference to the differences in nozzle diameter, layer height, and manufacturer. This is all explained further in the relevant "Material and their Settings" chapter of this book. I personally have my build plate temperature for PLA set to 55°C now instead of 60°C in order to help reduce "Elephant Foot".

The diameter is the diameter of the material and extruder you are using. This will either be 1.75mm or 2.85mm depending on your setup. If you purchase from a subpar manufacturer, you may get tolerances too large, so make sure you stick with what has been reviewed and tested to work. Most machines out there are 1.75mm today, but some companies such as Lulzbot still use 2.85mm.

Assuming you have your E-Steps dialed in, as explained in the "Over and Under Extrusion" chapter in this book, you will not need to change the flow from 100%. But, if you wanted to change your extrusion rates on the fly, you can change it in the flow section. 101% will extrude 1% more than what your current E-Steps are set to.

This is the section you can change if you are unable to flash your machine or give G-code commands. You can reduce the number accordingly if you are unable to change your E-Steps. This isn't ideal but it should have the same results.

Retraction should be enabled on the vast majority of your prints and will need to be tweaked based off of the material and if you are using a Bowden or Direct Drive setup (with the numbers shown being for PLA on a Direct Drive). Bowden machines will need higher numbers than I am showing.

Having your retraction dialed in is the number 1 way to reduce the stringiness and "hairy" prints. There are a few models that may require retraction turned off, but you will almost always want it on.

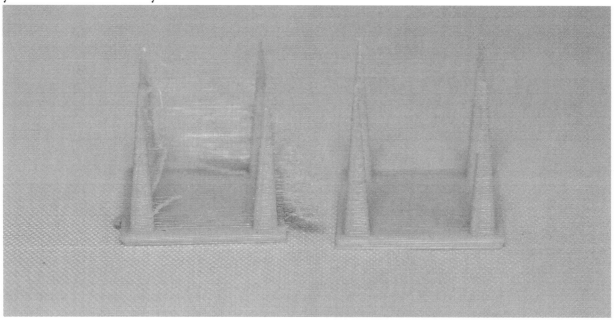

The print on the left is with retraction turned off, and the right is with it turned on to the settings I have shown above. Please keep in mind this model is designed to torture test your machine, and you may not need quite as high of retraction settings on every model. Going too high of retraction may result in an under extruded part.

The retraction distance refers to how far the material goes when retracting, retraction speed refers to how fast, and minimum travel refers to the amount of travel required for any retraction to happen at all. If you have a part with extremely small pegs (for instance - a very small fence on an architectural model) and they are still coming out "hairy" after using the settings I example, you may need to decrease this minimum travel number.

Bowden machines will need these numbers bumped up, as explained in the "Material and their Settings" chapter.

Particular materials also require different retraction settings. I have found that PETG is far stringier than PLA, requiring higher retraction settings. You can understand this further in the "Material Science" chapter.

It is very easy to clean up a minor amount of stringiness via a heat gun and a razor.

# Speed

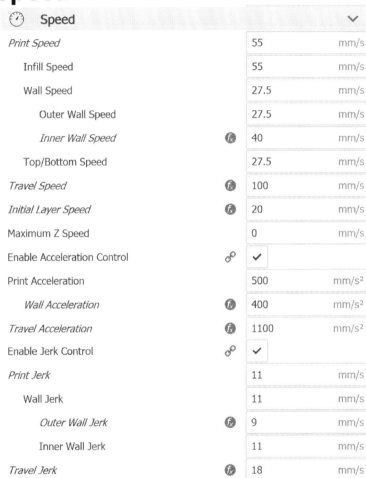

All of the numbers you see will need to be tweaked for Bowden machines, as explained in the "Material and their Settings" chapter. But these speeds will also have to be tweaked depending on your extruder and hotend setup. If you are using a non-geared extruder, you will need to run much slower than if you have a geared one. I am personally using a Bondtech BMG dual drive extruder with an E3D V6 hotend, so I am able to extrude fairly well at speeds even above what you see.

These are the settings that will be most tweaked depending on your machine, quality, and the material you are using. As mentioned elsewhere, if you are experiencing issues with the speed your machine is printing at, you should reduce it so that it is no faster than 100x the nozzle diameter. If you have a well-built geared extruder machine that is printing at mid-range (~50% nozzle diameter), you can actually get this number to 300x the diameter of the nozzle, but I would not recommend anything near those speeds if you are experiencing issues or extruder motor skips or rattling of your machine.

Keep in mind that the amount your hotend can actually successfully extruder will also determine your maximum print speeds. An E3D Volcano hotend can push out a lot more volume than a standard E3D V6, meaning it can have a higher print speed.

You should definitely see the video I published entitled "How Fast Can You 3D Print?" where I cover all of these details which you should know.

The infill speed should almost always be the same speed as your print speed, while your outer wall should be slowed down a bit to make sure it has the best surface quality. You will also want to make sure your initial layer is about 50% your print speeds, with it tweaked even lower if you are having difficulty getting that first layer to stick. A generally good range for this is anywhere between 15mm/s and 25mm/s depending on the material being used. There is no need to go fast on that first layer since it is the most likely layer to make the rest of your print fail if it does not get laid down perfectly.

Your travel speed is how fast the carriage moves when not extruding filament, and this can be bumped up fairly high, especially on Bowden machines. As long as your printer isn't rattling, you can likely get up to 100mm/s without much of an issue, even higher with a light carriage. I have recently been playing around with speeds of over 200mm/s since it should reduce oozing and will not affect print quality, but keep in mind these speeds may not even be reached without a high enough acceleration.

Acceleration refers to how fast your printer gets to your print speed, and jerk refers to the initial speed your extruder stepper will start at after a full stop. Your printer will accelerate at the highest rate possible up to that speed and then the acceleration value will take over at speeds above what is set for the jerk variable. In physics, "jerk" refers to something else, but this is what it refers to in 3D printing.

You can set your acceleration controls in your printer firmware, but it can always be tweaked right here in Cura. If you have ghosting/ echoing in your prints, a rattling machine, or ugly outer surfaces - reduce your acceleration and jerk. Reducing these will obviously slow your print down, but it will help immensely. Start with the numbers I show above for a direct drive machine and increase them if everything turns out fine. If not, there is likely something else that is wrong (such as a loose carriage or other issue explained in this book).

This is also where limitations for your machine come into play. You will never reach your print speed if your acceleration is not set high enough, or if there is not enough room to actually accelerate and decelerate. You can set your print speed to 1000mm/s, but without the space and high enough acceleration, it will never actually be reached.

As I went over further in my YouTube video mentioned above, I personally prefer to wait a bit longer for my print to complete and have my acceleration and jerk settings very low in order to guarantee a clean and successful print. You will likely hear others printing much faster than this, but if you are using a machine that cost under $1000, it is likely going to be hard for you to achieve those results.

# Travel

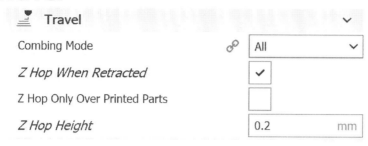

| | | |
|---|---|---|
| Combing Mode | 🔗 | All ⌄ |
| *Z Hop When Retracted* | | ✓ |
| Z Hop Only Over Printed Parts | | |
| *Z Hop Height* | | 0.2  mm |

Combing refers to the printer head following the path of the print rather than attempting to clear gaps. This will help prevent "hairy" sides of a print. When combing is set to "off", the extruder moves straight from the starting point to the end point and will always retract. Most of the time I will leave combing to "all", but there are specific times when I need combing turned off. When I work with very large layer heights – anything 0.4mm or higher, I will turn combing off. This is because the layers are so thick, that when the printer travels from one point to another, it will run into the infill. Even when I have "avoid printed parts when travelling" checked, the printer seems to want to run into the infill lines. You won't really notice this on low layer heights.

When combing is turned off, it will retract, do a z-hop, and then travel to its next position. As mentioned – this can add to your ooze and hairy issues, but sometimes it is needed. For instance, when I was using the E3D Super Volcano with a 1.4mm nozzle at 1.0mm layer heights, the print was just about impossible when combing was turned on.

Both avoid printed parts when traveling and avoid supports when travelling refers to what you think it would – the printer head steers clear of your print while moving from section to section. This will clearly add to print time considering the print head will not be taking the fastest path, but it will help avoid knocking your parts over. While it is not required to be on, I almost always keep both of these boxes checked.

Z hop when retracting refers to the amount the printer will raise in the Z-direction after retracting, as to not knock over small pieces when traveling between sections. If you are constantly getting parts knocked over even though you took all of the precautions mentions in the "Bed Adhesion" chapter, you may need to increase this number. The larger the nozzle diameter and layer height, the more you will likely want to increase this. Also refer to the "Parts Being Knocked Over" chapter if required.

If you ever hear some random loud clicks or noises during your print that you are having trouble figuring out where they are coming from, it may be from your nozzle hitting the print or support as it goes over it. Even if your print does not get knocked over, you will want to add a Z-Hop height and increase it until this does not happen. Almost every print you will want at least a minimal Z-hop height. For the vast majority of my prints, I have my Z-hop set to the same as my layer height and will tweak accordingly if needed. If the clicking continues – turn combing off.

Having these previous sections all turned on should definitely help with reducing issues related to parts being knocked over.

# Cooling

Cooling refers to when your active cooling fan will be engaged. Refer to the diagram of a 3D printer in the beginning of this book to know exactly which part I am talking about. This is crucial for getting the cleanest print possible on many different types of materials. If you are printing PLA without an active cooling fan, it is certain you are not achieving the best results you can.

This is not true though with specific types of materials, since you will reduce your layer adhesion. You need to know what material you are working with in order to understand if you need an active cooling fan on or off.

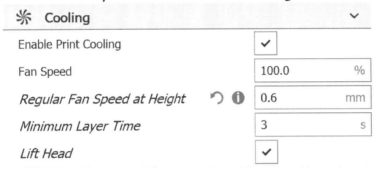

You do not want your active cooling fan to blow on your first layer since it can hurt with your bed adhesion. This is why I set the "Fan full on at height" number to 0.5mm – 0.6mm on most prints. It is rare that a material will call for a fan speed in-between 0 and 100%, so it is normally set to 100% on most prints.

If I am printing a large ABS part that comes to a small point, I may actually turn on the active cooling fan and turn this number to the height in which the point starts. If you have an active cooling fan on a medium-large ABS part, or any other high-warping material, it is likely you will end up with a failed print. This is why you will want the active cooling fan turned off for the majority of ABS prints, unless the geometry calls for it.

This active cooling fan can also play into your nozzle not maintaining a specific set temperature if the fan is blowing directly on your heater block, or if you are not using a silicone sock.

Minimal layer time refers to the amount of time required before starting a new layer. If a layer completes its tool path faster than this amount of time, your printer will pause until the time has passed before starting the next layer. This setting should almost always be accompanied with a "Lift Head" that you see right below it.

This "Lift Head" does just as you think it would. If a layer finishes faster than your minimal layer time, it will lift your extruder and pause until the correct amount of time has passed. For the example above, if a layer takes two seconds to complete, your nozzle will lift and remain there for one second before starting the next layer. This can add to the stringiness of your part but will make sure your top section is not a melted mess.

Most of the time you will not require this number to be higher than 5, since 5 seconds is long enough for the vast majority of materials to properly cool. If set to 1 second or lower, you will get very ugly, melted pointed tops. Any model that doesn't come to a single point will not even be affected by this number, unless set very high. If you are just printing one skinny part, you will notice that it may come out hairy due to constant head lifting from the minimum layer time not being hit. In these instances, you can print 2 or 3 of the model without increasing the print time at all, and may actually result in a cleaner print as well.

# Support

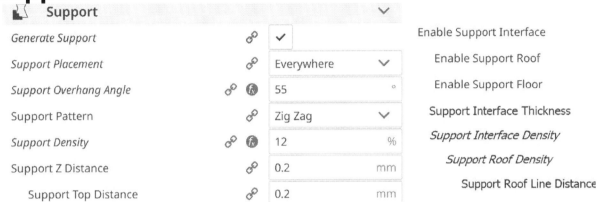

The overhang angle for support refers to the minimum angle required before support material is laid down, vertical being 0°. This may seem a bit confusing so it is best described by the image below:

Certain slicing software, such as the one for a Zortrax machine, will go in the opposite direction, having horizontal be 0°. We will be using 0° throughout this book, but if you are using an alternate slicing software, you may need to invert the settings I am describing in this section.

The general rule of thumb is support material will be needed on overhangs of 45° or greater. PLA can actually cleanly lay down angles of a higher degree if everything is set up properly and you are running an active cooling fan. There are models you can find on www.Thingiverse.com that allow you to test the highest angle your printer and material can achieve without supports. Just search for "overhang test".

Materials may actually be able to achieve different overhangs without the need for support depending on your other slicer settings, particularly your layer heights. This is covered a bit in the "Materials Science" chapter, as well as a video on my YouTube channel titled "How to Avoid Needing Support Material".

For ABS, I have this number set to 45°, and I will hone it in for any angles I notice scarring. In general, for most materials I will not go lower than 40° or higher than 60°.

You will usually want your support placement to be "Everywhere", unless the model you are printing was designed to only require "Touching Build plate". "Touching Build plate is what you assume it would be, it will only place support structures where they can easily touch the build plate. This is often not desired on most prints.

The support pattern I almost always have set to Zig Zag, though you can use Lines to save filament, or Grid to increase quality of the print, but when using the Support Interface explained later, it won't make much of a difference at all. The support density should be tweaked as well if you are not using the support interface.

Please refer to the "Experimental" section near the end of this chapter to find out how to reduce your support material even further.

Essentially, the support interface generates a dense interface between the model and the support creating a skin at the top of the support in which the model is printed, and is a newer feature on Cura. This is automatically done on Zortrax machines and is a great addition to Cura. In the first edition of my book this was not available yet, so I went over my support settings just using the normal support lines.

As you can see in the image above, there is this support interface in-between the normal support and the model. The image may be hard to see on your printed book, so don't forget to reach out to me at Sean@3DPrintGeneral.com for high definition color photos.

This means that the support pattern and support density will not affect the underside quality of your print when having this turned on, so I will reduce my support infill to as low as I can get it. Too low and your support may get knocked over during the print, which is why I like to keep mine at 10-12%.

I use this support interface on almost all main materials, but if you are using flexible filaments or materials with absurd layer adhesion, you will likely want this turned off. Removing parent support material can be quite difficult on many unique materials.

The numbers you see are what works for me on PLA for both a direct drive and Bowden extruder, and may need to be tweaked further for your machine.

If the underside of your print is still ugly after using my suggested starting points, either increase the support interface density and/or decrease the Z distance for support. If it is proving very difficult to remove this support material based off of my suggested settings, you should increase the Z distance for support. The support X/Y distance of 0.8mm seems to work just fine on almost all models and materials, and any closer the support material may be difficult to remove.

I recently created a video titled "Detailed Cura Support Settings" where I take a look at every aspect of this and show how it makes a difference in your prints. I spent a while on this video making sure to cover everything, so I really suggest checking it out if you are having lots of support difficulties.

# Build Plate Adhesion

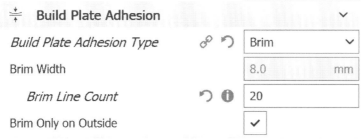

Having a skirt will allow for the material to purge a bit at the beginning of your print and for you to double check that the bed is level, but will not help to anchor your print. You will only need one line and you will want the start distance far enough from your print so that it does not interfere. A distance of 3mm works fine.

For roughly 90% of my PLA prints I only use a skirt, since there is no real problems with warping. But if you ever need a part to have enhanced plate adhesion, change this to a skirt.

If you are having difficulty getting your part to stick to the bed, or if you are printing with a high warping material, you will want a Brim, as mentioned in the "Bed Adhesion" chapter. If you choose "Brim", it will add the number of lines you choose touching the perimeter of your print. These lines are as thick as the line width you are using (which I keep as the nozzle diameter). So if you choose 15 lines and are using a 0.4mm nozzle, you will be adding 6mm of brim around your print.

This brim acts as an anchor to prevent warping and help bed adhesion, and is removed post print. I have "Brim Only on Outside" checked for most prints, because it will prevent extra brim from being laid on holes on the inside of your print, and only be printed on the outside to act as an anchor.

Keep in mind that a brim can be difficult to remove cleanly from some materials, one being PLA, which is just another reason I keep my settings to only be a skirt for the majority of PLA prints. A brim on ABS is much easier to remove than PLA.

Finally, your last option for platform adhesion, is to add a raft.

I honestly do not use this option often, but there are specific times I will. Many printers, such as the ones made by Zortrax, will leave an easy to remove raft on all prints. The Zortrax does it because the build plate is perforated and would leave an ugly underside to your print if it didn't. Other printers make this standard because they do not have a heated build plate. I will personally use a raft when I am battling with "Elephant Foot", as described in that chapter.

If you are printing a part that only has a lot of very small posts touching the build plate, you may want to consider adding a raft. Material has a lot easier time sticking to itself when printing than it does sticking to the build plate on its initial layer. By adding a raft with specific settings, you can make sure the bottom layers are nice and thick with plenty of adhesion, and then stick your print to the top of it. You can then easily pop the parts off without having to battle with cleaning off a brim.

These rafts are then removed after printing, but can damage your part if too close, and can leave ugly scarring if your part is too far.

## Special Modes

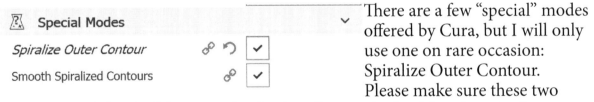

There are a few "special" modes offered by Cura, but I will only use one on rare occasion: Spiralize Outer Contour. Please make sure these two boxes are NOT checked for a standard print. I am only checking them in the example above so you can see the two options involved.

Spiralize the Outer Contour is basically "Vase Mode" for Cura. This will make it so only the outer wall and bottom layers of your part are printed. No inner walls, no infill, no top layers. This option should leave no seams on your print.

You will only want to use this when you are printing a Vase or something that needs similar properties. I have a Christmas tree that I printed large in this mode that looks great, along with a couple of vases given to my mother. I also use this mode when I need to print something transparent in PolySmooth, as covered in my

"Transparent 3D Prints" video. Other than rare use cases like this, it is likely you will want to keep this option unchecked.

# Experimental

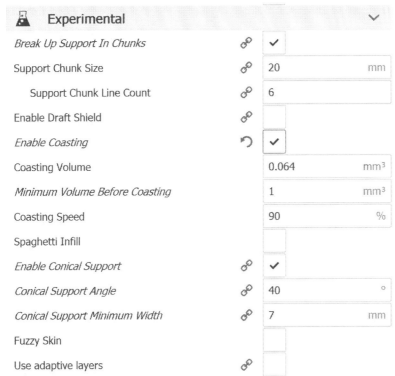

This section is constantly changing and is where "Ironing" once appeared a while back. I attempt to go over some of these on my 3D Print General YouTube channel, but Cura is always getting tweaked. I currently have 3 videos on experimental Cura settings, so refer to those for further information.

I have tried a few of these but have found the most useful to be Coasting, break supports in chunks, and conical support. Coasting is so useful that I expect it to be moved out of the experimental section in upcoming updates. I do not have coasting turned on for direct extruder prints, but always have it on for Bowden machines.

Coasting replaces the last path of an extrusion path with an oozed travel path. The oozed material is used to print the last piece of the extrusion path in order to reduce stringing. If you are experiencing "hairy" or stringy prints regardless of tweaking your retraction settings, you will definitely want to try this out. In fact, I have this turned on for almost every Bowden print that I do. The volume should just be your nozzle diameter cubed, and the minimum volume before coasting will make it so coasting is turned off for small areas. This is important to get to 0.8mm or above to prevent small parts from looking under extruded. If that is happening to you, go ahead and increase this number.

"Break Support in Chunks" does just as you would imagine. It allows there to be less support material that is easier to remove. You want to be careful breaking them into too many chunks, since you will just be printing in a "line" pattern rather than "zig zag".

"Conical Supports" is pretty awesome, as it allows the amount of support material touching your build plate to be less, and then grow at an angle until it is the size required for the underside of your print. If you go too low you can be battling with too small of a surface area touching the build plate, but the settings I have above work great. This can actually end up saving you a lot of material and time on large builds.

A "Draft Shield" builds a wall around your print in order to help trap air and reduce ambient air from getting to your print. This should, in theory, reduce the amount of warping and delamination you experience, I just personally have not noticed much of a difference at all. It may be worth you playing around with.

"Fuzzy Skin" randomly jitters the outer wall so that the surface has a rough and fuzzy look. This is a very rare use-case, but it works great to give something a grippy feel that looks stronger than it is. I have personally used this for handles on cosplay guns.

Adaptive layers is a very intriguing section, but I am unable to make it work right. It makes it so that you have smaller layer heights for high detail sections of your print, and larger layer heights for when detail is not needed. This should, in theory, improve your print quality and reduce your print time. The unfortunate thing it does not factor in is the need for different printing temperatures and speeds for different layer heights. I assume that in the future it will incorporate these things, but I personally do not use it for my prints for this reason.

## Settings on other slicing programs

Other slicing software may have these features in different sections, may call them something different, or they may not have them at all. For years Simplify 3D was the way to go if you wanted full control of your slicer settings, but as of the last couple of years Cura offers just about everything they do – free of cost. There are so many options available that I have well over half of them turned off. You can spend a couple of weeks just doing test prints to figure out what each one does, allowing for full customization.

I am definitely not paid by Cura/Ultimaker and have had zero contact with them other than really enjoying their updates to the slicing software. PrusaSlicer is also a new, free, slicer that is growing in popularity if you want to try something else out.

# Speed Limitations

Often, printer manufacturers will advertise print speeds that are either not really possible, or will result in a subpar quality print. There are limitations when it comes to printing fast, many of which have physical impossibilities.

There is no doubt that printing at larger diameter nozzles with larger layer heights will result in a print that completes in a shorter time than their counterparts, so this chapter will not really be covering this. This is in relation to the speed your extruder carriage is moving.

**NOTE:** Please keep in mind I always suggest erring on the side of printing slower, as you see throughout the rest of this book. I am just going to be going over the limitations involved with printing top speeds.

## Nozzle diameter limitations

This is a little vaguer than the rest of this chapter, but the diameter of your nozzle will limit you on just how fast you can extrude. This is due to bottlenecking between the extruder and the nozzle.

Just as with traffic when driving, attempting to squeeze material through a very tiny hole will have its own limitations in speed. It is difficult for me to give exact top speeds on this, but the smaller the nozzle diameter, the slower you are going to have to print. While I am able to print just fine with a standard V6 hotend on a 0.4mm nozzle at speeds of up to 100mm/s, I have increased difficulties going with a smaller diameter than this.

Pushing 1.75mm filament out of a 0.15mm nozzle diameter is going to have a lot of bottlenecking. With this extremely tiny nozzle diameter, I am forced to go down to just 20mm/s print speed. Any faster than this will have a lot of difficulty overcoming bottlenecking, resulting in a very under extruded print, if it doesn't just result in extruder skips or a nozzle clog.

A larger diameter nozzle will allow for faster extrusion without this bottlenecking occurring, though you will need to read the next two section to understand how that has its own set of physical limitations.

## Hotend limitations

This is a physical limitation that is impossible to avoid. A hotend can only extrude so much volumetric material per second. The material needs time to heat up and become viscous enough to actually come out of the nozzle.

Many hotends have a rating for just what volumetric throughput it can handle. The standard V6 hotend by E3D – likely the most common hotend on the market - has a max throughput of around 15mm3/s. This maximum throughput will change depending on the material you are using, but the maximum it can handle is roughly that volume of plastic per second.

Based off of that max rating, you can do some math to figure out the max speed the hotend can handle depending on the line width and layer height. You can essentially figure out how much volume of material is coming out per mm travelled. But, if this is a bit complicated for you, you can also check out a calculator online by Print Industries (PrintIndustrustries.com/pages/print-speed-calculator).

Based off of this 15mm3/s, the max speed for 0.2mm layer heights on a 0.4mm layer lines would be 240mm/s. This is far higher than you would ever want to go for your 3D prints, but you can at least see the physical limitations involved with a hotend. When bumping these numbers up to 0.8mm layer lines at 0.4mm layer heights, this maximum speed is down to 60mm/s (due to more volume being pushed out the nozzle per mm travelled).

Mind you those numbers are pushing the hotend to the max. I would error on the side of going for roughly 50% the maximum throughput rating for your hotend. This means that with a 0.8mm nozzle at 0.4mm layer heights on a standard V6, you shouldn't go above 30mm/s speed. This is when your hotend will really limit your maximum speeds.

If you plan on only dealing with a 0.4mm nozzle, then your V6 hotend will not really be limiting you on your maximum speeds. It is when you want to work with these larger nozzles that it will become a factor. And that is why the E3D Volcano and SuperVolcano exist.

The Volcano allows for up to 3x the maximum throughput of the V6, and the SuperVolcano allows for up to 11x the maximum throughput of the V6. These are the hotends you want to use if you want to print big parts with large layer heights. This way your hotend will not be the limiting factor on you printing fast.

So, if you ever see a printer manufacturer advertising print speeds of 150mm/s, you need to question the capabilities of the hotend, and with what nozzle diameter and layer heights they are referring to.

Please refer to my video titled "Taking it to the Extreme with the SUPER Volcano" for more information on hotend limitations and testing out these higher rated hotends.

## Extruder limitations

As covered in the "Extruder Stepper Skipping" chapter, your extruder itself is going to be limited to how fast it can spin. If you are using a non-geared extruder, especially one on a Bowden setup, you will never come close to printing at speeds where you actually require a higher rated hotend. When I am using an inexpensive printer with a Bowden non-geared extruder, I am really limited to just about 40mm/s max speeds when printing with a 0.4mm nozzle at 0.2mm layer heights.

Any faster and I will hear that annoying clicking of the extruder motor skipping.

When going with larger layer heights and larger nozzle diameters I am going to be forced to go much slower, due to the extruder motor needing to push out more volume per mm travelled.

Ever since switching to the Bondtech BMG on a direct extruder setup, I have never faced these limitations. I am sure there is a point where the extruder needs to spin too fast, but even when using the SuperVolcano with a 1.4mm nozzle and 1mm layer heights, I was still able to print 55mm/s without any issues, but my extruder gear was spinning extremely fast. You need to know the limitations of your extruder setup.

## Acceleration/Deceleration

If you hear that someone is printing at 300mm/s without an immense amount of modifications, you can almost be guaranteed they are never actually reaching that top speed. This is because the hotend needs time to accelerate to this speed, and then time to decelerate.

This is the main reason just doubling your print speed is not going to cut your print time in half. Your print time is going to have diminishing results the faster you set your print speed, in a pretty logarithmic fashion. This is where your acceleration and jerk settings are going to come into play.

Your jerk settings are for the initial speed your hotend will instantaneously start travelling at from a stop. This would mean if you set your jerk to 20mm/s, your hotend will instantaneously start moving at 20mm/s, and then accelerate from there.

So if you have a jerk of 20mm/s and an acceleration of 1000mm/s2, it will take your hotend 0.1 second to reach a speed of 120mm/s. This may not sound like a lot of time, but you have to factor in that most 3D models require a lot of starting, stopping and changing of directions. And your printer can't just come to a complete stop after travelling 120mm/s, it needs to decelerate, taking roughly another 0.1 second to stop.

When we bump that number up to 300mm/s, we are talking about a time of over 0.25 seconds to reach that speed with the same jerk and acceleration settings. You can imagine how your printer may never actually have a quarter of a second to accelerate and decelerate, meaning you would never actually reach 300mm/s.

You could of course bump up your acceleration and jerk settings, but that is when you are going to come into problems covered in the next two sections.

## Frame of your machine

The frame of your machine is going to really limit you on how high your acceleration and jerk settings can be. While Cartesian printers are the most common machines out on the market, they are also going to be the machines that limit you the most on acceleration and jerk.

And this is because on Cartesian printers your print bed is going back and forth in the Y direction. This heavy, large print bed constantly accelerating and decelerating is going to cause your machine to rattle. While this may not be much with low jerk and acceleration settings, the higher you go, the more extreme this is going to be. When I set my acceleration and jerk settings very high, my entire table was rattling all over the place, to the point things were falling over. You can see just what I mean on my video titled "How Fast Can You 3D Print?".

You can harness your printer to the print table, but your ghosting problems are going to increase due to the lack of vibration dampening.

This is a major reason people prefer CoreXY and Delta machines. Delta machines are far less common, but the one thing they have going for them is the increased acceleration possibilities. Your printer really shouldn't rattle much at all even with very high acceleration and jerk settings.

CoreXY machines have pretty much become the preferred frame for most makers out there, including myself. The fact the build plate is only moving in the Z-direction means you will experience exponentially less rattling. This lower amount of rattling will not only help to print tall skinny parts and not have parts be knocked over mid-print, but it will also help you to achieve higher acceleration and jerk settings without losing quality.

While I keep my acceleration to around 500mm/s2 on my Cartesian machine, I can bump that to over 1000mm/s2 on CoreXY without any loss of quality.

## Print Quality

Just about everything covered above are actual physical limitations involved with hitting high print speeds, but the one thing we haven't covered is print quality.

Assuming you are within the limitations of your hotend and extruder setup, a high print speed will not really decrease your print quality that much. The thing that will be decreasing your print quality the most is high acceleration and jerk settings.

The biggest issue is ghosting, which you can see covered in the "Ghosting" chapter in this book. Ghosting is mostly happening due to high acceleration settings on a frame that is rattling a lot without vibration dampening.

If you don't have a well-built frame, you have an increased chance of experiencing Z-wobble, layer shifts, and parts being knocked over. There are likely to be extra artifacts on your print that are hard to explain or fix due to the difficulty honing in your retraction and other settings.

This is why I always suggest going slower in all settings if you are having difficulty getting a clean print. I am sure you would be willing to wait a couple extra hours to be assured your print will come out with the quality you expect.

# Stepper Motors Overheating or Malfunctioning

This is a fairly broad printing failure but is essentially when one of your motors is not turning properly or is overheating. Many of these issues are covered in the "Layer Shifts" chapter in this book.

## Stepper motors overheating

A stepper motor can be running too hot for multiple reasons. If you have an enclosed printer and are running a long ABS print, not only will the stepper motors be getting hot from standard usage, they will be trapped with ambient air of 35°C – 50°C. Even if a print is being completed without any issues, you do not want to run your motors too hot so that they can remain as free of maintenance as possible.

Industrial grade stepper motors have magnetic cores which begin to degrade when they reach temperatures above 80°C. During warm days or prints on an enclosed machine, the stock stepper motor surface temperature will hover between 70°C and 75°C for long print durations at moderate extrusion speeds.

Unless you are using a pancake stepper, your stepper motor shouldn't overheat, so make sure you check you are within your Vref range. The way to test for this is explained in both the "Extruder Motor Skipping" and "Layer Shifts" chapter, in which calculating your ideal Vref and how to tweak it are explained. Going over your rated Vref can lead to overheating.

Along with reducing the current to the stepper driver as mentioned in next section, you can provide some external ways to cool these motors.

The extruder motor is one of the most common to overheat, so it can only be beneficial to add a passive heat sink. Increasing extrusion rates while maintaining a constant output temperature will require additional torque from the extrusion motor. This additional torque will require more power, which creates thermal dissipation through electro-mechanical inefficiencies – meaning this motor will become hotter the faster it runs.

After the extruder motor, the X and Y steppers are second most likely to overheat, since the Z will only move intermittently. The photo below is a heat sink on the X-axis motor.

You can either screw a heat sink into your motor, get thermal glue, or some use some strong thermal double sided tape to stick it right on there. These will increase the heat dissipation of the individual motor by expanding the area available for convective heat transfer.

I suggest to everyone that they at least put a heat sink on their extruder motor. You can touch your extruder stepper mid print and see just how hot it is getting.

Finally you can connect a fan that will actively blow on that stepper motor. You can wire this fan directly to the power supply on your board so that it turns on when your printer is on, allowing for cooling of any overheating stepper motor. This is not needed on most machines, but if you are running hot, this is a pretty surefire way to help remedy.

You should then also check to see if you are feeding out too much power from your stepper drivers, which can lead to overheated stepper motors.

## Stepper drivers overheating

Along with your stepper itself overheating, the stepper drivers can overheat. Most drivers will come with very small heat sinks that definitely help, and if yours does not, I highly recommend applying them. Though this helps, it is not enough in itself to entirely prevent stepper drivers from overheating.

As mentioned elsewhere in this book, you will always want 1-3 active cooling fans blowing onto your board. This can do wonders when it comes to overheating drivers and other parts on your board. All pre-built machines should have these fans standard, but they can burn out or be damaged over time. If you are building your own machine, you need to include these fans.

Just remember that if you do not have a filter on these fans you will see dust accumulate which can cause the fans to fail over time. Always make sure your printer is off when it is not being used to not collect unnecessary dust, and to clean these fans and your board periodically. Almost every pre-built printer comes with these fans on the board standard, so periodically check to make sure this is spinning well.

If still experiencing overheating, you will want to check that the current going to that driver isn't over the rated limit via the methods described in the "Extruder Motor Skipping" chapter, or in the "Layer Shifts" chapter. These stepper drivers are inexpensive, so if you are continuing to have a driver overheat, it might be smart to try and replace it. Just be careful – an overheated stepper driver will be so hot to the touch it can hurt you.

# Unlevelled X carriage

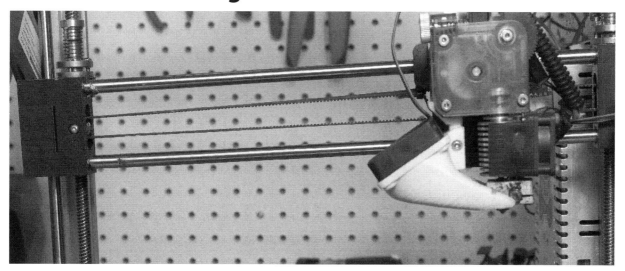

In the "Unlevelled Build Plate" chapter in this book I mention that it is important to level the right and left side of your X carriage in relation to how close it is to the build plate. These can become unlevelled over time, but you will see some massive differences if one Z stepper driver is malfunctioning.

If you notice your printer is looking like the photo above, you likely have a malfunctioning stepper (or stepper driver) for the Z-axis motor(s). It could also mean one of the parts on your frame is broken, so inspect closely.

This, as well as any other stepper malfunctioning, will have to be remedied as follows:

## Plug in a different stepper motor (or plug the current stepper motor into a different driver)

You can test to see if it is your stepper or driver/board that is malfunctioning by swapping the stepper motors. Unplug the stepper in question and take those same wires and plug them into a different stepper you know is working properly (either on your machine or a spare that you have on hand). Attempt to move the stepper again by moving the axis in question and see if it is working properly. If it is, this means you will have to replace the motor that was malfunctioning.

If when you plug in this different stepper that you know is working, and it does not spin when moving the axis in question, you have a problem with either your stepper driver or your board. This is assuming you have confirmed that all wires in question have continuity (as described above).

You can achieve this same outcome by using the motor in question but plugging it into a different driver that you know is working.

Replace a motor if it is the problem, and move on to the next step if it is working fine.

## Check the continuity and wiring of the stepper in question

With the frequent rattling and movement of your machine, wires can easily get caught mid print and become either disconnected or frayed to the point they are not providing continuity. The first thing you will want to do when you see a stepper is malfunctioning is to check the continuity of each wire.

If not visually frayed, you will need to take your multimeter and switch it to the continuity tab. Turn off and unplug your machine. Then unplug the connector for the stepper in question and its connector to the board.

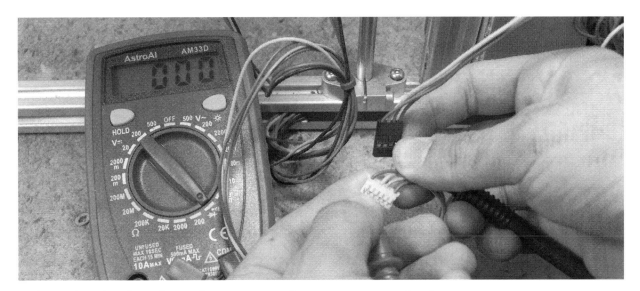

Take either lead and touch it to one of your wires inside the connector to your motor (be sure it is touching metal). Take the other lead and repeat the process for the connector that is going to the board for the same color wire you are testing on the motor side.

If you hear a beep, that means there is no break in that wire – there is continuity from the starting point of the wire to where it connects to the motor.

Continue the same process for each colored wire. If you notice that one of the wires is not beeping, that means there is a break in the wire somewhere. Follow that cord from the motor to the board and see if there is anything you can see with the naked eye (frayed, cut, or burnt out sections of the wire). If it easy to spot, cut that section, re-solder, and confirm that there is continuity.

If there is no physical damage you can spot with your naked eye, you will want to replace that wire entirely. Once you confirm all wires have continuity from the board to your motor, everything should be working properly again. If not, move on to the next step.

## Test your stepper driver by swapping it

Once you have confirmed that your wires all have continuity and that the stepper motor itself is working, you will want to test the stepper driver in question. This is simple and can be done with any spare stepper driver you may have, or by just testing a driver for a different motor you know is working.

Unplug the driver in question and plug your spare/new driver in. If everything works just fine, you know it was the driver that was malfunctioning. Always make sure you are using the proper stepper motor for your machine setup.

You will want to make sure that this new stepper driver doesn't overheat and get burnt out again. If you are using a different brand driver, you may need to figure out the proper Vref (as explained in the "Layer Shifts" chapter). If you have the proper fans blowing, and your new stepper driver over heats as well, you may unfortunately need a new board.

## Final fix - replace your board

Finally – if all wires are showing continuity, the motor is proven to be working fine, the stepper driver is functioning just fine - it's likely that you unfortunately have a malfunctioning board. Ramps boards are very inexpensive but some printers other boards such as a Rambo that may cost close to $150.

Once you have made it this far in your testing, and you made sure you are using all the proper parts, I can almost guarantee the issue remains in the board itself. Boards that require NANO fuses will not work at all if the NANO fuse is blown, so if you are able to heat your extruder and move different axis's, then it is not a NANO fuse problem.

Buy a replacement board, or get a free replacement if under warranty, and embark in the annoying process involved in unplugging and re-plugging everything (with your printer off and unplugged of course). Some machines can be extra frustrating to do this on because of the limited space you have. You unfortunately will not be able to just test the one motor in question until everything is wired and your board is flashed with the appropriate firmware.

I suggest you take a picture of your old board while wired so you can refer to it if you get lost connecting your new board.

Once everything is plugged in, and the correct firmware is flashed, test everything out. If all the proper tests above were taken, everything should now be working fine.

Remember to test all wires and motors before going this final route, since you don't want to spend your time and money only to have the issue occur again with the new board.

## Summary of Fixes and Precautions

- If motor is extremely hot to the touch during a print, add a heat sink. It is smart to add a heat sink to your extruder stepper regardless.
- If motor is still overheating, add an active cooling fan.
- If overheating is an issue that a heat sink or fan cannot overcome, check the Vref of the stepper driver and make sure it isn't over your rated amount.
- Add a heat sink and active cooling fan to an overheating stepper driver.
- Check current on stepper driver if still overheating.
- If motor is malfunctioning regardless of heat, check continuity of all wires from it to the board.

- Replace or fix all wires that do not show any continuity.
- Test a different motor or plug a different driver's cords into the stepper in question to test if the stepper itself is the culprit.
- If stepper itself is not working, replace it.
- If stepper is functioning, check the driver by testing a spare.
- If driver itself is not working, replace it.
- If all above fails, purchase and install a new board.

# Stripped Filament

If you are noticing that your filament is stripping during the print, it may result in a part that look under extruded. This is because the shaved filament will not be fed through the extruder.

Constant filament stripping without any cleaning being done can lead to your extruder slipping, due to the teeth on your hobbed gear/bolt becoming less sharp as filament wedges itself in between the grooves. All of this will cause further under extrusion and failed prints.

## Moisture in your material

The number one reason this problem will consistently occur is due to the material having absorbed too much moisture. When this first happened to me I did all of the steps below, but no matter what I did, the particular spool of PLA would just grind until it could no longer print. This was on a direct drive Titan extruder that I had checked multiple times for any problems.

Well, I eventually put a different spool of PLA on and it printed great. It ends up that the spool of PLA had absorbed too much moisture and could not print properly. You can notice this if you see bubbling when extruding, but another is if the material continually grinds down.

All filaments require you to store them in a low humidity area – either via vacuum sealing with desiccants, or being left with a dehumidifier set to around 25% (or just as low as it will go). You should make note of where you live, since this won't be nearly as much of a problem for those living in the desert, versus myself living in a more humid climate.

When writing the first two editions of my book I lived in Southern California where the humidity never rose very high, which meant I could be more lax with my handling of filament. Now that I live in Texas where the humidity is always higher, I need to vacuum seal every material when it's not in use.

If your filament keeps getting grinded until it looks like the photo above, you will either need to replace the spool, or get it dried out.

You can purge out the excess moisture a couple of ways – the best doing a minor vacuum purge after heating to a bit under the materials glass transition temperature. You can use your printer bed to place the vacuum on stop of as a means of heating everything.

Most of us do not have a vacuum, so here are the steps for what you can do with the tools you have at home.

First – check the glass transition temperature of the particular material you are using. PLA is right around 60 degrees Celsius, so you don't want to get it hotter than that. Turn your print bed to this 60 degrees (or slightly lower), and then place the spool of filament on the print bed. Cover it with a cardboard box (you can use the one it was shipped in). Make sure to throw in a couple of desiccants that have not been used. Leave it there for roughly 1 hour. The heat will help to evaporate the moisture from the spool, the desiccants will help absorb, and the cardboard box will help trap the heat while doing a minor amount of absorbing as well.

It took me 3 rounds (3 hours) of this and it fixed my moisture filled spool of PLA perfectly. I was able to print as if the spool was brand new without any grinding filament.

This may not always work, so you want to make sure to use the proper precautions to avoid ever having to do this. Nylons are much more likely to absorb moisture, and thus would be a bit more difficult to complete this process.

In fact, most materials just have a shelf life. Nylon material may only be good for a month or two even if you take the proper precautions. Even a year old PLA will just not be as good as it was when it was first delivered to you. Keep this in mind before you tear your hair out trying to fix a spool that you've owned and has been open for a year.

## Clean your extruder

As I mention in the "Good Practices" chapter early in this book, keeping your parts clean is important to have consistent prints without failure. This definitely includes your extruder.

If you are experiencing stripped filament, or would like to prevent it as best you can, grab a small wire brush and pick and clean out the teeth on your hobbed bolt/gear.

If these grooves are not defined, they will not grip properly to your filament. This can lead to filament slipping and stripping.

## Check idler tension

As mentioned for other issues in this book, you will want to make sure you have the proper tension on your extruder idler. Too tight of an idler can cause the extruder motor to skip if under powered, and to even cause filament grinding to the point of snapping when it is geared.

While grinded filament can occur from too tight of an idler, it can actually also occur from an idler that is too loose. This is because no consistent grip is attained by your hobbed bolt/gear, and certain rotations will just rub against the filament, rather than pushing it through your hotend.

It is important to get this tension right since it can cause various issues in the quality and consistency of your prints.

## Increase hotend temperature

I always recommend this with caution because if you go too hot, materials will easily get clogged in the barrel, causing you the need to read the "Nozzle Clogs" chapter in this book. But as mentioned in that chapter, running the hotend too cold for the speed you are feeding can lead to under extrusion.

In fact, it is smart to read the "Nozzle Clogs" section now if you haven't already. That is because a nozzle clog will certainly lead to stripped filament, meaning if you fix the nozzle clog, you may fix the stripped filament problem.

Your extruder stepper may be turning the proper amount of steps, but bottlenecking in the nozzle will cause your hobbed bolt/gear to just rub against the filament when the pressure is too high.

If you are under the high end of the temperature range for your material, you can attempt printing the same G-code at a slightly higher nozzle temperature in order to help the viscosity of the material.

Don't go over the materials temperature range, since running PLA at 230°C can give you further problems with clogging in the barrel and oxidizing material.

## Lower the speed/acceleration

Just like with the solution described above, lowering the speed and acceleration can reduce the amount of bottlenecking caused in the hotend/nozzle.

You can imagine that if you were to speed your extruder up 10 fold you will clearly grind your filament, since it cannot be fed through your nozzle at that speed since it cannot properly heat the filament (which is one of the benefits of a hotend like the E3D Volcano or Super Volcano).

You do want to make sure you have a properly cooled barrel and that you understand what material you are using in order to reduce the threat of heat creep. Certain materials have a very small range of temperature and speed they can properly be extruded at without a clog being formed.

If you would like a tutorial on how to reduce the acceleration on your machine, please refer to the "Extruder Stepper Skipping" or "Settings Issues" chapter in this book

## Printing fast on large diameter nozzles

You will need to slow down prints when attempting to print large layer lines on a large diameter nozzle with a standard setup. This is because the material needs a certain amount of time to heat and reach its proper viscosity to extrude. Since you are pushing so much material through the nozzle, it needs to be slowed down to prevent filament grinding.

If you will be printing on large diameter nozzles (Larger than 0.6mm) frequently, it is smart to upgrade to a hotend setup that is specifically designed to allow for high volume extrusion. E3D has their Volcano setup which is meant for just this purpose – printing fast with large diameter nozzles and layer heights. You will clearly need a geared extruder to even achieve these speeds, which is why they also sell their Titan extruder. You can use the Bondtech BMG in conjunction with a Super Volcano hotend for the fastest printing possible.

## Replace hobbed bolt/gear

Please keep in mind that cheaply made hobbed gear and bolts may not have the proper spacing, sharpness, and depth required to grab onto the filament. These components also wear over time, particularly if you are running carbon or glass filled materials. If you are experiencing constant filament grinding regardless of the steps you took above or the material you are using, you should purchase a new extruder hobbed bolt/gear from a reputable manufacturer. Choose stainless steel options over aluminum for this part, if available.

I currently use the Bondtech BMG extruder which actually has two gears grabbing onto the filament, rather than just one pushing against a bearing. This dual drive extruder has made it so that I haven't had any grinding or extrusion issues at all since purchasing it over a year ago. I cannot recommend this extruder enough, though it does currently come with a hefty price tag ($100 at MatterHackers.com).

## Summary of Fixes and Precautions

- Confirm the material you are using hasn't absorbed too much moisture. This is the most common reason for this.
- Replace filament, or dry out your material if it has absorbed moisture.
- Clean your extruder by making sure there is no filament stuck in the teeth of your extruder's hobbed bolt/gear on your extruder.
- Check to make sure you have the proper tension on your extruder idler.
- If you are below the maximum suggested printing temperature for your filament, try increasing it slightly.
- Reduce the speed and acceleration on your print. Make sure your barrel is properly cooled.
- Replace poorly made or worn-out extruder hobbed bolts and gears.

# Unlevelled Build Plate

An unlevelled build plate will mean that the nozzle is too close in some areas and too far away in others. If the bed is extremely unlevelled, there may be structural issues with the way the build plate is mounted to the frame, however, in most cases it is minor (less than an mm height difference from one corner to another). In these situations you just need fine tune adjustments to the spring loaded corner mounts of the build platform.

Many new FDM 3D printers come with an auto bed leveling system that actually works, and there are some third party bed levelling sensors that are useful, unlike attempts in the past. I go over these a bit further in the "Upgrades and Purchasing a New Printer" chapter, as well as a later section in this chapter.

The majority of my machines now have these auto bed levelers, since I find them worth the price when it comes to this annoying issue.

You can easily diagnose this problem by either running a bed calibration G-code, or by paying close attention to the first layer of your print. By getting used to what a print should look like on its first layer, you will easily be able to which corners are too close, and which are too far.

(Remember that you can email me at Sean@3DPrintGeneral.com with proof of purchase for high def photos and color PDF files)

The photo above is easy to diagnose this – the front left corner has the nozzle too far from the build plate and the top right corner is way too close. Somewhere in the middle the nozzle is the proper distance.

An unlevelled build plate, along with Z-height calibration, are the two most common failures when starting a new print. Most printers either have bed clips or some form of mechanical leveling system. These screws become loose over time, and even one long print can cause your bed to become unlevelled for the next run.

If you continue to only tighten corners without adjusting your entire bed, it can result in a warped metal build plate, and eventually constant layer shifts - as mentioned in that chapter in this book.

## Levelling left and right side before touching corner bed clips

Before you even bother adjusting the corner bed clips, you will want to level the left and right part of your X-carriage. Variations over time, moving your printer, as well as times that you home the Z axis too close to the bed, can all cause your two Z- rods to become unleveled from each other in relation to the X carriage.

Mind you that this issue should only be relevant to Cartesian machines. CoreXY and Delta should not have to worry about this.

If this is just a maintenance problem, and not an issue with your stepper motor (as mentioned in the "Steppers Motors Overheating or Malfunctioning" chapter), you can level this while your steppers are disengaged. Hold onto the left coupler that attaches the left threaded Z rod to its respective stepper motor. While holding onto the left coupler, twist the right threaded Z rod's coupler in the correct direction to level your X carriage. This is obviously only true when using dual Z leadscrews/ threaded rods.

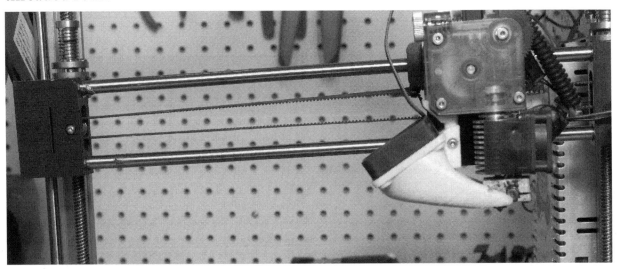

You can measure the distance from the bed to the X carriage rod on the right and left side of the build plate, and continue the above process until they are even. If you attempt to just tighten bed corers while your actual frame is off, it will result in further issues.

## Loosen/tighten corner bed clips

If you have confirmed that the left and right side of your X carriage are level to each other in relation to the build plate, and you are still experiencing an uneven first layer, you will want to play around with the corner bed knobs of your printer.

I always suggest that you loosen before you start tightening these corners. That means you should try to loosen the corners that are further from the nozzle rather than tighten those that are too close. So if one corner is too close to the nozzle, I would suggest raising the z-height slightly and loosening the remaining 3 corners until level. This is because you do not want to be in the situation where you cannot tighten a corner any further. This leads to a warped metal plate overtime and will cause layer shifts in the Y-direction since it becomes rough to move. This is not nearly as much of a problem on CoreXY machines since the build plate only moves down in the Z-direction.

This is not always possible though, because you can imagine the above situation where 1-3 corners are too close to the nozzle and the remaining corner(s) are as loose as they can go. You can always use a longer screw and larger spring on those corners, but if that is not feasible, you will want to tighten those corners that are too close to the nozzle.

On newly built, or strong framed machines, this can be as simple as doing a slight tweak while a new print begins. Printers that have a lot of build time racked up can lead you to having a massive headache going forward with the above method. If you are unable to level the build plate easily with the above two methods, I sincerely suggest entirely starting over. If you just over tighten, the build plate will move with a lot of resistance, which is not good for your printer and parts.

This means that you should take your build plate apart, make sure everything is assembled properly, and put it back together. Make sure that all corners have the same length screws and same exact springs and are all equally tight. Then confirm once again that the left and right side of your X carriage are level. Find the proper Z-height and then run a bed leveling G-code that you can easily find online if not provided by your printer (just search on Thingiverse for a bed level test). Starting from scratch like this can often make this issue go away.

If you still cannot level your build plate after all of this, you likely have an issue with the frame of your printer. Take the metal bed plate entirely off and lay it on a flat surface. You can then push on each corner to see if it has warped. If this is the case, you will need to order a new metal plate from your printer manufacturer.

If the plate is flat, confirm that your frame is built properly. This means that if you are using t-slotted aluminum rods, confirm that everything matches up in a 90° angle and that it lays flat on the tabletop you are using. Some printers have little feet that make sure your printer lays flat but they break off easily.

Confirm that all printed parts on your frame are not warped. Check to see that all bearings are popped into their holders and that everything is equal distance from each other. It would be smart to go over the "Mandatory Maintenance" chapter to make sure everything is working as it should.

If you are using an acrylic framed printer this problem will become more prevalent over time. All metal framed printers experience less warping and bending over time.

One or multiple corners of your build plate may not be laying perfectly flat because of the issues above.

## Larger layer heights/nozzle diameter can make this process easier

If you are using a 0.25mm or smaller nozzle with 0.1mm layer heights or lower, you will notice extremely slight variations in how level your build plate is. As mentioned in the "Z-Height Calibration" chapter, the lower the layer height and nozzle diameter, the more difficult it is to get your first layer to stick to the build plate.

On any print like this I would suggest increasing the initial layer height on your slicing program. Increase the first layer to be 0.2mm and you will have a much easier time leveling the build plate. The same is true if you are using a very small nozzle.

0.4mm nozzles can get most jobs done and will allow you to get that bed adhesion that is so hard to come by on 0.15mm – 0.3mm nozzles. On a 0.4mm nozzle I have 0.25mm or 0.3mm layer heights for the first layer, which can save you an immense amount of headaches.

A build plate on a printer using a 0.6mm nozzle with a 0.3mm initial layer height will be relatively extremely easy to level when compared to a 0.15mm nozzle with 0.05mm layer heights. On these small nozzles, always max out the initial layer height by multiplying the nozzle diameter by 0.75. You will still be limited to only 0.11mm for a 0.15mm nozzle, but it will at least be easier than going lower than that.

Please refer to the "Settings Issues" chapter for a further explanation.

## Do not frequently move your printer

FDM 3D printers are not meant to be travel ready and should stay in one spot as much as possible. Every time you move your printer, especially when traveling in a car, minor adjustments can occur that will require you to recalibrate.

The most common issue with moving your printer is having to readjust an unlevelled build plate. When we would take printers to fairs and events in the past, we would ALWAYS have to re-level the bed when setting up. Take care not to bump into, move, or vibrate a printer, even when it is not in use.

## Purchase an auto bed leveler

You can purchase a part that will allow you to auto bed level your machine. You will still need to get the proper Z-height, but your printer makes minor movements in the Z-motors to make sure the bed is level.

I personally upgraded my CR-10 to use TH3D's EZABL which will take a reading of the bed before printing to make sure that first layer is perfectly level. This part takes 9 points on the bed in order to get a mesh, though you can change this number to be more or less precise. After honing in the Z-off set, it then uses the Z-motor (or motors) to vary the height of the print as the nozzle moves. This means if one corner is too far from the nozzle when compared to another, the z-motors will tweak to make sure the nozzle is closer in that section.

This minor motor movement can be seen when looking closely at the first layer. I am extremely happy after upgrading to this since I no longer have to deal with this particular failure on this machine. I still have to make sure the Z-height is correct, but no more messing with individual corner knobs. And I promise you – an unlevelled build plate caused me far more frustrations in the past than I would like to admit.

## Summary of Fixes and Precautions

- Confirm the left and right side of your build plate are equally level to the X-carriage. This is only needed on Cartesian machines.

- If they are not, while stepper motors are disengaged, hold onto the left threaded Z-rod's coupler and twist the right threaded Z-rod's coupler until level.

- Loosen the bed corner knobs that are too far from the nozzle relative to the remaining corners. Tighten only when needed.

- Start from scratch by dissembling build plate and making sure all corners are equally tightened, using same sized screws and springs with equal amount of tension.

- If still experiencing issues, confirm that your metal build plate is not warped, the printed parts on your machine are not warped, and that the frame is put together properly.

- If any part is warped or off tolerance, you will need to purchase or print replacements.

- Increase your initial layer height, or even increase the diameter of your nozzle if you don't want to deal with this issue as frequently. A large initial layer height makes leveling the bed much simpler.

- Take care not bump into, move, or vibrate a printer - even when it is not in use.

- Upgrade to an auto bed leveler to prevent this problem from happening.

# Warping

The warping of parts is just about inevitable if you don't understand the material or machine you are using. Warping is when corners, or entire parts of the print curl upward due to uneven cooling of your part, or due to improper bed adhesion.

Both the first and second edition of this book were written before my collaboration with Nicolas of Polymaker and his "Material Science" chapter contribution, and because of this, I never fully understood why warping was occurring. Ever since working with them, it has helped my understanding immensely. I can't suggest enough that everyone checks that chapter out so that you know why warping is occurring – since it may help you to diagnose and fix the problem without reading on.

## Understand the "Bed Adhesion" chapter, "Z- Height Calibration" chapter, and the "Unlevelled Build Plate" chapter

You need to entirely understand all three of these chapters in order to even start to try and fix your warping problems. A print will have an exponentially higher chance of warping when either part of the print, or the entirety of the print, is too far from the build plate.

This is fairly easy to understand because the further the nozzle, the less bed adhesion that is involved, the higher chance it will curl up later in the print.

You will need a brim on any material that has a high shrinkage rate and high internal stress rate such as ABS. For large non-circular ABS prints, you will need an ABS slurry if you cannot maintain an ambient air temperature of around 45°C – all things covered in those three chapters.

## Understand the material you are using, and possibly use an alternative

Much of this is covered in the "Material and their Settings" chapter, so please review this as well when understanding your material needs.

You will almost never experience issues with warping when using a material such as PLA, because PLA has a low shrinkage rate and low internal stress of the material (though, to understand this better, refer to the "Material Science" chapter). Very large, highly dense PLA parts should use a heated build plate and a brim, but it is very uncommon to get warping with PLA on a level build plate.

ABS is an entirely different matter, being an amorphous thermal plastic with a lot of internal stress when extruding. Since ABS also requires a higher temperature for its build plate due to its higher glass transition temperature, the differential between the bed and the ambient air is also increased.

While ABS is great for its price and functionality, this factor may make it impossible for you to achieve certain parts on your machine without warping. This is why it is important to understand the factors and features you are looking for on your print and if you can use an alternative material.

If you require mechanical functionality and affordability, but do not care about acetone vapor finishing or a high glass transition temperature, you should definitely try out PETG. PETG is a great material for the vast majority of mechanical applications you were attempting to get out ABS, and has a very low relative warping chance. It also has a competitive price tag.

PETG has some serious adhesion when a bed is set to 70°C, and I have yet to experience major warping on a level build plate when using this material, though it is definitely possible.

If you require a high glass transition temperature from your material, I haven't personally found a great alternative to ABS. One of your best options would be Carbon Fiber Reinforced ABS by 3DX Tech. This material has a great glass transition temperature of 90°C and warps far less than standard ABS, while maintaining its ability to be acetone vapor finished. The biggest drawbacks to this material is the price compared to ABS, increased degradation of your nozzle, lower layer adhesion, and a lower bend to break ratio. The problem with most materials that have a high glass transition temperature is their likelihood to warp.

Certain nylon materials that do not have a high glass transition temperature will still have a high probability of warping. This is because they are semi-crystalline that take up less space when they are aligned (room temperature) than when they are chaotic (extruded). It is essentially crystalizing on your printer bed, and causing warping. More information on this can also be found in the "Material Science" chapter. For these nylon materials you will need to use a coat of PVA on a glass build plate, as described in the "Bed Adhesion" chapter. Polymaker has helped with this nature of Nylon with their PolyMide CoPA, which is advertised as "Warp Free". It still has the potential to warp, but compared other nylons, its far better.

I have attempted to print Polypropylene and Acetal (Delrin) in the past, to essentially no avail. Along with requiring a high temp hotend, Polypropylene warped on just about every print larger than a cubic inch, and Acetal was impossible to get any print started without using a sheet of cardboard on top of the build plate. They just do not want to stick to standard build platforms. Polymaker is currently working on a warp-free version of Polypropylene, so if you absolutely need that material for your 3D print, I would suggest checking to see if that is available.

Polycarbonate ABS has an amazing glass transition temperature of around 120°C but will require an enclosed environment on any print larger than a cubic inch. This material's warping probability is just too difficult to overcome on most machines.

Using an ABS slurry, as described in the "Bed Adhesion" chapter, can help with particular ABS blends to truly stick to the build plate.

## Print slower and increase printing temperature

This may not work for all materials, but for ABS you can help to reduce your warping issues by extruding slower and at a higher temperature. As Nicolas of Polymaker covers in his chapter, printing slower gives the material more time to release its stress. This means that a lower extrusion speed will reduce your warping problems.

The same is true with the extrusion temperature. Increasing the extrusion temperature means more motion within the material. More motion + time to release stress = less warping. Printing ABS as slow as possible on your machine, along with printing temperatures up to around 250°C, can help to reduce these internal stresses, and thus, reduce warping.

## Printing in an enclosed environment

When you are printing a part on a heated build plate you are automatically working in an environment with uneven ambient temperatures. When the room is around 30°C and your heated build plate is 110°C, there is a quick change in temperature for parts close to the build plate, yet exposed to the surrounding air. While internal stresses may be the biggest reason for your warping, this extreme temperature difference will also cause warping problems.

Printing in an enclosed machine allows for the ambient air to remain a bit hotter, due to the trapping of the heat given off by the build plate. This means you are closer to the glass transition temperature of ABS, allowing for more motion in the material and are giving it more time to release stress.

You can purchase a printer that is enclosed, or somewhat enclosed, which works pretty great if you can afford them. You can also build a DIY enclosure with laser cut acrylic and a few printed parts. Or you can find some other build that someone has posted instructions for online.

When printing a part with a high likelihood of warping in an enclosed machine, you will want to let the bed sit at its printing temperature for around 5-10 minutes to allow the ambient air to heat up. A good ambient temperature for ABS would be

45°C, and ideal up to 60°C. You obviously would not want to print PLA in that type of environment though, since that is right around its glass transition temperature.

Many issues arise when you allow ambient air to rise this high. Stepper motors and other electronics will overheat and cause your printer to malfunction. This is why you will need to have your power supply and board outside the enclosed chamber, have enough heat sinks spread throughout, and keep an active fan on anything that is heating too hot. E3D actually has a water cooled option now, but it is not very common. Read up on the "Stepper Motors Overheating or Malfunction" chapter as well.

Even then you may still experience issues, so be sure to understand some basic thermal dynamics and mechanical engineering before getting your ambient air to 50°C or higher.

To be honest – this isn't quite as important as it may have been. Due to there being so many material varieties, and from your now understanding of material sciences, you can likely avoid most warping problems even on an open printer.

## Delamination of layers

You may not consider this failure as "warping", but it has nearly all of the same reasons for happening. This is why it is not included in the "Poor Layer Adhesion" chapter.

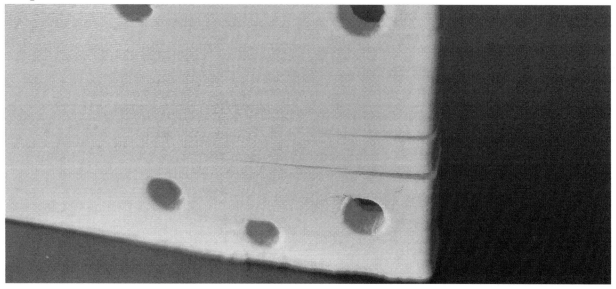

If you have incredible bed adhesion, such as when you use an ABS slurry, but are printing a large part in an open environment, you can experience delamination instead of warping.

Delamination is when two layer will separate from one another, even when taking in all the layer adhesion precautions. This is because of the same temperature gradients and internal stresses explained earlier, but occurs when bottom layers are stuck extremely well to the build plate.

The bottom of your print may not curl upward taking the entire print with it, but rather layer adhesion becomes the breaking point for this shrinkage/internal stresses.

If this is happening to you, you will need to check your settings or drastically change your environment/material being used.

I have only experienced delamination on very large PLA prints when the ambient air is quite cold, while it can be unavoidable on tall ABS prints not in an enclosed environment.

Your settings can be tweaked to help prevent this. The denser your part is on the inside, the more likely this will happen, so try printing your part with less infill and a couple more shell walls. Print slower and hotter to also help slow down the material releasing stresses and have more motion.

Finally, confirm that your E-steps are on (as explained in the "Over and Under Extrusion" chapter). If you are under extruding by a decent amount, you could potentially experience more frequent occurrences of delamination.

## Make sure the build plate is not losing heat mid print

If your board is overheating or you having issues with connectivity to your heated build plate, the temperature may drop mid print. If you only watch the beginning of your print and come back when it is finished, you may not even notice this is happening other than returning to a warped part.

Make sure your bed is maintaining its heat throughout the entire print, and if it is not, refer to the "Build Plate Not Heating" chapter

## Summary of Fixes and Precautions

- Read the "Material Sciences" chapter in this book before reading this chapter. It will help you to understand why warping is actually occurring.

- Make sure your bed is level and that your Z-height is correct when starting your print.

- Use your preferred method of bed adhesion. Some large ABS prints on a non-enclosed printer will require an ABS Slurry.

- Print slow and hot to give the material more time to release stress and increase the motion within the material.

- Print with a brim.

- Know the proper print settings for the material you are using.

- Attempt using a material with a lower shrinkage rate and internal stresses with similar applications (PETG, CFR-ABS, PolyMide CoPA, etc.).

- Use an enclosed 3D printer, or build an enclosure for your machine, but understand the possibility of parts overheating.

- Delamination occurs on taller parts that have good bed adhesion. You will need to reduce the density of your part, print an enclosed environment, or use a different material in order to fix this problem.

- Make sure the build plate is maintaining its temperature throughout the print.

# Z- Axis Wobble

When you are experiencing Z-axis wobble, you will see what looks like repeated minor layer shifts, sometimes with every single layer. If the wobble is minor, it may just look like the print surface is not clean. You can hone in all of the slicer settings properly, but it will not fix this issue. This is an issue with the frame of your printer and not an issue with settings.

## Tighten extruder carriage and hotend setup

This is probably the most common cause for a wobbly looking print. Your extruder carriage is moving and rattling constantly over prints and screws loosen over time. This is especially common on 3D printed parts, since their tolerances are not as tight as mass produced carriages and extruders. This will be far less of an issue if using an E3D Titan extruder with an E3D hotend on a $3,000+ machine than on a $200 stock Prusa i3 with printed parts.

This is because more expensive machines usually have higher end parts holding everything together. Lower end machines will use printed parts with minor tolerance issues, and may even use zip ties to hold belts and bearings in place. These zip ties can become stretched over time and results in a carriage that is not harnessed tight.

Frequently check to see if you can easily move or rattle your hotend/extruder setup. Lower the print temperature to room temperature and literally grab the hotend and try and move it around. Don't be rough, just give it a little rattle. If you see the carriage or hotend rattle or have free play, you will need to fix that in order to get rid of this problem. The machines that I have used that have this setup be extremely stiff result in the least amount of Z-wobble.

If you can, you will likely need to tighten the screws/bolts that hold the extruder or hotend to the carriage. If tightening doesn't fix the problem, check to see if your printed parts are worn out or off tolerance. If they are, you will need to reprint them. If not, you can move on to the next solution

## Replace old/worn out bearings and make sure they are harnessed tight

If your carriage is rattling when you manually try to move it, but your entire extruder carriage and hotend are tightly set up, your bearings may have become loose over time. This is far more common with plastic bearings than with metal ones, as you can imagine.

This is for linear rods, not for linear rails. Linear rails do not use bearings to hold onto and slide the carriages, they use rollers. They normally result in a stiffer frame, which is why many people prefer linear rails on their machines.

When doing the step above – rattling the hotend when at room temperature on a machine with linear rods– you should be able to see if there is a small gap in the bearing.

I didn't think this could happen until I replaced a 2 year old printer's bearings who was experiencing consistent Z-axis wobble, and it fixed the issue instantaneously. These were on Lulzbot TAZ 5 machines that used plastic bearings. The replacement bearings had no free play and gripped the linear rods tight.

If you are using a less expensive machine that uses zip ties or something similar to hold the bearings in place, you will need to replace these with new zip ties, or find a part online to print that will hold the bearings tight. I have come to prefer linear rails as of late just to reduce this ever becoming an issue.

## Ensure your hotend and nozzle is set up properly and tight

This process is explored in the "Built up Material in Nozzle" chapter, but can also show symptoms in a Z-axis wobble. Every hotend setup needs to be assembled in a slightly different fashion, but nearly all of them require you to not over tighten. This can lead to you leaving them too loose.

When the hotend heats, the metal expands and can cause your once tight nozzle/heater block to actually have minor gaps. This can lead to rattling of the heater block throughout the print, causing an ugly wobble in your print.

If you notice that your heater block is loose when hot, or that you constantly have to brush off the nozzle from excess material, you will likely need to tighten these parts.

I always suggest doing the final tightening of your nozzle and heater block when heated to 240°C, using proper gloves and tools. Remember that you have a high chance of burning yourself, so only do this with extreme caution. If you tighten the hotend/nozzle when at room temperature, you will find it won't be tight at 240°C.

You still want to make sure to not over tighten anything. I have broken quite a few heater blocks, nozzles, and heat break barrels due to over tightening. These parts, especially when hot, can easily snap under pressure. This hasn't happened to me in a while, but would occur when I didn't understand how careful I should be. When you are doing this, make sure to only tighten until you know that the nozzle and heat block are not loose and will not unscrew during the print – don't muscle it. Just make sure you do this when hot.

If you still are experiencing your hotend is rattling and you have made sure it's harness is tight, you will likely need to upgrade or replace your nozzle, heat block, or entire hotend. Poorly made parts will not have tight tolerances and can lead to these gaps in your threads. You can try to save money if you want, but I only purchase from reputable manufacturers for this reason. All of my hotends are from E3D, since they are one of the most respected companies in the 3D printing field.

## Make sure the build plate is harnessed tight

Just as with the extruder carriage and bearings, you will need to make sure your print bed does not have any rattling in it. This will NOT be an issue with CoreXY machines, since the bed only moves up and down.

When using a Cartesian machine, free-play or rattling in the build plate will result in Z-wobble, just as it would with rattling in the hotend. When not printing, and with the bed at room temperature, give it a good rattle up and down and left and right. The print bed should not have any movement other than what comes from the whole machine moving. If the print bed has some free play in the bearings or harness, this will need to be fixed.

On one of my inexpensive DIY machines, the build plate harnesses are attached to the bearings via zip-ties. These zip ties seem to stretch over about a month or two of printing, and so I will cut them off and replace them as needed.

Just as with the carriage, you will need to replace any plastic bearings that have become worn out over time (unless using a linear rail system).

Finally, make sure that the parts that are connecting the bearings to the build plate are securely tightened and up to tolerance. Take your glass or other print surface off, and then tighten all of the screws that are connecting everything. These, as with all other screws, will loosen over time.

## Tighten all belts

Other than confirming all harnesses are tight and that there is zero rattling on the extruder and build plate, the next most common reason for Z-wobble is a loose belt.

As explained elsewhere in this book, it is possible to over tighten a belt, but it is pretty difficult to do so on low end machines where the belt is just held together via zip ties. Both the X and Y axis belts should be very springy to the touch with zero-droop.

If there is any droop in your belt, you will need to tighten. For low end, non-upgraded machines, cut the zip tie that is holding the belt together, grab some pliers, and pull tight as you put on a new zip tie. Make sure the belt is tighter than it was and that the zip tie is pinching everything so that the belt won't slip.

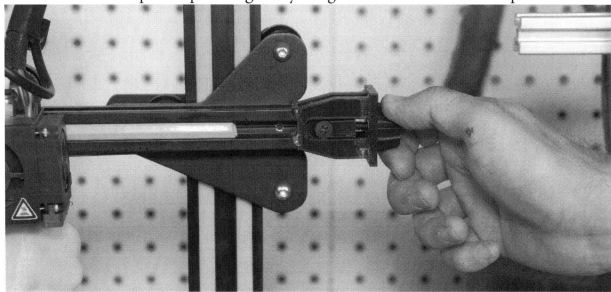

Even better than doing this would be to print a manual way to tighten your belts. There is likely a file on Thingiverse for your specific machine setup, you would just need to search. I have added such a way to tighten the X-axis belt on my CR-10 by a model designed by donnyb99 on that site. I disassembled the X-axis belt and where the bearing is connected, and then added this printed part. I can now easily tighten the X-axis belt via a simple turn on the knob.

Be careful when adding one of these, since you will now be able to over tighten, which I had mentioned is difficult to do without this. Just turn the knob until the belt is very springy to the touch. There is no real scientific way to do this, you just want to make sure there is zero droop whatsoever.

## Check for wobbly or bent rods

Using thin threaded M5 or M6 Z-rods instead of thicker M8 or M10 leadscrews will lead to a wobbly or bent rod over time. It is a major upgrade when you have a thick M10 leadscrew that is connected on the top and bottom of the frame of your printer, since you will experience far less z-wobble on a machine that will last over a longer period of time.

If you have these thinner threaded rods, just move your printer up and down in the Z-axis. You will actually be able to see this problem easily since the rods will wobble back and forth. This is exactly what happened on my DIY machine and I fixed it by upgrading to M8 leadscrews (just make sure you print all the parts you need before disassembling and upgrading). To get a full tutorial on this, please see my YouTube video titled "Upgrading your 3D Printer to 8mm Leadscrews". Almost all high end machines will use these thicker leadscrews.

There are some models on Thingiverse and elsewhere that help with this wobble in your threaded Z-axis rods, such as the "anti-wobble coupling" by toolson, and they actually work quite well. While this is true, they won't be able to fix an actual bent rod and nothing will be quite as good as actually upgrading to thicker leadscrews.

This is not common at all unless you frequently transport your machine. An actual bend in your threaded Z-axis rod will require you to replace it. I have only had to do this on one machine, one time in my history of printing, and it was on a thin threaded Z-rod.

While I have only had one fully bent rod, I have had plenty of ones that will wobble when moving up and down, and this is anything but ideal, leading to minor Z-wobble.

## Add an anti-backlash spring loaded nut

These are normally only meant for thicker leadscrews, and they help quite a lot to prevent any backlash when moving up and down in the z-axis.

This is slightly confusing as to explain, but with these springs and added nuts, you can expect a lot less rattling and prints looking as if they have Z-wobble. Please take note of the pitch of your leadscrew since you will need to make sure your anti-backlash parts are the same. The majority of 8mm leadscrews have a pitch of 2, but you will just need to confirm with your printer specs (or with the part you buy online when upgrading).

Also make sure you are able to actually use these on the printer you are adding them too. I bought a set that were too thick to add to the CR-10, and their holes did not line up, having me return the set. You also want to make sure you are able to get full use out of the Z-height on your machine. As you can tell from the photo of my anti-backlash nuts above, I am losing about 20mm of height on this machine since the Z-axis motors are on the top. I have added extenders to make up for this, but keep in mind where you add these and if you are reducing your max Z-height for prints.

These aren't needed for most machines, but they definitely help.

## Lubricate guide rods and threaded rods

Your X and Y axis guide rods should be smooth enough so that both carriages can move around freely (when using a linear rod printer). Your Z-axis guide rods (the ones that are not threaded) should also be smooth enough for the carriage to move in the Z-direction without any skipping or any bearings getting stuck.

Most printers use self-lubricating bearings, but even these will require lubrication after frequent printing. If your bearings are getting stuck or having trouble moving during the print, you can experience some Z-axis wobble.

Get some white lithium grease apply with a rag to these non-threaded guide rods. Move the carriage around on all axis's so that it spreads across your bearings. This should help with the issue.

Just another reason for linear rails, since it just has rollers resting on the rails that do not need to be lubricated.

Along with the smooth rods, you should also add a bit of lubrication to the threaded rods/leadscrews. Just grab some lithium grease on a paper towel and rub it up and down. You want to make sure these aren't entirely dry to the touch.

## Make sure the bed can move back and forth

# smoothly

As mentioned in the "Unlevelled Build Plate" and "Layer Shifts" chapters, if you over tighten one or multiple corners, you will have a lot of difficulty moving the bed back and forth (of course only on Cartesian machines). This difficulty to move may lead to stepper motor skips which cause layer shifts, but can also cause some Z-wobble. You will want to make sure your bed can move back and forth easily without a ton of friction. Follow the steps in those two chapters to help remove this problem.

## Is your part too tall and skinny?

This problem will not occur quite as often on a CoreXY machine, but on Cartesian 3D printers where the build plate is being moved back and forth, a tall skinny print may end up wobbling. You can use as much brim as you like with the perfect bed adhesion, if you are printing a tall and skinny part, it will likely wobble as the bed is moved back and forth.

This wobble will make the top of your print have this Z-wobble, while the bottom of your print looks just fine.

To be honest – there is no perfect way around this. You can manually design some anchors onto your print so that as it gets taller, it is held further in place, but just printing a very tall skinny part as is will likely result in this Z-wobble.

If I am unable to design in some further anchors, I am often forced to cut extremely thin display parts in two, to be glued together post printing.

Below is a summary of how to add a very simple anchor to your part via Cura.

## Anchoring Parts:

I am positive there are better ways to do this, but the easiest way would be to anchor your print that I know of is in Cura. I have rarely done this, but it definitely helps with a tall, skinny print wobbling back and forth. This is also explained in the "Parts Being Knocked Over" chapter.

Below is an example of two skinny swords from a Deadpool print that I made for my YouTube channel. When not adding any anchors, my Cartesian machine would wobble the build plate back and forth and cause the top half of these swords to look extremely ugly (if they didn't get knocked off entirely).

Cura now allows you to bring in a second model that intersects with your main print. They also allow you to print a part entirely as support. This means you can drag in a second object that acts only as support for your main structure.

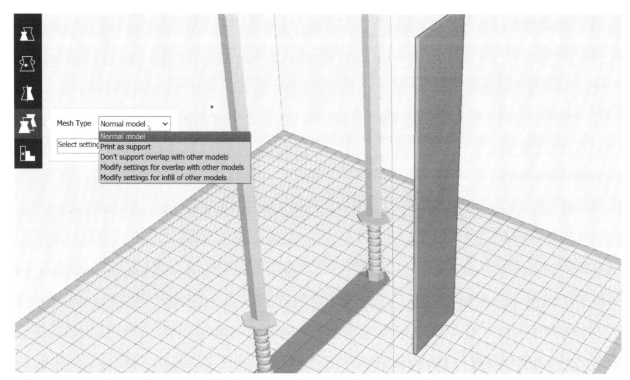

This rectangle in the example above is thin, so that it won't take up too much material, yet will extend the anchoring for the sword (I added a second sword to compare how it will slice). After bringing in a shape that will work for your model, you can choose the model and click "Print as support".

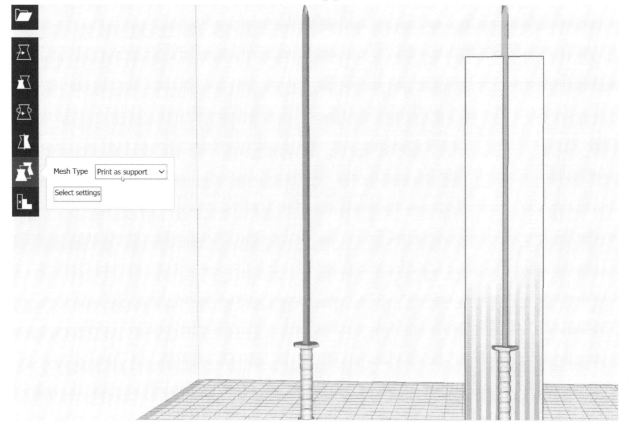

After turning the shape into "Print as support", you can then drag it over your tall, skinny print.

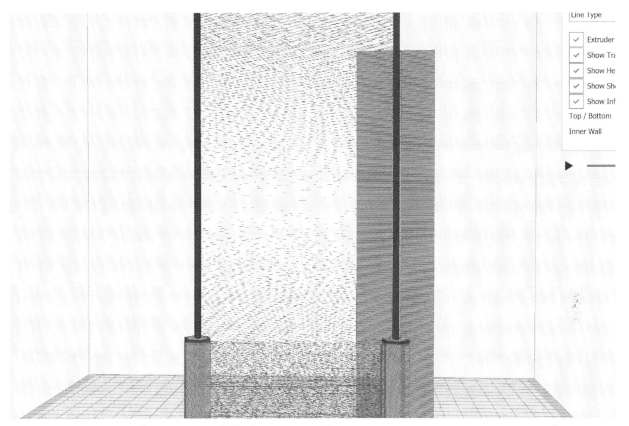

As you can see in "Layer Mode", this entire shape is now support structure that can help to anchor your tall skinny print to help prevent this wobbling back and forth.

As mentioned – there are many other ways to do this, this is just the simplest way since it allows you to do this right in your slicing software.

## Summary of Fixes and Precautions

- Tighten all of the bolts and screws that connect your extruder and hotend to your printer.
- Check to see if you need to replace printed parts on your extruder carriage.
- Reduce all rattling in the X-axis carriage.
- Replace old or worn out bearings on linear rod machines.
- Tighten your hotend setup while heated to 240°C, making sure to not over tighten.
- Remove all wobble in your print bed including replacing any bearings and tightening all harnesses.

- Tighten both the X and Y-axis belts. There should be zero droop.
- If using a thin threaded Z-axis rod, print a part that can help guide and reduce wobble.
- If possible, upgrade to a thick M8 or M10 threaded Z- axis rod.
- Replace any physically bent Z-axis rod.

# Z- Height Calibration

The Z-height calibration refers to honing in how far the nozzle is from the platform. This is determined on most machines by an adjustable screw that will run into an endstop. This is by far the most common mistake when starting a new print, but also the quickest to spot.

Along with many other printing failures, a combination of mechanical issues and slicer software tweaks can be the culprit. Even when using an auto bed leveler you will need to adjust this property.

## Too close to the build plate

(Remember if you are having trouble seeing the images to email me at Sean@3DPrintGeneral.com with proof of purchase, and I will send over high quality photos and a color PDF)

Having a nozzle start too close to the build plate can be very problematic for your machine. Not only can it prevent material from coming out – often causing a nozzle clog and/or extruder motor stepper skips – it can actually damage your printer.

When a printer starts to close to the bed it will grind away attempting to continue printing. This can cause your printer bed to be damaged by serious scratches, and can actually degrade your nozzle. This is just another reason it is essential to watch your first layer printing before leaving your machine unattended.

Over dozens of prints where some started too close to the bed, you can easily see this degradation in the picture. Yours will likely not be this bad, but this is used to show the extreme case.

This will cause you to have to purchase a new nozzle and possibly a new build plate. If you are using a PEI surface, this can be an expensive fix. Never let a printer continue if you notice it is too close to the build plate.

## Too far from the build plate

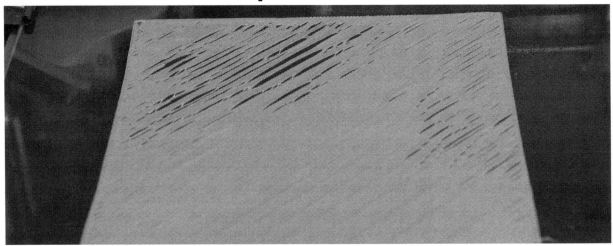

If you were to let your printer go when the nozzle is too far from the build plate, the headaches involved can vary depending on the distance. If only slightly too high, your part may be more susceptible to warping and will cause gaps on the bottom layer of your print. A little further and your print may get knocked off, and very far you will be left with a spaghetti monster to clean up.

Generally, having parts start too far from the build plate will not cause as much damage to your machine, but you will be left with wasted material and a cleanup on your hands. There have been rare cases in which this mess of material engulfs the hotend as it continues to print, and once cooled leads to a hotend being submerged in a solid block of plastic. The cleanup from this can be so extreme that it may warrant or require replacing hot end components. See the end of the "Built up Material in Nozzle" chapter for a further description of this.

# Mechanically adjusting Z-height (printer too far/ close from bed)

Most machines come with an adjustable screw or lever that will run into your Z-endstop when finding home (if not using an auto bed level sensor). If your printer does not have an adjustable Z-height, I highly suggest printing one.

Files for adjustable Z-height calibrations can be found on websites such as Thingiverse, you will just have to find the correct one for your machine.

Being able to easily adjust the Z-height is key, because over multiple prints these mechanical machines are very susceptible to slight variations (along with just having different initial layer heights). You will want this screw to have a spring keeping pressure on it in order to prevent as many minor turns as possible throughout the rattling of the printer.

You will want your nozzle to be in a starting position where you can slide a piece of paper under it, but so that it has some resistance. This distance will be tweaked depending on the initial layer height, as mentioned later in this section. I personally am able to tell what the proper z-height via sight is since I have done so much printing, but you can always go this piece of paper method as a starting point.

If this initial height is good, but the rest of your bed is not, you will want to read from the "Unleveled Build Plate" chapter of this book.

You will want to make sure to auto home, then disable steppers, and check this before starting a print because there are a lot of problems that can occur from letting your printer continue at the wrong Z- height.

# Initial layer height

The height of your first layer will drastically determine minor variations in your Z-height.

This may seem intuitive, but it is very noticeable when printing different degrees of quality parts. Printing in draft quality, or having your initial layer height be close to 0.4mm on a large diameter nozzle, will allow you to start prints much more simply than if you were to only be printing in very fine quality. This is because there is a lot of leeway on this thick initial layer.

This mean that changing your nozzle diameter and layer height can change your

Z-height calibration. Using a very fine 0.25mm nozzle will cause your printer to have to be much closer on the initial layer height than a printer with a 0.6mm diameter nozzle.

Always max out your initial layer height based off your nozzle diameter when using small nozzles. This means a 0.25mm nozzle should have an initial layer height of around 0.18, even if the rest of your print has lower layer heights. This will help you to find a good Z-height easier.

## Variations based on material/temperature

As with all materials, glass and metal expands when heated. This means that you should always be checking your Z-offset with the nozzle and bed heated to your desired temperatures. This also unfortunately means that you may have to tweak your Z-height based on what material you are printing with. Printing with ABS on a 100°C build plate will likely require a slightly different Z-height than printing with a low temp Nylon on a build plate that is 45°C.

## Changing the Z-height in the "Start G-code" by adding a Z-offset

Along with mechanically changing the Z-height, you can also change it by adding a positive or negative Z-offset to your start G-code. This is ideal for when you have specific settings based on what layer height, nozzle you are using, and material being extruded since you have a saved profile for each. Having a Z-offset for each material profile you have is beneficial because a heated build plate to 110°C will be closer to your nozzle than one that is heated to 50°C, due to the expansion of your bed.

I actually don't do this anymore since the auto bed leveler goes off of actual distance from the build plate, instead of an endstop that is attached to the frame. To do this though, you need to go to the Machine Settings on Cura, but it might be elsewhere on other slicer software. Right under the section in your start G-code of your Z axis finding home (G28 Z0), you will want to add your Z-offset with G0 Z<position> as shown below:

# Machine Settings

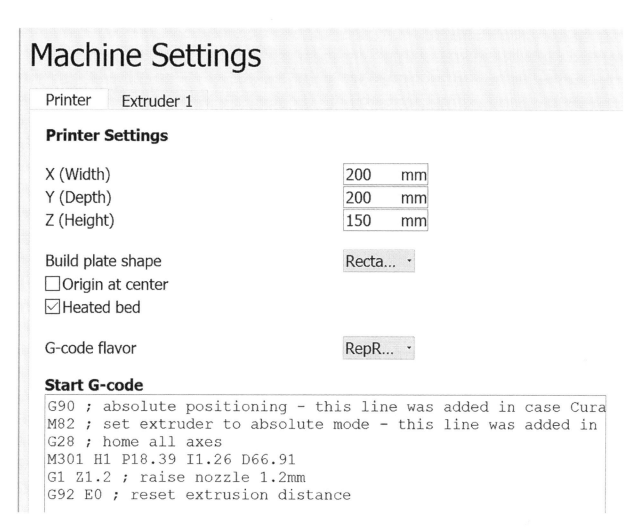

**Printer**    Extruder 1

### Printer Settings

X (Width)                           200    mm

Y (Depth)                         200    mm

Z (Height)                       150    mm

Build plate shape               Recta... ▾

☐ Origin at center

☑ Heated bed

G-code flavor                   RepR... ▾

### Start G-code

```
G90 ; absolute positioning - this line was added in case Cura
M82 ; set extruder to absolute mode - this line was added in
G28 ; home all axes
M301 H1 P18.39 I1.26 D66.91
G1 Z1.2 ; raise nozzle 1.2mm
G92 E0 ; reset extrusion distance
```

In the above example, the nozzle will raise by 1.2mm after finding home and before starting the print. So, if you found the perfect Z-height when using PLA, but you have noticed you have to raise your nozzle roughly 1.2mm every time you switch to ABS (which is pretty extreme), you could instead add this to your ABS profile when slicing parts. This should reduce the amount of times you have to mechanically adjust your Z-height, but will require you to tweak all of your profiles based on initial layer height, material being used, and nozzle diameter.

Here is a photo of what your print should look like when at the proper Z-Height:

## Summary of Fixes and Precautions

- Mechanically adjust where your extruder runs into the Z-Endstop (if not using an auto bed leveler).

- Print additional parts if your printer does not have an adjustable Z-height option.

- Make sure to auto home before starting a print to make sure your nozzle is not too close or too far when starting a print.

- Increase the initial layer height in order to have an easier time honing in on the correct Z-Height.

- Small layer heights and nozzle diameters can lead to a lot of headache honing in proper Z-height.

- Recognize that different temperatures can lead to different Z-heights due to the expansion of your build plate.

- Create unique profiles with Z-offsets in the start G-code to reduce the amount of mechanical adjust required (if not using an auto bed leveler).

# Tips if Still Not Working

While I tried my hardest for this book to be all inclusive for every printing error, there may be a unique situation not covered that you can experience, or at least one you cannot diagnose easily. Below are some good solutions if you can't fix your problem with any of the remedies described earlier.

## Turn off machine and power supply for 10 seconds and turn back on

This used to be a running joke at our facility because it was surprising how many times it fixed a problem. I would be frustrated for a half hour and someone would yell out "Did you turn it off and back on?" We would then laugh ironically as it actually worked.

For most problems it doesn't hurt to turn off your machine and power supply for 10 seconds and turn them back on.

## Check frame for sturdiness and loose bolts

If you have been printing for a while without confirming all bolts on your machine are tight, or you have an acrylic frame, you can experience minor mechanical shifts resulting in ugly or failed prints.

Periodically examine your frame for any bends or loose bolts and fix or tighten as needed. Review the "Mandatory Maintenance" chapter in this book for proper precautions.

## Flash firmware

This is another thing that is confusing but would work more often than I would think. Sometimes re-flashing the firmware onto a machine that was giving very strange failures would fix the problem. This isn't possible with a machine that hasn't been bootloaded (CR-10 from the factory as an example), but the vast majority of machines should be bootloaded with Marlin to allow you to re-flash your machine. To learn how to bootload, visit TH3D's YouTube channel and website.

I go over how to flash your firmware in the "Over and Under Extrusion" chapter, and elsewhere in this book. But if you do not have access to Marlin and the original firmware, you can also do a factory reset with the "M502" command. Just remember anything you changed (such as E-steps) since you got your printer will be set back.

I actually do not need to do this quite as frequently as before, but it doesn't hurt to do periodically if you are experiencing hard to explain issues.

# Re-slice G-code

There is a chance your G-code itself can be corrupted and you can fix your error just by re-slicing and exporting a new G-code. This is covered in the "Print Pauses Mid-Print" chapter.

# Switch filament manufacturers

The quality of your filament matters. You could spend a full week trying out all of the solutions described in this book and still not be able to achieve a successful print if you are using subpar filament, or just old filament that has absorbed moisture.

I don't even bother with filaments that do not have high reviews and aren't made by well-known manufacturers, since their quality control is frequently very poor. If you are buying a spool of PLA for under $15, you may have found a great deal, but it is likely the company just doesn't use high quality PLA or have good quality control. Always read reviews, or check the "Resources" chapter for some of my personal favorite manufacturers.

# Search online and on YouTube

If you are having a problem, it is likely someone else somewhere has experienced it. If you can search for your specific problem on Google to find a forum or a thread somewhere where someone has successfully fixed your issue. You can also search on YouTube.

I suggest subscribing to Thomas Sanladerer's YouTube channel since he covers an immense amount of 3D printing tutorials, and continually comes out with new videos. He has personally taught me a lot of what I know from these videos. His is definitely my favorite 3D printing tutorial YouTube channel.

If you purchased a machine from a manufacturer who makes a lot of printers, there is undoubtedly a review or two on YouTube. Just search your printer name and you will likely find them.

There is also the 3D printing Facebook group. There are currently over 87,000 members as of editing this book, and most are extremely helpful in diagnosing people's prints. I frequently respond to individual's problems, and love to read other's responses to help grow my own knowledge base. Be humble and state you are having trouble with a specific issue while including all relevant photos, and I can guarantee you will get some good suggestions. Just don't ask them what a good machine for under $300 is, since that has become a running joke over there.

# Send me an email

If you purchased this book and are still experiencing issues, feel free to shoot me an email anytime at Sean@3DPrintGeneral.com. I have helped many individuals just like yourself who just reach out to me, and a couple of those problems have made it into this new 2020 edition.  I may take up to a full business day to respond, but I will do my best.  The more detail and photos you have for me, the easier it is.

# Limitations Involved with 3D Printing

3D printing is not a perfect end-all solution for manufacturing parts, especially with today's technology. The RepRap project started as a dive into the unknown. Problems were addressed as they came and prints were considered a success if they were useable at all. These early prints would be considered unacceptable in today's terms.

I compare today's 3D printing market to that of using email in the mid 1990's. Most machines are not plug-and-play and require a bit of knowledge before you can even have one successful print. I'm not sure they will ever be to the point where you need no background knowledge to use.

Almost all 3D printing manufacturers, especially those on Kickstarter, will brag how their printer can be instantly used by anyone with any knowledge for high quality parts - but there really isn't a desktop machine like this. Every single printer will have its own limitations and difficulties.

## Unprintable models

I go over this in further detail in the "Model Errors" chapter, but the models you can print are limited to the capabilities of your machine, and 3D printing in general.

Walls and details that are thinner than your nozzle diameter/line width will not be shown on your final print. In the example above, Wolverine's claws get thinner than the line width I am using. This means the printer will not recognize them, and your final print will look like the image on the right. If you need text to show up in which the thickness of each letter is less than 0.1mm, you may not be able to find a desktop 3D printer on the market that can achieve this detail.

There are also issues involved with the need of support material. Since gravity will always be a factor, FDM printing will have problems printing clean overhangs. Not only will cleanliness of the underside of overhangs be effected, but you will not be able to print specific models since you cannot remove the support material.

You essentially will not be able to print any object entirely hollow unless it is a sphere or comes to a rounded top. If you want to print a giant rectangular cube, it will require at least 10% infill in order to have the top surface print cleanly. A true hollow rectangle would require support material, but there wouldn't be a way to remove it, meaning you cannot print one.

## Active patents that prevent innovation

One of the things that prevented 3D printing from reaching the masses sooner were a few integral patents. As with many blossoming industries, unused or all-encompassing patents that have a long life span can prevent people from innovating out of fear of being sued. Now that 3D printing has grown into such a lucrative market, there are countless patents that currently exist.

Some of these patents prevent innovation to enclosed build environments, some to build plates, and others that encompass entire sections or methods of printing. Many of these patents are actually expiring, which helps to contribute to the amount of inexpensive machines that are popping up on the market. Days where you were forced to spend $2,000 on a basic machine are no more. There may be innovations to these patents that still exist that are not currently even explored. We will hopefully see further innovation as these patents expire over the next 5-10 years.

## Print speed limitations

Barring a major change in the process used in FDM printing, there will always be a limitation to just how fast a part can be printed. The better the tolerances, the longer the print - there is no way around that.

Please refer to the chapter titled "Speed Limitations" for a more in-depth explanation than given below.

Speed is also limited by the material you are using and the size of your printer frame. Even if you had an extruder with an excessive amount of torque that grasps tightly onto the filament, there are limitations involved with melting each individual material composition. The filament needs to melt to a good viscosity before it can be pushed out of the small nozzle head, and this cannot be done instantly. Using a Volcano hotend will help, but there will always be this limitation.

The new E3D Super Volcano can actually extrude at speeds so fast, that they exceed what your frame is able to achieve. This is a great innovation but it will cause your frame (or stepper/extruder) to be the limiting factor.

The larger your printed model is, the greater the speeds you will actually be able to achieve as well. This is because your printer's top speed is limited to the space required to accelerate and decelerate your extruder. There is a limit to any machine as to what speed it can actually physically ever get to due to this space needed to accelerate and decelerate.

The last limitation is the frame itself. You don't want your frame rattling all over the place, which is why CoreXY and Delta machines can print faster than Cartesians without the frame shaking. A shaking frame will lead to an increased ghosting/echoing effect. This is especially true when you increase the acceleration a lot in order to achieve your top speeds. You should see my video titled "How Fast Can You 3D Print" to see more information.

Once again, refer to the "Speed Limitations" chapter for a further explanation.

If you require speed when 3D printing, you may want to consider an alternative 3D printing technology such as MJF or DLP over FDM. While significantly more expensive, these technologies were developed to drastically speed up printing and alleviate some other process limitations found in FDM.

# Upgrades and Purchasing a New Printer

3D printing technology is rapidly improving and even purchasing this book just two years from publication can have many of these failures fixed on stock new machines.

These are parts that you may want to think about upgrading on your machine, or what you should look for when purchasing a new printer.

## Auto bed leveling/auto bed tramming

Five+ years ago, the vast majority of manufacturers that offered an auto bed leveling system did not live up to their marketing. They were too mechanical and overall did not work much better than just adding a few extra end stops.

By 2018 you could purchase 3rd party auto bed leveling lasers, or buy a machine that comes stock with one. Many of these work quite well and can save you an endless amount of headaches that I describe in the "Unlevelled Build Plate" chapter.

When using one of these sensors, your extruder will travel to different sections of your build plate at the start of a new print. The sensor will be able to tell variations in how level your bed is and will change your printer firmware to automatically tilt your model accordingly to compensate. These don't actually "level" the build plate, but rather make minor variations in your initial z-height.

I personally use the EZABL by TH3D Studios, which can be purchased and added to your machine for roughly $60 at TH3DStudio.com (confirm it works on your machine first). This was a great upgrade since I always have a level build plate now.

Surprisingly, even inexpensive machines are now adding these. I have a $200 Tina2 sent to me by WEEDO for review which actually has one of these stock as well. I would never have expected this to be the case a couple of years ago when I released the first edition of this book. If you are spending over $500 on your machine, it should hopefully come with one stock.

These sensors will be mounted to your carriage, and you can find a model for your printer setup on Thingiverse. You should watch videos on TH3D's YouTube channel, since Timothy covers a lot of issues and setup guides for adding this to your machine. I also have a quick video where I go over this on my YouTube channel titled "Paid Upgrades for the CR-10".

## Get thick threaded Z-axis rods

A great improvement to think of when buying your next printer is to see how thick the threaded Z-axis rod/rods are. The thicker the rod and the better it is housed into the frame, the longer your printer will last without having tolerance issues.

Thick M10 threaded Z-axis leadscrews on a printer usually means the printer will come with a higher price tag, but it is definitely a great upgrade. Many well-built CoreXY machines have a single thick M10 leadscrew which the build plate moves up and down on. Inexpensive Cartesian machines will have a single M5 threaded rod, while better versions will have two M8 leadscrews.

I have a video in which I go over this exact process titled "Upgrading your 3D Printer to 8mm Leadscrews" on my YouTube channel.

## Upgrade hotend

Many high end printers come stock with a well-made hotend. There are quite a few options out there, but I always suggest buying from a reputable manufacturer - do not try and save money by buying cheap knockoffs.

All metal hotends do not need a Teflon tubing going all the way to the heat break, meaning you can print much hotter materials. Having the Teflon tubing go all the way to the heatbreak will make it so you can't print as hot without deforming the tube. All metal hotends fix this issue.

I have personally standardized to E3D hotends, and it honestly seems like most of the 3D printing community has as well. They are well made, all metal, and have a variety of nozzle options. The extremely popular and well-made Prusa MK3S, Lulzbot TAZ machines, all the way to the expensive Raise3D machines all use E3D hotends stock.

E3D has a wide array of nozzle diameter choices, are well- made, and seem to experience minimal amount heat creep. And if you do experience a nozzle clog, they are easy to disassemble. You can see all of these options over at MatterHackers. com

If you find a different hotend that you prefer, you should definitely go for that. Just make sure you watch any relevant reviews first and be extremely cautious of attempting to save money from off brand versions.

Replacing a poorly made or very old hotend can drastically reduce failures, increase the amount of materials you are able to print, and improve the quality of your parts.

# Well-made geared extruder

A stock extruder without any added gear ratio cannot print nearly as fast as a well-made geared extruder. You can print the parts for a geared extruder, but there are manufacturers that produce these extruders with some added benefits to the tolerance and quality.

Without a gear ratio you will be limited to only printing stiff materials, since any flexible version will not really be possible. The same is true with nozzle diameters. Attempting to print on a nozzle with a diameter smaller than 0.3mm will almost certainly require a gear ratio. Both of these facts are even truer when using a Bowden printer instead of a direct version.

For instance, E3D also makes their Titan Extruder. This is a well-built, light, geared extruder.

My personal favorite, as mentioned elsewhere in this book, is the Bondtech BMG dual drive extruder. This extruder not only has a 3-1 gear ratio, it also has two sets of teeth gripping onto the filament, rather than just one pushing against a bearing as with all other extruders. If you can't print with one of these extruders, you likely can't print with any extruder. Unfortunately it costs $100 right now, but I am very happy I upgraded.

These can be used with a Bowden setup with an extra part, or can be used on direct drive machines with an E3D barrel without any extra parts needed. I bought mine over at MatterHackers.com.

Ever since switching to this Bondtech extruder, and setting it up to be direct instead of Bowden, I have been able to print every material and in every nozzle diameter with zero issues. Definitely worth it in my opinion.

**NOTE:** As of editing this book, a new extruder/hotend combo has been announced by E3D called Hermes. This is a part that has both the extruder and hotend as one unit, meaning it will reduce the weight and space it would take to have them as separate unit. But that isn't the best part, as E3D has joined Bondtech as making this extruder dual drive.

I have yet to test out Hermes, but the results I have seen from people in the community really astound me. People are able to print extremely difficult flexibles, such as Ninjaflex, at ridiculously high speeds. While I normally limit my speeds to around 25mm/s for Ninjaflex, the examples I have seen have had the Hermes printing it at up to 100mm/s - something I once thought impossible. Be sure to research this extruder if you plan on upgrading your machine.

## Cartesian vs CoreXY vs Delta

There are benefits to each of these types of printers, but the vast majority of machines you will see on the market are Cartesian, with CoreXY being the second most common. When I say CoreXY, I generally mean a gantry system, and CoreXY is one type of these gantry systems. You can also find it in an H-Bot variety, I will just refer to the bed moving down as CoreXY as to not confuse you further.

Delta printers seem to be able to print the fastest, but are difficult to calibrate and must be tall if you want to print wide objects. Personally, I do not have extensive experience with delta machines. There will be less tutorials for these types of machines vs. Cartesian and CoreXY.

CoreXY printers have been growing in popularity and they definitely have added sturdiness and benefits. I personally like CoreXY machines the most for quality, but have a bit more experience on Cartesian models, due to them being more popular over the past decade. Printers such as the Zortrax M200 and Makerbot Replicator 2 are CoreXY machines.

CoreXY machines have the benefit of not moving the build plate back and forth. This constant moving of the build plate will not only have extra wear and tear on your printer, but can result in parts getting knocked over easier with an increased chance of ghosting.

Because of this, CoreXY machines have become my favorite type of printer. When looking to purchase a new printer, it is worth seeing if you prefer CoreXY (gantry) over Cartesian.

# Enclosed machine

I go over this added benefit in the "Warping" chapter in this book, but it is highly beneficial to purchase a machine that has its build area at least somewhat enclosed when printing with warping materials. This way you do not have to worry as much when wanting to print in materials that have a high internal stress. You just need to make sure your board is not enclosed with the printer, since you don't want that overheating.

Personally, I only have one enclosed machine. I do not use extremely high warping materials very often, and my open frame does a good job for the vast majority of my prints. For me, spending the extra money on an enclosed machine is not really worth it. You will need to determine if it makes sense for you, or if you can get away with printing non-warping materials (including the warp-free technology that Polymaker now offers).

# Metal frame

If you haven't noticed already, I highly suggest purchasing a printer with a strong metal frame. Acrylic framed printers will not hold up over time and, in my opinion, it is entirely worth upgrading to metal.

I will not bother with acrylic machines or any printer that is not sturdy. It's all metal or nothing for me now due to the headaches I have had in the past.

# V-Slot Aluminum Extrusion

3D printers on the market are increasingly offering v-slot aluminum extrusions for their frame instead of linear rods. These rails use a stiff, aluminum rail along which the carriages slide. It accomplishes this with rollers that roll on the rails. This is opposite a linear rod printer where the carriages are attached to a smooth rod via bearings.

The vast majority of printers a couple of years ago used linear rods, but it seems to be changing. This is due to an increasing amount of makers preferring v-slot aluminum extrusions. Aluminum rail printers are often much stiffer and more precise with smoother motion. I personally prefer aluminum extrusion and linear rail printers now, though it does depend on the particular machine.

## 24V instead of 12V

Most inexpensive 3D printers come with a 12V power supply and output. Buying a printer that is 24V will come with a few added benefits. These include a shorter time required to heat your build plate, more torque to your stepper motors (reduces extruder stepper skipping and allows for faster prints), and results in less noise produced by your stepper motors.

If you are building a printer from scratch, just make sure any upgrades you purchase are rated for 24V. If you are converting your printer to 24V, you will need to change your hot end heater cartridge, your heated build plate (or at least the wiring to it if your build plate can handle 24v), and you must remove a specific diode on a RAMPS board. If you are doing this upgrade yourself, you must watch tutorials and be sure you are confident in what you are doing. If not confident, don't do it.

Keep in mind a 24V machine is likely going to be more expensive than their 12V counterparts, though that is not always the case. Do some research on the particular machine you plan on purchasing and if it being 24V is beneficial to you.

## 1.75mm vs 3.00mm Filament

This debate has been going on for years and there is still no specific answer, though it seems that 1.75mm has slowly won. I have extensive experience using both, and personally I like to use 1.75mm more.

3.00mm filament (more accurately it is 2.85mm filament) has a tighter tolerance in its diameter than 1.75mm filament does. This should theoretically mean parts should come out cleaner and you should experience less nozzle clogs, but I do not notice much of a difference in this vs. 1.75mm printers. You can print parts a bit faster though because less torque is required on your extruder stepper since less distance is required to extrude the same amount of material. This means your extruder can turn slower when dealing with 3.00mm filament (possibly leading to less extruder motor skips).

The biggest issue with 2.85mm filament is with its want to curl back onto its spool. When you are near the end of a 2.85mm PLA spool, you can experience an extensive amount of breaks in the filament due to it wanting to curl back into a circle.

This is far more annoying than you can imagine if you haven't dealt with it yourself. This factor alone has made me prefer 1.75mm filament, since it is far easier to manipulate and you don't ever have to throw away spools that still have 30 grams of material on them. I see no quality differences with 1.75mm and the headaches involved with using it are far less. You may prefer 2.85mm, I have just come to like 1.75mm.

# Poll Results

I actually held a poll on my Twitter page to see what people refer the most. Everyone has their own reasons for liking one of the options below, but I figured I would see what the majority of people like.

While there were only about 40 participants, the results were as follows. I will hopefully have a larger sample size later, but this is just so you can see what people think.

I asked what their preferred method of each of these were:

**Build Type:**

Cartesian: 14%

CoreXY: 79%

Delta: 7%

**Extruder Type:**

Bowden: 0%

Direct: 100%

**Filament Diameter:**

1.75mm: 91%

2.85mm: 9%

**Extruder Brand:**

E3D Titan: 33%

Bondtech BMG: 67%

**Hotend:**

E3D V6: 47%

E3D Volcano/SuperVolcano: 47%

Slice Mosquito/Mosquito Magnum: 6%

**Frame:**

Linear Rail or V-Slot Aluminum Extrusion: 89%

Linear Rods: 11%

So it seems that the average person in this polling agrees with my personal favorite methods. I have come to like CoreXY more than Cartesian, Direct over Bowden, and rails over Linear Rods. By the time you read this book there may be new hotend and extruders that people like (such as the Hermes I made a note of), so always see what is popular by looking at new videos and reviews online.

# Resources

Below are some great resources you can use to help you in your 3D printing exploration.

## Video Tips and Tutorials

The 3D Print General (Myself) YouTube Channel

Thomas Sanladerer YouTube Channel

3D Maker Noob YouTube Channel

CNC Kitchen YouTube Channel

Joseph Prusa YouTube Channel

Maker's Muse YouTube Channel

Make Anything YouTube Channel

3D Print Nerd YouTube Channel

Teaching Tech YouTube Channel

CHEP Filament Friday YouTube Channel

TH3D Studio YouTube Channel

## Other Resources

Facebook 3D Printing Group (very helpful group of people)

TH3DStudio.com

## Free 3D Models For Download

Thingiverse.com

MyMiniFactory.com

Cults3D.com

GrabCAD.com

Yeggi.com (compiles 3d models from many different sites, including those that cost money)

## Free Software

Cura for slicing parts

Prusa Slicer for slicing parts

Tinkercad.com for editing .stl files

MeshMixer for editing models

Autodesk Fusion 360 for editing and creating models. Just sign up as a "Start-up or Enthusiast" to not pay legally

3D Builder for Windows 10 for editing models

Repetier Host for directly connecting to printer

Octoprint for connecting multiple printers to a network

## Places to Purchase Printer Parts

3DPrintGeneral.com – where I link to many of the parts I use. I do not sell them, just link to where you can purchase them.

MatterHackers.com – my favorite for finding reputable parts

Amazon.com – be careful to not accidentally purchase off-brand from a non-reputable seller

TH3DStudio.com - Tim makes sure all of the parts he sells are of high quality and sourced properly

Fillastruder.com for E3D parts in the United States

E3d-online.com for Europe

Prusa3D.com

Newegg.com

DigiKey.com

Mouser.com

## Reputable PLA ABS and PETG Manufacturers

Polymaker

Hatchbox

AIO Robotics

Proto-pasta

Prusament

Esun

IC3D

Overture (I have begun using this a lot due to its low price)

## Reputable Unique Material Manufactuers

Polymaker

3DX Tech

taulman3D

MatterHackers

NinjaTek

Proto-Pasta

ColorFabb

Fiberlogy

## My Favorite 3D Printers (Pre-Built)

$ - Creality CR-10 or Ender 5 (best price for what you get, though you may want to do upgrades). There are many clones of this style of build that are all at a great price point as well.

$$ - Prusa i3 MK3 (highest praise in the community. A real workhorse)

$$$ - Lulzbot TAZ Pro (was my favorite printer, though there are so many other options now available that are less expensive)

$$$ - Zortrax M200 or higher (great surface quality)

$$$$ - Ultimaker 3 or higher (easy to use, I personally do not like this for the price, but good for newbies and educational settings)

$$$$$ - Raise3D (large, enclosed printer. Great for real production but not necessarily for personal use due to its price)

There are many other printers that are great that I haven't tested, just make sure you watch review videos before purchasing.

## Places to Order Prints

SD3D.com

Shapeways.com

ProtoLabs.com

Visit all3dp.com for their article on "Best Online 3D Printing Services" for a more expansive list.

# About the Author

Sean Aranda began his 3D printing explorations by becoming the Operations Manager for SD3D in early 2015. Along with adding innovations to the 3D printing industry, SD3D is a production service provider for everyone from inventors to large businesses. With over a dozen FDM machines and a few hundred clients, Sean was able to amass well over 50,000 hours of successful printing.

Sean was also able to receive extensive experience with material variations and profile settings required for a successful print, since SD3D offers over 16 different types of FDM 3D printing materials.

While he had a very basic background before starting at SD3D, Sean's knowledge of printing failures grew rapidly as he helped all clients get a usable 3D print within the promised timeframe. Whenever a printer failed or had a malfunction, Sean was in charge of all maintenance and repairs.

Sean has also authored a much smaller graphic handbook for 3D printing called The A-Z 3D Printing Handbook, which has amassed well over 5,000 downloads. This is the third edition of this book, the first two selling thousands of copies helping the community to achieve consistent, successful prints.

Since releasing the first edition of this book, Sean has been growing a 3D printing channel titled "The 3D Print General" where he goes over fun prints and in-depth tutorials. In these three years of videos he has easily added another 25,000 hours of successful printing with his half dozen machines. These videos are meant to fill in the gaps from this book and to show first hand examples of how you can fix your 3D printing failures. Many of the topics covered in this book have been covered on this YouTube channel in a 5-10 minute video.

A lot of what you are reading in this book is from shear testing over the course of two years of full time manufacturing across dozens of machines and countless hours for his YouTube channel, as well as updates that have occurred in the three years since. It also includes any issues that readers of those first two books have contacted him on – but were not in those editions.

But it definitely wasn't all trial and error, the 3D printing expert, co-founder of SD3D and editor of this book, David Feeney, was always around to educate.

# About the Editor

One of the few people you will meet with a drastic amount of more 3D printing experience than Sean is David Feeney. David is an experienced manufacturing engineer, project manager and entrepreneur. With six years of direct experience in the automotive and industrial equipment industries as a manufacturing engineer and project manager, David understands the needs of the target client extremely well.

Prior to co-founding SD3D, David worked at Aptera Motors as a project manager for over a dozen electrical and mechanical engineers. David later worked as a manufacturing engineer for the Large Compressor Set and Mechanical Drive (LCSMD) division for Solar Turbines. In this role David was solely responsible for fixing any design or manufacturing issues prior to hitting the assembly line on over $100 million worth of equipment annually. David holds a bachelor's of science degree in mechanical engineering from San Diego State University and is EIT accredited with the California Board for Professional Engineers.

Mr. Feeney is the head of the technology upgrades at SD3D and is utilizing his hundreds of thousands of hours of successful 3D printing by helping to advance the entire industry. Visit SD3D.com now to find out more!

Whether you are new to 3D printing, or you have dozens of successful prints under your belt, this book is going to help you!

Sean Aranda and David Feeney have hundreds of thousands of successful 3d printing hours combined, so let them help you achieve consistent clean prints.

Made in the USA
Middletown, DE
08 April 2020